Business Analysis FOR DUMMIES®

A Wiley Brand

by Paul Mulvey, Kate McGoey,
and Kupe Kupersmith

FOR DUMMIES®

A Wiley Brand

Business Analysis For Dummies®

Published by:
John Wiley & Sons, Inc.
111 River Street
Hoboken, NJ 07030-5774
www.wiley.com

Copyright © 2013 by John Wiley & Sons, Inc., Hoboken, New Jersey

Published simultaneously in Canada

For general information on our other products and services, please contact our Customer Care Department within the U.S. at 877-762-2974, outside the U.S. at 317-572-3993, or fax 317-572-4002. For technical support, please visit www.wiley.com/techsupport.

Wiley publishes in a variety of print and electronic formats and by print-on-demand. Some material included with standard print versions of this book may not be included in e-books or in print-on-demand. If this book refers to media such as a CD or DVD that is not included in the version you purchased, you may download this material at http://booksupport.wiley.com. For more information about Wiley products, visit www.wiley.com.

Library of Congress Control Number: 2013937659

ISBN 978-1-118-51058-2 (pbk); ISBN 978-1-118-51061-2 (ebk); ISBN 978-1-118-51063-6 (ebk); ISBN 978-1-118-51064-3 (ebk)

Manufactured in the United States of America

10 9 8 7 6 5 4 3 2 1

Contents at a Glance

Table of Contents

Introduction

● ●

*O*kay, so you bought this book looking for hints about performing business analysis. Or maybe you're still in the bookstore thinking about whether this book is going to be of any value to you as a business analyst. (Hint: It is.) You may be working as a business analyst now or wondering whether it's the right job for you.

As a career path, business analysis is a good option. Companies today need business analysis performed so they can solve problems, take advantage of opportunities, make sure they're chasing the most cost-effective solutions, and streamline efficiency. The good news is that the skills needed to address these concerns are learnable. With even basic knowledge, you can immediately help a company reach its goals. You can make a difference today in the success of your (or someone else's) business.

However, one of the challenges you face as a business analyst (BA) is that it isn't black and white; the standard BA answer to almost any question is, "It depends." Business analysis deals with a lot of variables and changing conditions, which means you have to practice a lot to get good at it. The more you experience, the better you get. *Business Analysis For Dummies* brings together a lot of experience in one place to help you get a head start and jump in right away.

About This Book

Part of business analysis is about setting general expectations for the project results and being educated in various techniques and principles, and this book is right in line with that philosophy. No book about business analysis can possibly explain every situation and every approach you may find yourself in. You have to do a certain amount of figuring it out as you go along.

What this book does give you are tools and techniques you can use to set your expectations. We provide tips and starting points for communication with stakeholders and even explain what business analysis terms like *stakeholder* mean. This book is a reference tool you can turn to in order to understand what particular aspect of business analysis you're looking for. The beauty of it is that you don't have to read through the entire book cover to cover to get the information you want out of it. You can simply open to the table of contents, find what you're looking for, and head directly to that section without passing Go or collecting $200.

Here's a taste of the useful reference material you can expect to find in *Business Analysis For Dummies:*

- How to determine whether someone is giving you a solution disguised as a requirement and how to find the root cause of the problem (Chapter 6)

- Why you have to understand what is driving the business to undertake the project and know whether proceeding is a good decision (Chapter 8)

- How to create multiple solutions for a problem (or take an advantage of an opportunity) and recommend which one the business should undertake (Chapter 9)

- How to find and maintain the boundaries of a project so you know exactly what you are (and aren't) working on (Chapter 10)

The great thing about this book is that we let you know exactly what information is vital and what's nonessential. We've packed the main body with all the stuff we think you really need to know, but you can skip items like *sidebars* (shaded boxes) and Technical Stuff paragraphs. These bits are interesting, but you won't miss out on vital information if you choose to pass them by.

All web addresses appear in monofont. As you read, you may note that some web addresses break across two lines of text. If you're reading this book in print and want to visit one of these web pages, simply key in the web address exactly as it's noted in the text, pretending that the line break doesn't exist. If you're reading this as an e-book, you've got it easy — just click the web address to be taken directly to the web page.

And one business analysis-specific note: We use *BA, business analyst,* and *business analysis professional* interchangeably to describe the person doing this type of work — just as these terms are used in real life. Know, though, that "business analyst" is a general descriptor rather than a professional title. Business analysis is performed at all levels of a company. Even mom-and-pop shops need to perform business analysis, but they don't necessarily hire an outside business analyst; someone on their staff performs the business analysis work. In this book, that person is as much a BA as someone who has "business analyst" printed on her business card.

Foolish Assumptions

Business analysis is full of assumptions (though BAs have their own definition of *assumption*). Seeing as how we're so accustomed to assumptions, we make a few about you as our readers:

- You need to perform business analysis to do your job, whether you have the title "business analyst" or not.

✔ You know how to read documents and search for information (the fact that you're reading this book to gain information confirms that assumption).

✔ You can (or need to learn how to) ask tough questions, communicate with people both electronically and face to face, and get up in front of a group to present an idea.

✔ You're constantly willing to increase your business analysis skills and to look at different ways to accomplish things.

Icons Used in This Book

Look for these familiar *For Dummies* icons to offer visual clues about the kinds of material you're about to read:

This icon points out good advice relating to the subject matter you're reading about. Skimming these paragraphs gives you some seriously good suggestions that can help you utilize resources efficiently and make your work just a little easier!

The decisions you make and information you present can have a profound impact on the business. For that reason, we highlight important business analysis concepts and principles with this icon. Consider these bits the extra-important paragraphs you'll want to come back to.

Read these paragraphs to avoid BA pitfalls that may result in poor customer satisfaction and solutions that just don't hit the mark.

This icon appears beside information that's interesting but that won't impair your understanding of business analysis if you skip it.

The Anecdote icon calls out our attempts to show you how a particular BA technique has been applied in the real world. We have had more than 50 years of experience among us, so we want to share our success (and horror) stories with you so you can benefit from (or just chuckle at) them.

Beyond the Book

In addition to the material in the print or e-book you're reading right now, this product also comes with some goodies you can access on the web. No matter how diligently you prepare, execute, and follow the business analysis guidelines we offer in this book, you'll probably come across a few situations that stump you.

Check out the free Cheat Sheet at www.dummies.com/cheatsheet/business analysis for an overview of a project's lifecycle; 15 indicators that can point you to areas that are ripe for process improvement; and a checklist that helps you perform a business impact analysis, which lets you target the project worthy of your efforts and the business's resources.

Head to www.dummies.com/extras/businessanalysis to find pointers on conducting a requirements review, a process that gets you to the heart of an issue by asking one simple question, and advice for developing a good relationship with your project manager.

Where to Go from Here

The book is about as modular as you can get with business analysis, meaning you don't have to read one chapter to understand what happens in the next. If you're looking for a specific keyword you heard a manager use or a new technique you saw another BA use in a meeting, you can use the index or table of contents as your guide and skip right to the appropriate chapter to read about it.

We've organized this book so that you can jump in wherever you want, so if you want to skip to the end and read the short chapters in Part V first, go right ahead. You find lots of good information presented in easy-to-digest nuggets there, and who knows — these pearls of wisdom may inspire you to go back to find the more detailed, how-to info in the main chapters themselves.

If you're totally new to business analysis, start at Part I. Chapter 3 is a good landing point if you want to brush up on the people side of the business. Want to find out about making a business case? Head to Chapter 9. For help figuring out what the problems are to begin with, your starting point is Chapter 6. If you need to cut right to the chase and implement solutions effectively, try Chapters 12 and 13.

The easiest way, though, to use the book is to just start turning pages and read the content! And because the true value is in how you apply it to real life, don't be shy about making notes in the chapters, highlighting information, and putting flags on the pages. Whether you're using sticky notes or your e-reader's highlighter function, this book is one of the first tools in your BA toolkit; refer to it often!

Part I
Getting Started with Business Analysis

In this part . . .

✔ Discover the value of business analysis and the impact it has on your organization.

✔ Pick up the key skills you need to be a business analysis professional.

✔ Get familiar with the different levels on which you perform business analysis and recognize the challenges associated with each.

✔ Meet the people you work with and understand how to best interact and communicate with them.

Chapter 1

Business Analysis in a Nutshell

In This Chapter

▶ Grasping what business analysis is and why it's valuable

▶ Tracking a business analyst's role and skills

▶ Introducing industry guidelines and certification options

*1*n today's competitive world, companies must always be at their best, maintain an edge, and capitalize on opportunities for growth. Business analysis is a deliberate attempt to review operations to ensure that business is moving along as well as it can and that the company is taking advantage of opportunities.

Basically, *business analysis* is a set of tasks and activities that help companies determine their objectives for meeting certain opportunities or addressing challenges and then help them define solutions to meet those objectives. Sometimes, companies hire outside, independent business analysts (BAs) to come in and perform the analysis. Other times, they may call upon an employee to perform BA tasks internally regardless of whether he has a business analyst title. No matter which category you fit into, this book lays it all out for you.

In this chapter, we give you a very broad overview of what business analysis is, introduce you to the business analysis lifecycle, and explain what the job entails.

Defining Business Analysis

According to the Business Analysis Body of Knowledge (BABOK) version 2, business analysis is the "set of tasks and techniques used to work as a liaison among stakeholders in order to understand the structure, policies, and operations of an organization, and to recommend solutions that enable the organization to achieve its goals."

Translation: Your goal as a BA is to understand how companies work and to enable companies to reach their potential by helping them articulate and meet goals, recognize and take advantage of opportunities, or identify and overcome challenges. All of which is a pretty tall order. But the task becomes more manageable — and understandable — if you think of it as having two distinct parts: the goal and the process.

- ✔ **The goal:** The *goal* addresses why you're doing the analysis in the first place — perhaps to improve a company's revenue and services or to reduce its costs. Think of the goal as the purpose of the project. In order to determine what the real goal is, you often have to employ the most frequently asked question in the world of business analysis: "Why?" Although we go into much deeper detail later in the book about discovering the goal of a project, the process really can be as simple as asking "why" until you've gotten to the root of the issue. (This fact is one reason we feel a 4-year-old is the best business analysis professional around.)

- ✔ **The process:** The *process* involves understanding the how — that is, understanding what the solution needs to do, what it should look like, and the people or systems that interact with it. The process requires you to grasp where the company is today and where it needs to be in order to achieve the goal. During this part, you determine what the solution should look and feel like and how to make sure it's used after developed. To develop the process, you basically break the goal down into manageable pieces that you and the company can execute. Those manageable pieces make up the solution.

In business analysis, you do not actually perform the activities to build the solution, nor do you actually manage the process to build the solution or test the solution. Instead, you identify the activities that enable the company (with your expert help, of course) to define the business problem or opportunity, define what the solution looks like, and define how it should behave in the end. As the BA, you lay out the plans for the process ahead.

Knowing Your Role in the Basic Business Analysis Lifecycle

Business analysis work is done at many levels within a company. From the chief executive officer (CEO) and vice presidents to the line managers, individuals throughout the company use business analysis activities throughout their day.

Because folks at all levels view things in terms of a *project* (a set of steps to accomplish something), explaining business analysis activities as part of a project lifecycle (as shown in Figure 1-1) is easy. Although these tasks fall in a general order, they're somewhat fluid, as we discuss in later chapters. For now, get to know this cycle; it's at the crux of all things business analysis:

1. **Plan the project.**

   Planning includes creating a work plan or at least thinking through an approach for the analysis effort on a project, encompassing all the activities you do and the techniques you use. As the BA, your primary role during planning is determining the scope of the effort; if you're a more senior BA, you may be involved in project estimation and resource planning. These additional tasks are detailed in Chapter 11.

2. **Scope the project.**

   Defining and documenting the project scope requires you to understand why the project has been initiated (the *project statement of purpose*) and the goals of the project (the *project objectives*). As the BA, you hold folks to the project boundaries and analyze the business problem without jumping to a solution. This step includes clearly identifying the opportunity or problem the company needs to address. Chapter 9 includes information on how to develop a business case, which also discusses the problem definition. For more on scoping, flip to Chapter 10.

3. **Elicit, analyze, and communicate requirements.**

   This step is the bulk of what business analysis professionals do at the project level. As the BA, you actively partake in understanding the real business needs and finding the root cause of business problems, as well as communicating requirements to the intended audience. This task involves categorizing the requirements and knowing how detailed they have to be to ensure your project is solving the right problem. We discuss requirements in Chapters 5 through 8.

4. **Design the solution.**

   BAs aren't typically responsible for this activity; rather, they collaborate with the solution team to develop a solution. Because solution design isn't a core business analysis activity, we don't cover it in this book. However, the fact that design doesn't fall to you doesn't mean you should walk away when the designing starts. Having the BAs available to support the design and development team is important.

5. **Build or buy the solution.**

   Based on the activities in Steps 1 through 4, the business and project team make a decision to build the solution internally, have a group outside the company build it, or buy a prepackaged solution. During this time, your role is to ensure the solution still meets the business need stated in the project objectives and the business requirements. In addition, you may also start writing test cases and test scenarios for the next (test) phase.

6. **Test the solution.**

As the solution is being designed and built, you need to validate that the business needs elicited during the project are being met. You collaborate with the test team, either as an active tester or by working with the testing team to ensure the solution meets the stated requirements and other project documentation. You can find out more about how to test solutions in Chapter 14.

7. **Implement the solution.**

After a solution is built, you need to help make sure the business uses the solution. You actively work with project stakeholders as the solution rolls out, perhaps as a change agent (advocating the need for change) and/or to train new users on the system. Part of the implementation may be eliciting metrics surrounding usability, noting how quickly they are adapting to the new system, and gauging customer satisfaction. We cover implementation in detail in Chapter 15.

8. **Conduct a post-implementation review.**

After the solution has been implemented, you need to make sure the goals outlined in the project are being met. If they aren't, another project may be necessary to address the gap. We detail post-implementation review in Chapter 14.

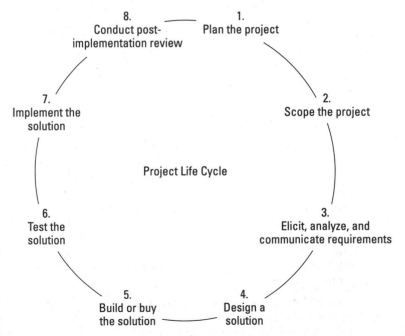

Figure 1-1:
A generic project lifecycle.

Illustration by Wiley, Composition Services Graphics

Don't confuse the post-implementation review with a "lessons learned" process. The latter generally discusses how you can do the project process better, not how well the solution works for the business.

Looking at the Value of Business Analysis

A popular perception of business analysis is that it makes businesses do business better. It's simple but true, and BAs are the people who function as the liaisons between the problems and solutions to make businesses everywhere do business better. Here are just a few of the ways that your performance as a BA can help an organization:

- ✓ **Setting expectations:** BAs help stakeholders define a solution for their problem. After a solution has been defined — whether that solution is to build a four-bedroom, wheelchair-accessible, three-car-garage house or to improve a business process to reduce costs — expectations are set. The stakeholders (the future homeowners, the business owner/executives, or whoever) expect that whatever actions follow will result in the solution that was identified.

- ✓ **Improving estimation:** Most people don't like surprises when it comes to time and cost estimates. Performing business analysis helps define what needs to be accomplished. Having this clearer picture lets organizations do a better job of estimating what their solutions will cost and how long they'll take to implement.

- ✓ **Better aligning projects with goals/objectives:** Because business analysis professionals work on both the "why" and the "how" pieces, they can see when a solution is no longer aligned with the goals and objectives.

Kupe was working on a project where the goal was to reduce employee time on a specific process for a utility company and therefore reduce salary costs associated with that process. He identified many parts of the process that could be automated, thereby reducing employee hours spent on the process. At one point, Kupe asked how many people performed a particular part of the process and how often, only to find that one person did it three times per year. Automating that part of the process would cost $10,000 . . . and save approximately 30 minutes of work time and $12 in salary cost per year. Automating this part of the process didn't align to the goal of reducing costs, so Kupe convinced everyone not to automate.

If you discover that the project work is no longer adding value to reaching the goals and objectives of the company, one of the best things you as the BA can do is cancel the project.

✔ **Managing scope creep:** *Scope creep* refers to the phenomenon of bringing in new requirements after everyone agrees on what should be included in a project. In companies where projects are going on all the time, scope creep is going to happen. Gain buy-in on the project scope from all impacted people as early as possible. Then, when scope creep happens, you can show the impact the new requirements would have so the business can make an informed decision.

For example, say you're on a project where you're solving a productivity issue for one department of a company; halfway through, the company wants to include another department. In this case, you have to review the original scope with the company and outline how the added department will change the project so the decision-makers can determine whether to proceed with the change.

✔ **Reducing project defects:** Business analysis activities detail the rules, process, and user interactions of the solution. This level of detail helps provide clear direction for the people developing the solution and those testing the solution to help ensure that defects are reduced and caught before the solution is implemented. In a solution that enables customers to buy products from a website, for example, one of the required conditions would be that the customer must enter a complete address; the BA would then elicit requirements surrounding the expected experience from the customer's viewpoint: Does the company cancel the order? Do the customers receive an error message? If so, what does the message say?

✔ **Smoothing the transition to production:** *Transition* as it relates to projects is all about moving from the development and test environment, where you're building the solution, to the production environment, where the users are actually using the solution. Good business analysis includes ensuring the solution will be used in production, which you do by getting the organization ready for the change and developing a rollout strategy.

✔ **Reusing requirements and reducing duplicate solutions:** For every initiative, BAs should be careful not to duplicate requirements underway in different areas of the company. Because you often develop many solutions at the same time for the same goals and objectives, companies may well be working on multiple projects trying to accomplish the same thing.

Kupe was working at an energy company that was trying to improve the operations of its four real estate divisions. Each division was independently trying to address the same need: updating the real estate database. By looking outside each individual group, Kupe and a team suggested combining efforts that could save time and money by focusing on one solution rather than four.

✔ **Improving communication within the team:** Business analysis activities boil down to communication. One of the BA's main roles is to elicit and communicate the true needs of the business so the right solution can be delivered. Making sure everyone has a clear and consistent understanding of what needs to be accomplished helps ensure all sides are working together to accomplish the goal.

✔ **Increasing customer satisfaction:** BAs help address the inevitable changes a company goes through and can help mitigate any problems customers may feel as a result of those changes. One of the biggest ways you as a BA can help is by facilitating communication of the changes to customers. For example, if the company wants to make a change to its services or product, you can help it determine what the impact on the customers will be and how to effectively communicate the upcoming changes to those affected.

Considering the Skills of a Successful BA

When performing business analysis, you need to be equally proficient in several skills so you can apply them at different times based on the project you're working on. But you can't stop there; you also have to know when to use which skill. The following sections spell out a few skills you need to succeed at business analysis.

Outstanding communication

Communication is integral to everything in business analysis, so you need to be great at it. BAs operate at the intersection of business problems and business solutions, which means you have to be able to communicate with two groups of folks that sometimes seem to be speaking different languages. We cover more on communication in Chapter 3.

Detailed research, analysis, and recording

BAs need to have the curiosity for understanding processes, procedures, and systems. They shouldn't be afraid to ask questions. If you're consistently the person in the room with your hand up when a presenter asks for question, you just may be cut out for work as a BA. Even if you know the subject matter well, you can still ask questions to understand it in more depth and detail.

That curiosity helps you understand what each person needs from the project. The key isn't just asking questions of other people; it's wanting to understand all aspects about how something works or what the underlying problem is. Such curiosity could lead to conducting research on your own to figure out where the problem exists and then analyzing the issues and barriers that would create an effective solution.

Time management and information organization

If you ask a true BA when analysis is done, his answer will be "Never!" However, the reality is that you have a limited time to complete your project, so to be successful, you have to be able to effectively manage your work and be good at setting priorities. Because you'll be dealing with a lot of people and a lot of information, you need to be good at organizing all the information in a way that lets you recall it when needed to support your communication. You need to understand which pieces of your elicited information are relevant to which stakeholders and how you are going to use what you found to communicate your results.

The ability to see the big picture

If you get close enough to an impressionist painting, all you see are brush strokes. Only as you move away from the painting can you start to see the image of a cathedral or a picnic. Being able to step away from the project at hand and see the big picture is crucial for any business analysis practitioner. You must be able to work on a project while understanding how that project fits in with other projects in the organization and continues to meet the business's overall objectives. This macro view is a particularly important skill because the BA is typically the only person with this vital perspective. You're the one who can keep efforts relevant, synergistic, and efficient.

Once, a project Paul was a part of was being worked on by several smaller areas (or *silos*, in BA lingo) within one organization. He studied the entire end-to-end process — including the different silos — and discovered that multiple silos were creating the same data stores when having just one for everyone to access made more sense. Focusing on the big picture allowed Paul to catch the issue in time to get things back on track.

Customer-focused and value-driven perspective

To be a good BA, you must always keep in mind what your customer needs from you. That probably seems like a no-brainer, but keep in mind that we're not just talking about external customers who purchase your organization's products and services; we're also referring to internal customers from other departments and even to those on your project team. With any of these customers, you have to make sure that whatever you produce provides value to the customer and to the project you're working on.

A large BA toolkit

Abraham Maslow, the famous psychologist, once said, "I suppose it is tempting, if the only tool you have is a hammer, to treat everything as if it were a nail." This concept led to the *law of the instrument,* or overreliance on one familiar tool.

As a business analysis professional, you need to avoid falling victim to this law. By having a large toolkit, you can apply the right tool to the situation at hand. You have to know which tools work best based on the context and the situation. For instance, if you're trying to model data, the best tool is to use an entity relationship diagram, not a workflow (more on data modeling in Chapter 13). If you need to show your stakeholders what your solution would look like in real life, you use a prototype (Chapter 4). On the other hand, if stakeholders just need the nuts and bolts and bottom line of the project, you want to make sure you can write a strong business case (Chapter 9). If you're trying to make sure your project stays on track and doesn't go out of bounds, you use your scoping diagram (Chapter 10).

In addition to the business analysis techniques covered in the book, you need to have a good grasp on the types of solutions specific to your business or field. For example, if you work in an area that develops web applications, you want to be familiar with and stay current on the features and functions that technology can deliver.

Flexibility

Don't worry; nothing about business analysis requires you to take yoga classes. The flexibility we're talking about here is the way you respond to changes on a project. Flexibility is important because the question isn't whether changes will occur on a project; it's *when* changes will occur. You need to be able to roll with the punches calmly and change gears swiftly.

Scope can be expanded, new features discussed, and possibilities tossed around, all of which may lead to change. Refusing to change along with the project doesn't bode very well for you as the BA or for the project team as a whole and may cause project defects. In fact, you probably have to be the most flexible because you're at the center of the communication. You have to be able to adapt to changes on a project and adjust accordingly. The more quickly you accept the change, the more time you have to steer the project in the new direction.

Flexibility isn't just about being adaptable to changes to project requirements. You often have to be flexible when the human aspect of your project (such as team members) changes.

Getting to Know the IIBA BABOK

In 2003, a group of professionals involved with business analysis got together with a mission to help promote the profession, certify practitioners, and have a space for the community to share experiences and learn from each other. Thus, the International Institute of Business Analysis (IIBA) was born. Today, IIBA is responsible for maintaining the *Guide to the Business Analysis Body of Knowledge (BABOK Guide)*. The *BABOK Guide* describes business analysis areas of knowledge, associated activities, and the tasks and skills a BA must do/have in order to be effective.

The *BABOK Guide* isn't a BA how-to manual (which may be what led you to purchase this book). Instead, it's a framework of six areas of knowledge:

- ✔ **Business analysis planning and monitoring:** Figuring out which activities are needed in order to perform the effort contained inside the project scope

- ✔ **Elicitation:** Getting information from stakeholders

- ✔ **Requirements management and communication:** Engaging the project team, sponsors, and stakeholders to keep them informed of project progress, scope alignment, changes to the scope, and the explanation of requirements

- ✔ **Enterprise analysis:** Finding and clarifying the real need to meet the strategic goals of the enterprise

- ✔ **Requirements analysis:** Classifying and prioritizing requirements in order to develop the solution

- ✔ **Solution assessment and validation:** Assessing which of the potential solutions best fits the business need and assessing the performance and effectiveness of the solution

In addition to these knowledge areas, the *BABOK Guide* covers another, equally important area that isn't considered a knowledge area: underlying competencies. *Underlying competencies* are skills an effective BA should have in order to perform as an effective business analyst. They consist of analytical thinking and problem solving, behavioral characteristics (such as ethics, trustworthiness, and personal organization), business knowledge, communication skills, interaction skills, and software application knowledge. (Many of these are the same as/related to the essential skills we discuss in the earlier section "Considering the Skills of a Successful BA.")

Pursuing Business Analysis Certification

Why get certified? This is a question BAs are still discussing on business analysis chat forums, and there are a lot of reasons why. Basically, though, it comes down to showing you have the requisite skills and experience to be effective in performing business analysis in the industry. In other words, a certification verifies that that a third party — the IIBA — has recognized you have "the right stuff."

The IIBA began offering certifications in November 2006 and provides an industry certification that measures a BA's knowledge of the BABOK. IIBA currently offers two levels of certification: certification of competency in business analysis (CCBA) and certified business analysis professional (CBAP). You can find the specific requirements on the association's website at www.iiba.org.

Many training vendors also offer certifications based on IIBA's business analysis curriculum. For example, B2T Training's curriculum aligns with the BABOK and helps prepare individuals for both IIBA certifications and B2T Training certifications.

You can find a lot of different certification programs, and the money and time you spend on them varies widely. For example, some certificate programs offered by training providers test your knowledge; the cost of earning the certificate is typically included in the cost of taking the courses. Here's what these programs often entail:

- ✔ You need to take a certain number of courses designated by the training provider.
- ✔ You may have to pass an exam after each course.
- ✔ You get your certificate after completing the courses and passing necessary exams.

Some certification programs involve a little more effort from the student, including prerequisites such as the following:

- ✔ You have to have had a certain amount of work experience, complete with references.
- ✔ You have to have had some formal BA training.

Other training providers have programs that both test your knowledge and incorporate a competency portion where you must show you can perform the work. These programs have a combination of tests and demonstration.

Evaluate certification programs and select the appropriate option based on your corporate and personal professional goals.

Chapter 2

Breaking Down the Different Levels of Business Analysis

In This Chapter

▶ Identifying the different levels of analysis work

▶ Comparing and contrasting analysis efforts at each level

▶ Identifying the key people and critical challenges at each level of analysis

*E*ssentially, you perform business analysis at four main levels within a company: the enterprise level, the organizational level, the operational level, and the project level. When taking on most projects as a business analyst (BA), you perform analysis on one level only, although analysis at any level always needs to support the company's overall goals, mission, and objectives. Most often, multiple projects come together to meet multiple operational goals, which then meet multiple organizational area goals, which in turn meet the big picture strategy of an enterprise.

All parts of a company — including your and others' analysis projects — need to work together to optimize efforts and maximize success. This criteria means that even if you set out to analyze on just one level, you may end up analyzing on any and all levels during your project. As we mention throughout this book, being a BA requires a lot of flexibility and fluidity, beginning with the level at which you work.

In this chapter, we detail the characteristics of each level and provide examples of when you may need to perform them. We also point out common challenges and explain how all the levels relate to each other.

Checking out an Overview of the Levels

Each level of analysis is distinct from but related to the others in a hierarchy that builds from the top down, as you can see in Figure 2-1. The topmost level — enterprise — contains just one entity, but the bottom level — project — has many entities. The concept makes more sense if you break it down by level, starting at the top:

- ✔ The *enterprise level* offers the biggest picture of a company. It's where you do the most strategic work and where the highest-priority and most-visible projects usually reside.

- ✔ The *organizational level* is the collection of distinct business areas or general regions that make up a company.

- ✔ The *operational level* features the various tasks — often divided into specific departments or divisions — performed in order to run an organization.

- ✔ The *project level* is the level at which you execute projects to deliver support or enable the company's organizational areas and/or operational functions to achieve their objectives.

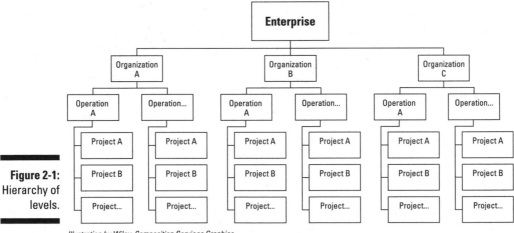

Figure 2-1:
Hierarchy of levels.

Illustration by Wiley, Composition Services Graphics

The levels aren't always so clearly defined, however. Figure 2-2 shows a structure that's more like a matrix for a fictional technology company called Computer Central. Before analyzing a potential opportunity or problem within a company such as this one, you must identify how the company levels interact and know where your project exists among them.

For example, say Computer Central develops a new piece of hardware for one of its existing market segments to support the enterprise's strategic objectives of having a larger presence. At an organizational level, the company is concerned with the development and delivery of the new product. At the operational level, it's concerned with marketing, shipping, and accounting for the product sales. And finally, this hardware initiative results in multiple projects that reside across the various organizational and operational levels (and ultimately, the enterprise level).

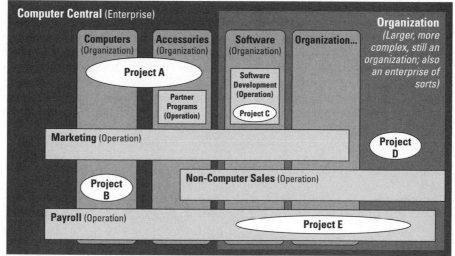

Figure 2-2:
Matrix of
levels.

Illustration by Wiley, Composition Services Graphics

Going to the Top: The Enterprise Level

When we talk about the enterprise level, we don't mean a deck on the spaceship from *Star Trek;* we're referring to the level at which strategic company decisions happen and then trickle down through the company, impacting policies and procedures at all levels. The enterprise level is the collective whole of a company viewed from the highest perspective — such as a parent organization — and contains more than one organizational level. For example, think of a company like Turner Broadcasting System, Inc. It has organizational levels that include news networks such as CNN and entertainment networks such as TNT and Cartoon Network. Even smaller independent companies, such as a law firm or a department of the local or federal government, make decisions on an enterprise level.

This level of analysis is often the starting point for a brand-new project and provides context for your requirements analysis and solution development (more on this topic in Chapter 5). When you analyze at this level, you can reveal to companies where they have a gap or are operating ineffectively. Enterprise-level analysis also enables you and the company to determine whether the company should go into a new business area or expand an existing area farther (like how Apple grew from just selling computers to offering MP3 players and tablets) and whether the company should purchase or sell to another company (such as when Google purchased YouTube). Performing enterprise analysis involves big-picture thinking to positively and strategically impact the entire company.

When doing analysis at this level, you most often work with the senior leaders of the company, such as the chief executive officer (CEO), chief information officer (CIO), chief financial officer (CFO), and chief operating officer (COO). This level of leadership is referred to as the *C level.* Most organizations have departments that focus primarily on enterprise strategic planning and development that consist of executives and marketing, research, and financial analysts. Depending on the strategic initiative, individuals from other levels, such as organizational or operational, may also be involved.

BAs don't often work at this level until much later in their careers, so your main task until then is to make sure your work on the lower levels always supports this level.

Doing business analysis activities at the enterprise level

Enterprise-level analysis focuses on optimizing interactions across multiple organizations within a company to benefit the whole. Business analysis activities that take place at this level include the following:

- ✔ Defining the *business needs* — the rules that govern the company (see Chapters 5 and 8)

- ✔ Eliciting goals and competitive product analysis (Chapter 7)

- ✔ Mapping *as is* (current) state and *to be* (future) state company processes and process reengineering (Chapter 13)

- ✔ Defining the *business case,* or the reasons you're going forward with a project (Chapter 9)

- ✔ Defining *solution scope* — what the boundaries of your project are (Chapter 10)

- ✔ Determining *solution approach,* or the way to solve the problem at hand (Chapter 12)

Overcoming challenges at the enterprise level

Working with senior leaders in any size company comes with challenges. For starters, you typically can get only a limited amount of time with these folks; in large organizations, they may be spread across different offices, which makes getting the group together when necessary extra difficult.

For this reason, you need to have clear goals regarding what you want to accomplish in every meeting with senior leaders. You need to be very confident in your techniques and have a plan for how you'll approach each interaction. Know each leader's preferred communication style and use it during meetings with them, while providing them with updates, and in presentations related to the initiative. See Chapter 11 for more on creating a stakeholder communication plan.

Another obstacle at this level is access. You may need access to market and competitive information or financial information (including salaries) that is typically confidential and not shared openly with everyone in the organization. If you aren't authorized to receive info you need, you have to get creative. Find someone who does have access and have her provide the answer in a format that doesn't give detailed confidential information but provides enough to perform your analysis.

For example, Kupe worked on a strategic initiative analyzing a core process that spanned multiple business areas of a company. One of the pieces of information he was analyzing was the cost of doing the process. including salary information he didn't have access to. To get what he needed, Kupe just asked individuals who had access to provide him with a total salary number for groups of individuals across the business areas.

Moving to the Organizational Level

The organizational level is the level just below enterprise; it refers to the company's general areas or large regions. Organizational analysis focuses on optimizing the activities and processes within these individual organizational silos as opposed to the interactions between them (which is the domain of enterprise-level analysis).

Depending on the organization's size, a separate strategic group may work to define goals and prioritize projects within the organization. As a BA, you need to spend some time with this group to understand the goals and priorities within the organization and properly plan your projects. The people you interact with at this level of analysis are one layer below executive leaders —

most likely directors or VPs of the different business areas. Their main focus is on their specific domains. Think about the division of Microsoft responsible for the Xbox. The leaders of that business area (or organization) probably don't put much thought into how the sales of Microsoft Office are going; their concerns relate only to Xbox.

When you're doing analysis at the organizational level, understanding the enterprise-level goals helps you prioritize and plan efforts at the organizational level. Say one organization within a company brings you on to develop and roll out a new piece of hardware, but you discover that the enterprise has placed a higher priority on rolling out a different product for a different market segment. In this case, the organization may not want to fund the project or support its development after all, given the priorities on the enterprise level. Even if the enterprise approves the project to begin with, the project may be stalled during the development.

Fulfilling duties at the organizational level

The activities you perform on this level are generally the same as at the enterprise level, but the scope and specific problems you solve are different. You can imagine the organization areas as enterprises of their own that roll up to the parent enterprise. For example, say a company has a strategic plan at the enterprise level to broaden its market reach by increasing the number of computers it sells. The company has three organizations: one that sells computers, another that sells computer accessories (such as keyboards and monitors), and a third that sells software products. On the organizational analysis level, you work with each separate organization to develop a strategic plan specific to each area. Those plans then fit together into the broader picture to meet the ultimate goal of selling more computers.

For each organization, the business analysis tasks you do include the following:

✔ Conducting strategic plan development for the organization (flip to Chapter 9)

✔ Facilitating strategic goal setting sessions and performing competitive product analysis specific to an organization, using competitive analysis as an elicitation technique (Chapter 7)

✔ Defining success metrics for the organization and aligning them with the strategic direction of the enterprise (Chapter 9)

✔ Understanding how workflow is used to implement changes in process reengineering (Chapter 15)

✔ Replicating enterprise analysis activities, including

- Defining business need (Chapter 9)

- Assessing capability gaps (Chapter 9)

- Process mapping the current and future states, using workflow as a tool to identify and define your processes (Chapter 13)

In the end, these efforts need to tie back into the goals and strategy of the larger enterprise.

Dealing with organizational-level obstacles

The big challenge you encounter when performing organizational analysis is that the leaders of each organizational unit may not care about integration points among other organizational units throughout the company. These leaders own and control their domains and are responsible for the success or failure of their specific areas. You may identify gaps and overlaps among the organizations, but each individual organization may decide those gaps aren't its problem, especially if it's currently working efficiently and successfully as a stand-alone entity.

We aren't saying that the organization leaders don't care about the enterprise's goals and needs; the leaders are rewarded and judged based on how their organizations perform, so that's where their focus is. If an effort takes a leader's time away from her organization and she doesn't know how it will help her particular area, she'll be less inclined to play along. You can mitigate this situation by always reminding each organization leader how the project will positively impact her personal area. Demonstrate the project's relevance and importance as it relates specifically to each leader's domain, and your work will be infinitely easier.

Also, if an organizational-level project makes changes to processes or systems that impact another organizational or operational level, it can cause conflicts and expand the scope of analysis necessary for the project. Although the project may result in resolving a problem for one organization silo, it may actually cause a problem for another silo. As a business analysis professional, you're responsible for highlighting the potential conflicts and identifying how the scope will increase so the leaders of the organization can make an informed decision on how to move forward. They may decide not to expand scope because doing so may result in problems for another organization. That outcome is okay; you did your due diligence and explained the consequences to the leaders so they could make the decision they needed to.

Drilling Down to the Operational Level

The operational level is another step down in the hierarchy, so now you're getting into more specific areas here, such as departments within the company's regions or divisions. In an entertainment company, for example, you find the programming division (which leads the effort to purchase, create, and schedule programming) and the network operations division that gets the shows on the air.

Most organizations that have large initiatives resulting in multiple projects set up program managers or departments to manage the entire rollout of the initiative. At this level, you work with individual department heads or line managers, such as the sales director or the head of marketing. These folks are responsible for a specific process or multiple processes within an organization.

Knowing your tasks at the operational level

At this level, you should focus your business analysis efforts on developing a *program* (a group of projects that allow the operational area to achieve the goal of the organizational or enterprise level initiative). For example, to roll out a new hardware product to a market segment, you'd launch several projects, including developing a marketing campaign, updating systems that support the purchase of and payments for the product, and incorporating new processes for product delivery and maintenance.

Some of the BA's activities on this level are similar to those for the enterprise and organizational levels we discuss earlier in the chapter, in that leaders at this level are concerned with the goals and strategy for their departments. However, more-detailed analysis activities take place here:

✔ New project or product business case development or project proposals (see Chapter 9)

✔ *Feasibility studies* — understanding whether the organization can really accomplish an objective with a particular solution (Chapter 8)

✔ Process modeling across operations area — diagramming with workflows (Chapter 13)

✔ Product definition — using elicitation to uncover the requirements making up the product (Chapters 6 and 7)

✔ Project vision definition — identifying the direction for the project and putting boundaries around the solution (Chapter 10)

✔ Creating and managing project metrics/measurements — creating an effective plan (Chapter 11)

Note: At this stage, while you are working on a document that will be involved in a project, you are at the operational level. The documents you work on will turn into projects (probably), but you get involved with them at this point.

✔ Transition requirement development — moving from planning into implementing and understanding all that implementation entails (Chapter 15)

Taking on operational-level challenges

Operational leaders tend to look only at their own areas and at being more efficient and more effective to help reach the organizational goals. The operation managers may have a sole focus on their departments, but they also need to understand how they fit into the organizational goals, which fit into the enterprise goals.

This risk extends beyond the higher-ups as well. At the operational level, company employees are responsible for supporting the ongoing operational needs of the business and have very little time to work on new initiatives or provide innovative ideas for improvement. They need to do things like sell advertising, program shows, and keep the business running. This load alone isn't an easy task at any company, so asking them to stop and think about where they can improve or add another product to the mix adds stress for them.

However, after a company identifies and launches an initiative (like your project), you must engage these individuals in refining the current processes. Eventually, these employees will be responsible for supporting the new processes, so their participation now is key.

Learning as much as possible about the enterprise and organizational goals and strategy helps you as a business analysis professional to guide and advise the operation leaders. Use this knowledge to support the operation leaders' improvement. If you know their business well, you can help drive the initiative forward while allowing the employees to stay engaged with both the project and their regular operational responsibilities.

You can accomplish this balancing act by spending time observing the work done in the operations area and asking questions of the people who work in the business. A great time for this interaction is over lunch with employees, where you can get to know them better, find out more about their business, and understand what drives them. If you follow this strategy with your operational leaders, you can better represent them on projects. And as for observation, just ask to sit and watch how someone does her job. People love showing what they do and how they do it!

Getting a Handle on the Project Level

The project level is the lowest level of analysis and is where most of the business analysis work at companies happens (because each enterprise has a handful of organizations, many operational areas for each organization, and many projects per operation area); Figure 2-1 earlier in the chapter shows you a graphical breakdown of this alignment. Therefore, the business analysis profession is highly focused on the project area.

The people you deal with on a regular basis at this level include your solution team members, your project managers, development staff (if you're on a software development project), and quality assurance analysts. On the business side, you work with subject matter experts and users of the solution. Understanding the people you work with on the project is important, so in Chapters 3 and 11, we provide more information for conducting stakeholder analysis.

Tackling activities at the project level

A project delivers a solution that's meant to enable the operation area to achieve its goals. For example, if a computer company wants to sell more laptop computers and has made a decision to start selling them directly to consumers rather than through retail stores, it needs to initiate a number of projects in order to implement the new goal, such as creating a website where customers can search for items, order products, and track their orders.

Because this level is where BAs do most of their work, the rest of the book focuses on this level of analysis in great detail. For now, you should know that although your team can take different project approaches to deliver your project or solution (as we discuss in Chapter 11), the activities you perform at this level remain the same:

✔ Planning your analysis work for the project (see Chapter 11)

✔ Scoping the project — understanding a business case, creating and maintaining the requirements scope for a project (Chapters 9 and 10)

✔ Eliciting and analyzing the business problem or opportunity and understanding the true business need (Chapters 5 through 8)

✔ Eliciting, analyzing, and communicating the solution requirements (Chapters 12 and 13)

✔ Verifying that the solution you're building addresses the need and helps the business reach its goals (Chapter 14)

✔ Developing transition requirements — moving from planning into implementing and understanding all that implementation entails (Chapter 15)

At first read of the preceding bullets, you may think that this book's organization doesn't match up to the project activity chronology. But there's a method to our madness. Even though planning is the first thing you do on a project, it requires a certain amount of foundational understanding. As BA trainers, we actually teach our planning class late in our curriculum because our students need to know all the techniques available before they can plan.

Rising above project-level hurdles

Much like at the operational level, getting time from the key project-level people you need is difficult. These folks are doing the work day in and day out. They're paid to work for the business, not to work on your project. Although helping improve the current state of the business is part of their jobs, getting the time you need out of them is tough if they're behind on their day-to-day work. To overcome this challenge, concentrate on collaborating with your peers and building good relationships with your teammates. Find out everyone's strengths and determine as a team how to work well together. Remind folks (including yourself) that on projects, everyone is part of a larger team. Head to Chapter 11 for more on getting stakeholders involved.

You need to be aware of how your project fits into the bigger picture of the business. As a business analyst, you're in the perfect spot to see when a project is no longer aligned with the higher goals of the enterprise. Don't lose the forest for the trees. Build spots into your project where you do a sanity check — that is, you make sure the project is still aligned with operational, organizational, and enterprise goals. These goals can change during the life of the project, so if you don't periodically stop and check, you can drive yourself (and everyone else) crazy when you realize later that you've just completed a project that no longer adds any value to the company!

Chapter 3

Identifying and Working with Stakeholders

In This Chapter

▶ Understanding who participates in projects

▶ Knowing the people in your neighborhood: your stakeholders

▶ Figuring out how best to work with various stakeholders

▶ Striving toward effective communication

*S*takeholder is a generic term for a person or a group of people who have an interest in an initiative and will be affected by it (directly or indirectly) or have influence over it. In other words, your stakeholders may not necessarily be a part of your project team, so you may have to think outside the box when identifying them.

Consider a project to create a new application to support order fulfillment. Obviously, the order fulfillment, warehouse, and distribution departments are stakeholders, but how about the internal technical support desk? They aren't part of the project team, but they'll be impacted by the initiative because they'll field technical support questions when the system rolls out. This role makes the people in this group stakeholders.

In this chapter, we discuss working with different stakeholders as you perform business analysis. Some of them are internal to the company, while others are external. These people have many unique titles, but what they have in common is that they're all relevant to the project in one way or another. We explain how to understand who these people are, how to figure out their degree of involvement in the project, and how to best work with them.

Reviewing a Who's Who of Potential Project Participants

Many roles are required to complete a project successfully: management roles (for providing information) and other roles (for creating and delivering the right solution). *Note:* Even though we use common job titles to categorize the different roles, don't get hung up on the titles. It's more important that you recognize what roles are needed for what purpose. The titles used in your company may be different.

Starting at the top with management

The people on the management side hold titles such as executive sponsor, account manager, product manager, and project manager. These people manage the project and business areas and are generally the highest-ranking member of the project.

Executive sponsor

The *executive sponsor* is the *raison d'etre* of the project or initiative — the person who initiates the project, has a vision of what the end product should be, and comes up with the project to accomplish it. The project may be integrating a commercial off-the-shelf (*COTS*) tool or improving the efficiency of a claims process. The executive sponsor also provides the funding for the project (after all, he's the one who wants it done, so he has to pony up the money).

An executive sponsor

- Approves project scope and signs-off on requirements
- Is most interested in high-level information and how it relates to the funding of the project
- Generally isn't concerned with the detailed, day-to-day operations and minutiae of the project

 If a stalemate regarding the project's direction ever occurs, the buck really does stop at the executive sponsor. Why? Simple: He's the one paying for the project.

Account manager/product manager

The *account* (or *product*) *manager* may hold a higher-level manager title, but this person defines the overall requirements and marketing approach for the product. Account/product managers are representatives of the external customer; they're the intermediaries between the external customer and the business, finding out what the customer wants and creating product requirements based on that information.

The account or product manager

- ✔ Makes decisions regarding project direction
- ✔ Reviews project requirements and may also review overall project requirements with the executive sponsor and guide/advise him on sign-off
- ✔ Generally has decision-making authority
- ✔ Is more involved with the project than the executive sponsor

Note: Don't get caught up in the exact title of the person performing this role. Someone with the title of project manager or some other title may play this role.

Project manager

The *project manager* (PM) is responsible for managing the project, including the project plan, the project scope and deliverables, and the *work breakdown structure* (WBS). The WBS is the detailed task list outlining who is responsible for each task, the amount of time to complete, and the dependencies each task has on another. During project execution, the PM ensures the project scope continues to align with the project objectives, and he raises any concerns with the adjusted project plan, including any missed dates or expired deadlines.

As the project moves forward and new opportunities or product features are discussed, the PM ensures that changes in scope are relevant to the scope and align with the project goal. The PM will probably look to you for help with understanding the impact that a scope change has to the project; he then reports those scope changes in terms of the project impact to the executive sponsor.

A project manager

- ✔ Identifies and staffs the appropriate project team members
- ✔ Creates the project plan for the overall project and seeks input on the requirements plan from the business analyst
- ✔ Reports on status for the entire project
- ✔ Manages the project risk plan and executes risk responses if a risk is realized

✔ Addresses and overcomes project barriers affecting completion of the project

✔ Looks to the BA for updates on the progress of the requirements phase

✔ Manages the project change control process, working with the BA to address project impact during change control

Sometimes, you may find yourself playing the dual-role of BA/PM, which can be a challenge because of the natural conflict between roles. The BA function focuses on analyzing items of the project; the PM function focuses on meeting the project dates. If you tend to like one role more than the other, be careful not to concentrate on one at the expense of the other.

Seeking subject matter experts

Subject matter experts (SMEs) are —surprise! — experts in the particular business or solution area you are working in for your project. These are the people you interview in order to craft your business requirements. You work with two kinds of subject matter experts: *domain experts* and *implementation experts.*

Domain subject matter experts

Domain SMEs are the people who provide project objectives, potential problems, and risks from the business perspective. They're businesspeople, and their job is understanding the business.

To get to the right domain SME for your project, make sure you understand the subject matter expertise and who can best explain it. For instance, if you're looking for information about a flight management system, you probably want to talk to a pilot, but if you're interested in the maintenance of that system, you want to talk to an aircraft mechanic. In any domain, make sure you're asking the person who actually performs the job. Other people may have an idea about how it's done, but the best person to ask is the person who performs the process.

Domain SMEs also set the priority of the project objectives and the requirements based on what they need to accomplish from the business perspective. You may help them prioritize by giving them guidance on impacts and analysis, but ultimately, they own the business area and the prioritization. Understand that addressing the most critical business requirements (business needs) is the value attached to the prioritization on the requirements, so it's very important to understand the difference between the business requirement and a solution.

A domain SME

- ✔ Provides information about the business and specific business terms

- ✔ Provides detailed requirements related to business processes and data

- ✔ Offers suggestions as to potential solutions to the business problem or opportunity related to the project

- ✔ Assists in defining project scope

- ✔ Works with the BA on user interfaces, business processes, data, and business rule definition

- ✔ Reviews detailed requirements documents, user interfaces, business process diagrams, and other deliverables to validate that the project and solution is right for the business

Because domain subject matter experts typically work within the problem area for a long time, they often figure out work-arounds and solutions to their problems and want you to use them as the project solution. Don't take their word for it, though; forge ahead with your process. You may find that the SMEs' solutions are viable in the end, but you must give them a fair analysis.

Implementation subject matter expert

The implementation SME is the one who provides technical expertise on how to develop a solution to solve the business's problem. In a software environment, you're talking about someone like the developer, lead developer, or software architect. In a warehousing business area, it may be a logistics expert or warehousing engineer.

Implementation SMEs provide possible solutions to solve the business problem and can respond and provide guidance about other possible solutions. For example, if a solution or screen design may not be possible with the current limitations of tools, the implementation SME will work to guide the solution team down a path to create a feasible solution. Generally, the majority of the resources come into the project at the phase when you're creating some sort of project solution.

An implementation SME

- ✔ Guides the project team on possible solutions to the business problem

- ✔ Works with the BA to create user interfaces and makes sure the interface supports the real work of the business

- ✔ Ensures that the suggested solutions are feasible from an implementation perspective and provides guidance on the impact of alternate approaches

Adding project support personnel

Project support personnel are those who support the project in various ways as it moves along. They're usually not assigned as 100 percent full-time resources on any one project; rather, they function as specialists supporting multiple projects within an organization. They allocate their time based on the project priority within the organization. Think of these people as advisors or consultants.

For instance, unless you're building an application to support the legal department, you probably don't need to understand the legal department's business processes. But a few members of that department may be stakeholders within your project. They may give you guidelines about how long to store customer data or what types of customer data you're allowed to store. You may have to run a solution the group comes up with by legal to get it approved. Of course, legal isn't the only department that falls into this category. If you're designing user interfaces for external customers, you may need a usability engineer or information architect.

 You can understand where the project support people are within the organization, to what extent you need their advice, and how much time they have to support your project by looking at the organizational chart or by asking other stakeholders and even BAs who are in other areas of the business.

Project support personnel

✔ May be involved in providing the group with constraints for the solution, based on what the team is designing

✔ Are assigned to your project and act in a consulting capacity

✔ Are experts in the subject matter they're working within and are brought into your project as a *project support person* (PSP)

✔ Guide the project team within their particular advisory subject matter area

Organization change management professional

The *organization change management professional* facilitates acceptance of solutions, creates the change management plans, and advocates the need for the change. Usually, you find organization change management professionals assigned to big, highly strategic, company-wide projects such as switching 4,500 account executives to a new sales system.

As a BA, do you find you do these things? You probably answered yes, and you're right: On many projects, this role usually falls to the BA rather than to a separate resource. See more on this in Chapter 15.

Regulators

Regulators are the people and organizations creating guidelines and possibly constraints on your project and solution. Think of them as the legal department within your organization; they specify what you can and can't do with your project. You may be implementing a solution to ensure that your organization adheres to industry or government regulations. Additionally, they may guide how you have to produce some of your deliverables. In the case of the armed forces, for example, certain documentation must conform to U.S. defense standards in order to be accepted by the customer. Similarly, communications companies must adhere to guidelines imposed by the Federal Communications Committee (FCC). The regulators also impose audit standards around the project.

Technical writer

The *technical writer* writes the software manuals, online help and web page help text, and user training manuals. The tech writer understands both how the solution functions and the audience who will be reading the produced tech manuals. Technical writers are mainly concerned with requirements such as the workflows (or process maps/diagrams) and the external agents or actors (the people who will be using the system). Although they deal with technical "stuff," they support the project only when necessary.

Turning to technical personnel

The technical personnel are those resources (the corporate way of saying *people*) on a project who help address how technology supports and fulfills the business requirements. If the solution for your project is a technical one, they build the solution. The earlier they are involved in the project, the better. They can provide guidance if the suggested solution isn't technologically feasible.

Some of the duties technical personnel perform include designing the solution and system security, system architecture, and network architecture. They also create the interfaces with other computer systems and databases.

Technical personnel also assist the testing effort by unit testing the programs and modules they write as part of the proposed project solution. They make sure the modules work well independently prior to integration testing. They may also help with integration testing.

Technical personnel

- ✔ Are interested in how the software needs to support the business need.

- ✔ Need to understand the business and solution requirements so they can code a solution that matches what the business needs.

✔ Interact with the BA to fully understand the needs of the business.

✔ Work best with others who have some technical knowledge. You don't have to be able to speak in computer programming language, but you do need to know the basics that are relevant to your project.

Make sure the technical personnel's efforts support the original business requirements and functional design. You don't want the technical personnel to develop a solution that does not address the business need. A programmer who states, "I know what the business needs better than the business does," isn't the kind of programmer you want on the project. He'll program what he thinks the business wants even though the business states something completely different. The best way to overcome this issue is to bring the programmers in during the design phase or earlier. Then they can offer suggestions and make the user interface work within the boundaries of the system. When they're involved early, they have a stake in the solution (because they helped design it) and will be hesitant to change it unnecessarily during the course of the implementation.

Usability engineer

Usability engineers primarily design user interfaces. People in this position have experience with how humans interact with machines, and they bring insight to the field of man–machine interface. If you're working on a *customer-facing* application (an application used by public consumers versus internally or on the backend), you're probably more likely to have one of these people on your project. Think of Apple. Many people think Apple's products are easier to use than a competitor's product, and that's because Apple has people that understand how users interface with a product and address that need to make it easier.

Usability engineers also assess usability for user interfaces they didn't necessarily design and may assist with testing for defects that may inhibit usability of the solution.

Quality assurance personnel

Quality assurance (QA) personnel are responsible for assuring the team delivers a quality product. On a project, their first initiative is to review the project requirements and write test plans. These people are a very big help for the BA, so you want to befriend them early on in the project. They look at every requirement to make sure they can test it and verify it. If they can't verify it, then the requirement is not clear enough. This will mean the technical team won't have clarity on how the solution should address that requirement. By looking at your requirements early on, they can filter out ambiguous statements such as "The software should be easy to use."

QA folks are also responsible for setting up the test environments, writing test cases, executing and overseeing testing activities, and reporting and following up on defects.

Database administrator

The *database administrator (DBA),*sometimes called a *data administrator*, looks at data from an enterprise-wide perspective. The project you work on will most likely use data. Instead of creating a brand-new database, the DBA looks to see where data already exists within the organization and whether it can be reused for the project. He also provides data-naming standards and conventions.

As a BA, you may consult with the DBA on logical data modeling techniques. Your job isn't to design a database, but you should work on the logical relationships from a business perspective. The DBA can help with that from his data knowledgebase. A DBA generally wants to help because he's ultimately responsible for designing the physical database.

Identifying the Stakeholders in Your Project

The project participants also have project-related roles and duties that are separate (although related) from their professional responsibilities (which we lay out in the earlier section "Reviewing a Who's Who of Potential Project Participants"). Just like actors in a play, stakeholders have roles in the project. Someone may have the title of Retail Sales Person Level 1, but they're the SME for the retail sales project, which ends up being their role in the project.

You use two main steps in identifying your cast of stakeholders: a *stakeholder list* and an *RACI matrix*.

Find your stakeholders

The first thing to do is look for all the stakeholders (anyone who impacts or is impacted) on the project. A stakeholder is a group or person who has interests that may be affected by an initiative or has influence over it. Stakeholders can be found anywhere for a project. If you identify a group or department, make sure you identify the correct individual stakeholders within a stakeholder group. Someone has to be the point person.

Here's how to create a stakeholder list:

1. **Analyze the project documentation.**

   Look for people, groups, departments, customers, and project team members affected by the project. (For info on how to successfully analyze documentation, visit Chapter 7). *Note:* Go directly to Step 2 if no documentation is available.

2. **Pull project team members together to brainstorm about other affected parties that aren't included in the documentation.**

3. **Make a stakeholder list.**

   Your list should include the stakeholder, whether he has sign-off authority, and how he's affected by the project (his *stake*).

You may also want to include a "Notes" column in your stakeholder list to keep track of effective ways of communicating with the stakeholder or other reminders (see Figure 3-1 for an example of how to lay it out). Just be careful about what you write and with whom you share the notes; you don't want your personal notes to be taken the wrong way or end up in the wrong hands.

Name	Title	Role	External Agent	Sign-off Authority	Notes
John Smith	VP of Marketing	Executive Sponsor	No	Yes	Wants big picture, bullet points
Jane Brown	Project Manager	Project Manager			Prefers daily updates
Marcia Karmak	Sr. Business Systems Analyst	Business Analyst	No	No	
Jim House	Marketing Administrator	SME, Marketing	No	No	Will validate/review and advise the executive sponsor on the requirements
Dave Stringent	QA Analyst	Quality Assurance	No	Yes	
Outside Advertising Agency	Ad execs	SMEs, content creation	Yes	No	
Bob Smith	Sr. DBA	Database Admin	No	Yes	Knows system interfaces and data feeds inside and out

Figure 3-1:
A stakeholder list is a good way to keep important details organized.

Illustration by Wiley, Composition Services Graphics

Using the RACI matrix

Another tool you can use is an RACI matrix. *RACI* stands for Responsible, Accountable, Consulted, and Informed. It's basically a chart that shows the different responsibilities people hold on your project. By thinking through the chart and presenting it to the project team as an official deliverable, you can help everyone understand who's doing what on the project.

You and the stakeholders should create the matrix together to ensure that it's accurate and that everyone is on the same page.

Here's how to assemble an RACI matrix (check out Figure 3-2 to see an example):

1. **List all the actions or responsibilities needed for the project along the left side of the page.**

2. **List all the stakeholders for the project along the top of the page.**

3. **Fill in each box with *R, A, C,* or *I* to describe the person's level of responsibility.**

   Each letter corresponds to a level of responsibility:

   - **Responsible:** The actual person performing the work. For instance, in the case of the requirements package, the BA is generally responsible for the work. For the technical documentation, it's usually the implementation SME.

   - **Accountable:** The one ultimately answerable for the correct completion of the deliverable or task and who delegates the work to the responsible party. This person also approves (signs off on) the deliverable or task. You can specify only one accountable for each task or deliverable.

   - **Consulted:** Those whose opinions are sought, typically SMEs, and with whom you have two-way communication. Your project support personnel are typically consulted parties.

   - **Informed:** Those who are kept up-to-date on progress. This communication is usually one-way — for example, the BA informs the external stakeholders that the requirements phase is complete.

4. **Distribute the matrix to all stakeholders**.

   This dissemination keeps everyone on track and informed.

Roles aren't 100 percent exclusive. Remember, these roles are just parts in the overall project play. Just like some actors play multiple roles in films (Mike Myers in the *Austin Powers* movies comes to mind), stakeholders on a project may wear multiple hats and play different roles.

Task	Executive Sponsor	Project Manager	Business Analyst	Business SME	QA	Usability Engineer	Regulator (Legal)	DBA	Tech Writer	Technical Personnel
Obtain funding for project	A	I								
Create business case	R	A	C							
Create requirements phase estimates		A	R	C						
Create design phase estimates		A	R							C
Create build phase estimates		A				C	C	C		R
Create implementation phase estimates		R/A	C						C	C
Create WBS (Project Plan)		R/A	C							C
Elicit business processes and requirements	I	A	R	C						
Design Solution		A	R	C	C	C	C	C		R
Create Implementation material		A		C					R	C

Figure 3-2: Create and distribute an RACI matrix to keep all stakeholders on track.

Illustration by Wiley, Composition Services Graphics

Playing (and Communicating) Well with Others

As the BA, you need to be able to figure out the best way to communicate with each team member. Your communication and interaction styles with each team member vary based on your relationship. The tips and communication styles we discuss later in this section are just a starting point. Treat each team member as an individual, do what you can to get to know him well, and communicate with him accordingly; it goes a long way in making your BA work successful. For example, if you develop a really good relationship with an executive, your communication style is going to be a lot more intimate (and, therefore, probably more fruitful) than with a team member you don't know as well.

Because communication is at the heart of everything a BA does, spending time honing your communication skills is important. Even the most experienced business analysis professional can find something in this section to improve about the way he shares information.

Targeting your communication to the various stakeholders

A message is only as good as how it's received. Take the time now to get familiar with the ins and outs of different stakeholders; it pays off in dividends down the line.

Working with executive sponsors

On a project, the executive sponsor is the your most important stakeholder. He controls the funding for the project, has expectations about what the project will deliver, and will decide if the project is successful or not. Following are some good questions to think about asking the sponsor to find out what the sponsor needs or expects from the project and the project outcome. Knowing the answers to these questions definitely contributes to project success:

- ✔ Does the executive sponsor have a clear vision of the desired state?

- ✔ Does he or she understand what it will take to get there?

- ✔ Is he or she expecting measurable results? And if so, what are the metrics?

- ✔ Will he or she encourage people to express concerns?

- ✔ Has he or she considered aligning rewards to support the change?

- ✔ Has he or she defined success as a business outcome as opposed to a systems implementation?

- ✔ What is he or she expecting after the project is complete?

- ✔ How often does he or she plan to interact with the project team?

You may not work directly with your sponsor. If that is the case, you'll work closely with other management and need to gain this information from them.

Dealing with domain SMEs

The first thing to understand about domain SMEs is that they're there to do the business of the business. If they sometimes seem to give you short answers or want to just get to the solution quickly, it's because they want to get back to doing the business. So how can you best work with them?

- ✔ **Keep your interactions with them short and to the point.** Look to Chapter 6 for detailed ways to get information from them and notes on which techniques work best based on the size of the group.

- ✔ **Put yourself in their position and learn their business area.** The best strategy isn't to walk in and ask SMEs for their requirements; rather, it's to ask them about their business problems. Because they know the subject so well, they're highly likely to give you solutions.

- ✔ **When you approach them, establish a rapport.** You can briefly talk about the project to set the stage for the discussion topic, but very quickly go into having them explain what they do in their business area related to the project scope.

- ✔ **Keep it in their world.** Don't stray off onto other topics, even if they're project-related. You aren't solving your project; you're solving their business problem.

- ✔ **Proactively notify them about the project and what it's all about.** They'll want to tell you all about their experience with the process and probably will give you many ways to fix it.

- ✔ **Keep it simple.** Use the business area's language rather than project-oriented BA language.

Conferring with project support personnel

Because project support personnel are not fulltime members of the team, you need to be as efficient as possible with their time. Here are a few tips on how to do that:

- ✔ **Proactively point out what you need from them.** Don't make them search through loads of documentation to find what is relevant to them.

- ✔ **Make it short and sweet.** Project support personnel are most interested in how your project interacts with their particular area of support. Don't over-explain all aspects of the project; focus on how it impacts them.

Just like the technical team, don't commit project support people's time or involvement with a project before understanding their time constraints. Asking other parties for information helps establish your credibility as a liaison.

Talking to technical personnel

Although your primary job as a BA is to understand the intricacies of the business, you need to have some technical knowledge so that you can communicate effectively with the tech folks. Here are the situations in which this knowledge can help you:

- ✔ When you have to understand their explanations so you can offer dialogue on the solutions.

- ✔ When you need to validate the solution team's understanding. If a given time estimate seems way off or they say the requirements can't be met, you need to have enough knowledge to recognize that fact and to question their assumptions. In questioning their assumptions, we mean having a good debate so the team comes up with the best solution for the business need.

Don't commit the team to providing a particular solution without consulting the team first. If you want the team to be committed to delivering a solution, the team members need to be part of the process that came up with it.

The same concept applies to the quality assurance team as well. You don't need to be an expert in quality assurance, but the more familiar you are with the processes followed and the techniques used, the more relevant your conversations with them will be.

Using active listening to your advantage

No matter which stakeholder or project team member you're working with, you need to understand active listening in order to be a great communicator. Communicating is vital to a BA's success, but sometimes people forget that listening is just as important as — or maybe more important than — talking (or texting, e-mailing, or even writing this book).

Active listening refers to the level of engagement you have with your communication partner. It involves not only listening but also performing actions that assure your partner that you're truly engaged in listening. Here are some great active listening tips:

- **Listen to the speaker's entire message.** In today's time-is-money environment, you may be tempted to interrupt the speaker because you "know" what he's going to say. But if you don't hear the entire thought, you may miss something important.

- **Ask questions to understand what the other person says.** Open-ended questions are great for eliciting, but when you need to actively listen and confirm, you should ask a closed question that requires only a yes or no answer.

- **Paraphrase to confirm what you heard.** When you paraphrase, use phrases such as "So to let me understand what you're saying . . . ." or "If I heard you correctly . . . ."

Overcoming common barriers to effective communications

We live in a time when so many barriers — some of which even seem to be socially acceptable — hinder communication. The more you understand how these obstacles can get in the way, the more you're prepared to overcome them and be a great communicator. You can find many great communication tips to overcome barriers and exhaustive books on communication topics (check out *Communicating Effectively For Dummies* by Marty Brounstein [Wiley]), but we list some of the most common suggestions here:

✔ **Try to minimize outside distractions so you can focus on your stakeholder completely.** Mobile phones and their land-line brethren, for example, are great communication tools, but when the phone goes off, let it ring. Better yet, turn it to silent or off completely when you're with stakeholders.

If you're expecting an important call, notify the person who comes in and sits down that if that call comes through, you'll have to take it.

✔ **Be aware of and address culture and language differences directly.** As a BA, you work with different people all the time, so it's practically a given that you'll work with people who have different cultures — maybe even languages — from you. And culture and language aren't just about nationality; they can also be about the company itself. When you join a new project, take time upfront to observe how people speak, carry themselves, and interact. Share a bit about your communication style, too. Doing so sets the foundation for open dialogue later down the road if a misunderstanding occurs over words.

Note any special needs and be sure to check in throughout the project to make sure your stakeholders understand you and that you understand them. For example, perhaps a stakeholder is hard of hearing. To prevent that person from missing out on important information, maybe you always come to meetings with pretyped notes or an agenda so everyone can follow along.

✔ **Don't let your past experiences determine your future.** Just because the previous project data administrator was a real jerk doesn't mean the next one will be — or vice versa. Each person has his or her own unique personality. Consciously remind yourself to not let prior experiences with others get in the way of your current relationship.

✔ **Keep meetings from running too long.** Do you how long a meeting can be before people check out and start doing something else? Two hours? One hour? Each company's individual culture dictates the actual number, but from experience, we can tell you that 1 to 1.5 hours is generally about the maximum period people can stay focused without drifting off to e-mail and other tasks. That number is even less if the meeting is a teleconference. If you have to conduct meetings longer than 1 hour, work in a 10-minute break every hour.

One final pointer to facilitate effective communication: Always ask the stakeholders how best to communicate with them; don't automatically assume you know their preferences.

Understanding and responding to verbal and nonverbal messages

Most people believe that words are *the* communication of the message when, in fact, words make up only 7 percent of the message. Tone of voice and nonverbal communication make up the other 93 percent. As a BA, you should be familiar with the positives and pitfalls of common verbal and nonverbal communication, such as the following:

- **Be precise, direct, and accurate in your communications.** Don't be vague or confusing. If a message is unclear, the receiver interprets it negatively 90 percent of the time. Consider your reaction when your boss leaves you a voicemail at 4:30 on Friday telling you he wants to see you Monday morning. Chances are you go through the entire weekend trying to determine what you did wrong, and then when Monday comes around, he tells you a stakeholder passed along an "atta-boy" that he wanted to communicate to you. So you were worried all weekend for nothing. That's what happens when communication is unclear.

- **Be aware of distracting nonverbal communications.** Unnecessary movements, words, and even sounds take attention away from you and decrease the effectiveness of your communication. Think about how you present. Do you stand there comfortably and calmly or do you rock back and forth, look at your watch, and rattle change in your pocket? Know your habits and then seek to remove them as a barrier to the communication process. You may even need to enlist the help of a video camera so you can see yourself presenting, or have a friend to give you feedback. After all, you don't want people to remember you for the number of times you looked at your watch rather than for the actual content of your presentation.

- **Make sure you spell-check everything.** The effect of misspellings or typos may be more powerful than you realize. To you, it may just be a misspelled word, but if it's in a slideshow presentation, you may have just lost your audience. Don't believe it? If you've ever seen a misspelled word in a presentation, what did you do for the remainder of the meeting? You look for misspelled words. Yup. That presenter lost his audience.

Instead of rereading your own communication, have an independent person read it. That person doesn't know what it's supposed to say, so he's more likely to catch mistakes you missed.

Just as you need to be aware of the nonverbal messages you send, you also need to take note of the nonverbal messages you're receiving. If you notice a disconnect between what the stakeholder says and the message he's sending nonverbally, take some time to figure out where the disconnect is. Say, for example, that he's telling you he's very open to your suggestions, but his folded arms and curt tone imply otherwise. You can take a moment to check in with him after the meeting, after everyone else is gone, or maybe send an e-mail later. Maybe he actually isn't okay with the changes, and your check-in gives him a chance to express that. Alternatively, you may find out that his nonverbals had nothing to do with the meeting but rather with a personal matter. Either way, following up and clarifying anything that doesn't match up is always a good idea.

Fostering Strong Relationships

How do you build strong relationships with your stakeholders? Be an excellent communicator. Consistently look for ways to improve the communication process and keep checking in with stakeholders to see whether you're hitting the mark. Head to the earlier section "Playing (and Communicating) Well with Others" for details on communication skills and read on for information on strengthening relationships.

Building trust and respect

When taking on large projects, stakeholders are often tasked with double duty for their current daily job as well as this new project. For that reason, building rapport with stakeholders is crucial. Show them that they are appreciated and respected. Here are some ways to foster trust and respect among stakeholders:

- **Make the best use of people's time.** Don't call them into meetings that they don't need to attend. By understanding and respecting their involvement, you become a more trusted advisor.

- **Refrain from speaking negatively about team members.** Even if you know inside information about a team member, keep it to yourself. And if someone wants to gossip with you about someone else, don't engage.

- **Don't break trust if information is given to you in confidence.** This point is especially important if the knowledge in question is something you need to know but other people can't, such as a *consultant rolloff plan* (the plan that's in place to reduce the number of consultants as the project nears its end).

- **Don't assign them timeframes in which to complete tasks; ask them for estimates.** In this way, you don't overcommit the stakeholders or the technical team. When assigning action items or tasks, ask the person who will actually be doing the task how long it will take. By having him give you the estimate himself, you avoid overcommitting him. And having him give you a time makes him more likely to stick to that time than he would be if you assigned one.

To build rapport, find a common bond between both of you. What do they display on their walls — golf pictures? If you like golf, too, you have your "in." You can also "feel their pain": See whether you can sit beside them as they do their job (or even perform the task yourself) so you can experience the business "pain" firsthand.

The more you learn about each side (business and technical), the more you have a sense of whether an estimate by either side is way out of line. When that happens, you're in a better position to speak from confidence and question it, and the stakeholders are less likely to be offended by your challenge because it's based on your genuine understanding of their side.

Generating consensus/gaining buy-in

One of your responsibilities is to help keep the project moving forward. Times will occur when stakeholders do not agree on requirements. Getting everyone on board to support the scope and requirements for a solution can be difficult, but it's possible. Although not all team members may get their preference right out of the gate, they'll be able to support it. Consensus is tough; to be successful, you have to understand the motivations for each stakeholder and what's really important to them.

To gain buy-in, let the stakeholders share their ideas. People who've had the chance to speak their minds are more likely to buy in to a decision even when they're not totally convinced that solution is the best.

Even when one ultimate decision maker exists (which is often the case), you can't just go to that stakeholder to get the scope of the project and all the requirements and move on. Others are impacted, and they can easily sabotage or slow down the process if they don't buy in. Not getting buy-in is a cause for scope creep. Imagine a director making a decision about project scope without including his management team in the decision process. Chances are one manager (or many managers) won't agree with that decision and try to slip their scope items throughout the project. You need to recognize when people haven't bought in to a decision. You may need to step back and gain buy-in before moving forward in the project.

Part II
The BA Toolkit: Tools, Terms, and Techniques

Business Requirements

Stakeholder Requirements

Technology ("technical") Requirements

Solution Requirements

Functional Requirements

Non-Functional Requirements

Transition Requirements

Learn how to use the Five Whys analysis technique to uncover the root cause of an issue at www.dummies.com/extras/businessanalysis.

In this part . . .

✔ Discover the different software tools available to make your business analysis more efficient and effective.

✔ Explore the differences between a *need* (the problem to be solved) and the various types of *requirements* (the solutions intended to address the problem).

✔ Discover the processes and techniques you can use to elicit meaningful information from stakeholders.

✔ Select which analysis techniques work best given your audience.

✔ Figure out what a business's real problems are and set yourself up to solve them.

Chapter 4

Talking about Tools of the Trade

*B*usiness analysis professionals (BAs) have specialized tools to help them accomplish the work at hand and perform their business analysis work more quickly and effectively. You can improve your productivity in two primary ways — facilitating efficiency and enhancing effectiveness — and commonly used business analysis tools always serve one or both of those objectives. BAs typically use general or specialized tools that fit into five different categories: communication, collaboration, definition, innovation and idea capture, and requirements management. The first two are general tools and support productivity across all business analysis activities, while the last three are specialized and focus more deeply on enabling particular activities and achieving specific analysis goals. In this chapter, we overview the different types of tools out there and help you think about their benefits so you can identify the ones for your business analysis needs.

We don't, however, give you the brand names of different tools because technology products and options change at the speed of light. Tools that were big players two years ago have slipped, and others that were hardly a blip last year now are very powerful. Business analysis tools and the vendors that provide them change faster than in any other industry. To find our recommendations, check out the Resources section on our B2T Training website (www.b2ttraining.com), where we maintain a current list of tools for reference. You can also do a web search by typing "software" + "workflow modeling" (or your topic of choice) + "vendors." The list that pops up will be immediately relevant and pretty much guaranteed to include whatever two to three tools we'd choose to highlight at that moment.

Productivity tools aren't a substitute for sound business analysis. Used poorly or for the wrong reasons, tools may create more problems than they solve.

Examining Communication Tools for Every Situation

Communication tools are the most basic of all the productivity tools. In fact, you probably use most of the common communication tools in the following sections every day, whether you're performing analysis or not.

Talking about your options

Several tools facilitate urgent transfer and delivery of messages. These choices are good for situations where you can't be face-to-face in the moment but still need someone's real-time attention:

- **Text messaging:** Great when you just need to share information quickly or ask an immediate yes/no/opinion question that really can't wait.

- **Chat or instant messaging:** The electronic equivalent of sticking your head into someone's office. It's a helpful relationship builder for remote colleagues, but if your question is more than one or two lines long or the chat will take more than two minutes to complete, switch to phone (or e-mail, if the matter requires less-immediate attention).

- **Phone calls:** Tone of voice plays a significant role in communicating effectively, so picking up the phone is the best way to go when you can't meet in person but need to discuss a potentially sensitive topic, convey understanding, or build teams and strengthen relationships.

When you need to communicate directly with a specific person but immediate connection isn't possible or appropriate, try one of the following:

- **Voicemail:** Great for getting an important message or question delivered to a specific individual with appropriate tone of voice.

  Most voice mailboxes are private, but this setup isn't always the case. When in doubt about privacy, leave a brief, general message that conveys the topic and requests a return call.

- **E-mail:** Useful for longer messages, sharing attachments, and tracking communication history. E-mail often gets information and some media transmitted most quickly, but actual communication speed depends on how frequently the recipient checks or receives e-mail and her initiative and interest in writing back.

- **Postal mail (snail mail):** Useful in situations where a hard copy is important — like if special paper, binding, or color printing is needed — or you need the recipient to sign and return papers. If documents are long, stakeholders may find reading a physical document more convenient than an electronic one.

Some tools are built for group communications, allowing people to correspond at their convenience without an influx of e-mails. Recipients connect when they have time and desire. Be aware that a delay occurs between posting and receiving information, so these tools aren't ideal for time-sensitive messaging:

✔ **Message boards:** One person posts a message or question, and others respond. Good for discussions on specific, single-topic items, for issue and risk management, and for gathering feedback on specific requirements prior to decision-making.

✔ **Social networking tools:** Corporate/inter-office/private networks similar to message boards. However, they feature multimedia and significantly more interaction. They're terrific for relationship-building and idea-generation.

When you need to share information with large audiences but discussion is less appropriate, these one-way communication tools may be effective:

✔ **Public broadcast television or radio:** Despite being used very infrequently in the business analysis world, these media can be still helpful in getting a message out to public audiences where appropriate. You can recommend using these options to solicit potential focus group members, request volunteers for market research or solution user testing, or to distribute particular marketing messages.

✔ **Video:** Video is useful for getting info out to large audiences while incorporating tone of voice and body language. It's especially useful during times of managing change because it's great for building situational understanding, communicating commitment, inspiring solutions and implementation efforts, and ensuring that all audiences get the same message.

✔ **Webinar or web conference:** With or without a video component, these options are great for building understanding, commitment, or action. They're useful for change efforts, as well as solution demonstrations, requirements walk-throughs, or information previews. They can be tailored to small or large audiences and can include document display and multimedia. Although audience participation is possible in webinars, large audience discussions are difficult to manage without a special producer.

In some circumstances, you may need to communicate with people who are hearing-impaired. Tools such as captioned telephone, teletypewriter (TTY) or telecommunications relay services (TRS) can help.

Choosing the right communication tool

The communication tool or method you choose should be appropriate for the audience, content, purpose, and message giver of the communication (as a BA, you may create communications for others to deliver). When evaluating communication tools, consider the following:

- **Number of people involved:** What works well for 10 people may not work well for 80.

- **Type of info to be shared:** Are you sharing verbal or visual information? If it's visual, do you share text, illustration, photos, or video? Some tools are better suited for visuals than others.

- **Amount or volume of info being communicated:** A few paragraphs of information may need 20 minutes and a different communication method than a 40-page document requiring 2 hours.

- **Frequency of exchange:** Consider "why," "how often," and "for what purpose?" Depending on your need, the solution may be a weekly team meeting, team members communicating project information three times a day, or a sponsor giving quarterly updates to solution users.

- **Desire/need for discussion or response:** Your approach may differ if communications need to be two-way/back-and-forth versus one-way outbound, such as for announcements or content broadcast.

- **Sensitivity of the message and expected audience reaction:** You may need to take privacy and security into account:

  - **Privacy needs:** Sometimes people react unexpectedly when hearing about organizational impacts of solutions, so think about how best to deliver messages so people hear them as intended. Consider whether it makes sense for group members to connect individually (personal reactions held more privately) or as a group (reactions are more public and experienced with the group).

    Sensitive topics may be best discussed in real-time instead of being sent over e-mail to be read alone and interpreted. Set up individual calls or a conference. For larger groups, use a conference call or video/web conference, followed by an e-mail to emphasize key message points.

  - **Security needs:** How sensitive is the message? Implement information protection methods where appropriate. If privacy is required but conversation or conferencing isn't possible, be sure to use security encryption on e-mail. Also consider document settings that disallow printing or forwarding of materials. If you're using phone or web conference, disable settings that allow participants to initiate or save recordings of the session.

✔ **Need for live communication:** Phone or conferencing tools are good choices for situations where information and reactions are discussed immediately. If topics need review or thoughtful consideration before discussion, use a delayed or off-line approach. For instance, send information ahead for prereading, but discuss it later in a different communications setting.

✔ **Interest in recording or reviewing communications later:** Sometimes getting everyone you need together at one time is impossible. If you want to ensure everyone hears the same information, consider recording the session and sharing it in an encore performance.

Trying Collaboration Tools

Collaboration is critical to business analysis success. It's about working together with other people to accomplish common goals whether you're all in one location or dispersed across many. To collaborate well, team members must understand the goal and purpose of the collaboration and actively contribute to the efforts by freely sharing info, talents, and context. The good news is that tools are available to help with that! Although collaboration tools don't supply your team members with an individual desire to contribute (a key collaborative ingredient), they can eliminate the big obstacles and facilitate the most-critical working-together needs.

Collaboration tools' primary purpose is to help people work together. They give you a place to work together, providing features that enable collective contribution and work-product development. Tools come in general or specific forms, enabling people to make progress toward a goal at the same time *(synchronously)* or at different times *(asynchronously),* virtually or in person.

Collaboration places are typically represented in one of two forms:

✔ **An event-type place:** A room where collaborators "go" (remotely or actually) to attend a synchronous collaborative session such as a meeting, a presentation, or a training opportunity

✔ **A repository-type place:** A display or data storage area where collaborators can display, store, or request contributions, including notes, comments or documents (tangible or electronic), folders, web pages, or text/ multimedia information or databases

Each kind of place can be physical or virtual/electronic. The following sections discuss the pros and cons of each setup.

Physical places

Employ physical places when you have face-to-face or *collocated* collaborators (those who work in the same building), because everyone is in the same setting and can easily meet and see the information whether they're collaborating synchronously or not. The downside is that you can't access information stored or displayed physically while working from home or traveling away from the office, unless additional support is provided (like shared copies of stored or displayed information).

Face-to-face collaboration is especially valuable when issues are complex or teams or team members are new. If some of your collaborators have never worked together before, or if you have a particularly challenging topic to manage where constructive debate and resolution require a view of body language and vocal tone, then consider a set of initial in-person working meetings.

Live meetings must be designed to get the team comfortable with their project topic as well as each other. Team members should spend a good deal of time on building relationships, cultivating trust and openness, and exploring and resolving the most critical or contentious project issues.

Of course, in-person collaborators also typically need electronic storage or event options in cases where not everyone who needs to work together is present at a given time.

Electronic places

If you're working with a dispersed and/or virtual team, electronic places are absolutely critical for you. Electronic repositories in particular (such as through a wiki or shared network drive) are useful when you're hosting asynchronous collaborations and for keeping deliverables and outputs available for future reference.

Team members that can self-retrieve information from a repository tend to be much more engaged and effective than those who get stuck waiting for another team member to send information out to them.

Virtual collaboration works well when your collaborators have worked together before, share a sense for each others' work style and personality, and feel a trust-based, collegial relationship. That doesn't mean people need to have met in person before, but they must have had a positive prior experience together. Lacking that, they need a simpler problem to solve and an agreement that all participants will approach collaboration with a spirit of positive intent and openness and an initial giving of trust (instead of reserving trust until someone earns it). That history or start-up agreement provides collaborators a foundation on which they can successfully discuss and debate their project issues without animosity.

Popular virtual collaboration tools provide key techniques and experiences typical to in-person collaboration, so you should look for features such as the following:

- ✔ Recording or viewing notes such as you would on a flip chart
- ✔ Drawing on a virtual whiteboard together
- ✔ Viewing the same thing at the same time, whether that's a computer screen, document, presentation, demonstration or simulation, or an individual
- ✔ Seeing which team members are present or speaking and/or seeing their faces
- ✔ Chatting or discussing topics and getting or giving feedback vocally or in writing
- ✔ Splitting into break-out groups for focused discussion and then coming back and sharing results with the larger group

You can also use specialized collaboration tools among your fellow BAs to improve your own analysis productivity and quality.

Investigating Innovation and Idea Capture Tools

Companies can lose a lot of time and money chasing ideas and testing concepts in the pursuit of innovation, so they need to successfully identify and distinguish the good ideas from the not-so-good as efficiently as possible.

Innovation and idea capture tools capture and categorize information at any level and allow companies to get really good and important ideas identified quickly and easily. These tools are best used for enterprise analysis, before any projects or products officially begin. They allow analysts and business or product leaders to more effectively analyze feedback and respond to input from a variety of sources at once by consolidating information and providing new perspectives.

Some questions facilitated or (sometimes) answered by innovation and idea capture tools are

- ✔ Where do we put all those ideas?
- ✔ Which ideas should we consider?

✔ What issues or products do they relate to?

✔ Which ideas are important?

✔ Where did those ideas even come from?

✔ What's been done (if anything) so far to drive the idea forward?

After the information is captured within the tool, you and the team can analyze it by

✔ Capturing, sorting, and categorizing information

✔ Identifying patterns in the information, such as emerging issues or trends

✔ Prioritizing the information and ideas according to relevance, importance, impact, or value to different audiences

✔ Identifying opportunities to improve services, products, or brand perceptions or to grow revenue lines across the business

The following sections introduce high-, mid-, and low-tech tools and suggest some features you may want to look for in various options.

Tools that provide idea or innovation support may alternatively get grouped into other specialized BA tool categories instead of being labeled innovation tools, so be sure to explore other places where you may find great innovation support, including early requirements definition, solution visualization or modeling, business case development with portfolio prioritization, and project management.

Looking at the technology spectrum

From a low-tech perspective, whiteboards and sticky notes are always great if you have to tackle brainstorming or elicitation. Each person puts her ideas on the notes (or board) and sticks them up on the wall, and then team members evaluate the collection of notes, rearranging ideas into groups or categories and determining how best to leverage the information next. Sticky notes are also great when you need to perform scoping analysis, data and process modeling, requirements management planning — you name it.

From a mid- to high-tech perspective, the best tools are software-enabled solutions. Each tool works in a slightly different way. Some options include single or multiuser web-enabled tools, interactive whiteboards and smartphone apps, enterprise software as a service (SAAS) tools, and single-user computer tools.

Considering specific features

Look for mid-tech tools that provide help with collaborative generation; fast-capture or collection; organization; development; and evaluation of ideas, such as mind-mapping. If you need brainstorming aid features (such as leading questions or generation of visual associations), these tools can help as well. Just keep in mind that, after you've captured this information, you and the team have to analyze it, perform the critical thinking, and come to informed decisions on next steps. Following are some of your options.

Listening tools

Generally, users (such as external customers or internal employees) manually enter information (like suggestions and feedback) one idea at a time into innovation and idea capture tools. But if you need more-automated solutions, look for higher-tech tools that offer listening capabilities or customer collaboration web pages. *Listening tools* tap into social media outlets; listen for key words, product names, and brand references; and then import and compile that information within the tool for evaluation and review. Collaborative web pages allow companies to discuss specific product ideas directly and in more detail with customers or customer groups who care to give more constructive or forward-thinking feedback.

Tools that track and grow ideas

If your analysis efforts are going to continue beyond the discovery of the idea, look for tools that track and grow the discovered ideas. Different tools may address a broad or niche set of innovation activities. For instance, in solution development, innovation happens throughout the lifecycle as ideas progress from conceptual into solution decisions and from feature decisions into concrete design.

Application lifecycle management tools

If you need to carry your ideas forward to completion without having to transfer the data and maintain traceability back and forth between systems, look for *application lifecycle management (ALM) tools* — a growing trend in the business analysis world.

These tools support requirements elaboration and definition from start to finish within one tool, eliminating the need to switch technologies as concepts develop. They enable business teams, software teams, and project governance boards to work better together through complete business solutions and software. These suites start with the initial ideas, suggestions, or customer complaints and then move them through innovation opportunities all the way into development management.

Discovering Definition Tools

Definition tools help you define requirements as productively and effectively as possible. (For details on what constitutes a requirement, head to Chapter 5. Chapter 13 has more on the techniques for analyzing requirements mentioned in the following sections.) Some requirements are best defined by using only text, while other requirements are better served by graphical or visual definition. Definition tools support one or both of these styles, which we cover in the following sections.

Textual definition tools

If you need to define things like glossary definitions, project descriptions and objectives, and stakeholder analysis information, use a textual definition tool. Usually, BAs use word processing applications or spreadsheet programs to compile this information into paragraphs and tables; however, the information often turns into extraordinarily long documents.

If you'd rather go for brevity, opt for index cards, markers, and sticky notes, which keep the bits of information manageable. Agile teams frequently use this approach to define *user stories* that capture the essence and goal of the requirements without getting too bogged down in tool or process overkill. They capture details about requirements on the index cards and then sort and organize the cards across conference room tables or tape them up on walls. (In this context, *agile* refers to a group of software development methods where requirements and solutions are developed through collaboration. Head to Chapter 11 to find out more about agile teams.)

Quite a few electronic tools provide features and functions to define stories that mimic the look and function of the index cards! If you like that angle, look for tools with features that organize and define the requirements, acceptance criteria, and resulting project tasks in usable views and prioritized order.

Modeling and diagramming tools

When you need visuals, use modeling and diagramming tools. Models and diagrams frequently seen in business analysis efforts include the following:

- ✔ Business process flows and logical models of all flavors, such as
  - Swimlane diagrams
  - Decision models or diagrams

- Data models (entity relationship diagrams)

- Organizational or operational models

✔ Scope diagrams, such as a context data flow diagram

✔ System context or architecture diagrams

✔ Use case diagrams

✔ Process decomposition diagrams

You can create these items by using low-tech paper and pencil or markers on a flip chart, which is very efficient. However, that result may not be particularly neat, formally presentable, or appropriate for your audience. In that case, some mid-tech tools speed your ability to create and update diagrams yourself with a computer; they feature buttons and menus for drawing standard shapes or creating clean lines. Some tools allow you to record *meta data* (data about data) with fields that define information about the boxes, lines, or information you've drawn on the diagram. Collaboration with mid-tech tools is manual, where one person drives the tool while others watch or contribute suggestions for the driver to address and incorporate.

Opt for high-tech tools if you need to take it further. They have features for defining, modeling, elaborating, reviewing, simulating, and collaborating — all within a single tool or suite of tools. These modeling and diagramming tools provide features fused with other options that support definition by

- ✔ **Creating diagrams for you:** They generate items such as process flow diagrams based on a word, language, or grammar analysis of your textual requirements.

- ✔ **Providing templates and techniques:** They allow you to enter information in one manner while the tool translates the information for display in another manner.

- ✔ **Offering workflow or notifications about requirements:** Team members concerned with certain requirements get updates or changes the instant those items are documented but not any they don't care about.

- ✔ **Designing process code or generating development code based on the process models or design diagrams you create:** This feature increases team efficiency.

- ✔ **Creating or providing a central storage place where requirements can be more easily shared or reused across projects.**

- ✔ **Linking together and tracing all different kinds of requirements from and to one another:** You can track requirements from original need to implementation/destination. Advanced features offering traceability ensure more complete requirements definition and enable you to perform gap and impact analyses around the solution, especially valuable on very large projects. (Check out Chapter 12 for details on requirement traceability.)

Prototyping and simulation tools

Prototyping is a type of definition and modeling tool, but rather than modeling process and manual workflow, you're modeling screens and application work flow. Prototyping tools enable analysts and designers to imagine and illustrate what the software screens and applications will look like before they're built, by leveraging drawings and *wireframing* (mockup) capabilities. When designed, users and stakeholders can review those prototypes and provide feedback early in the lifecycle rather than toward the end.

Prototype tools can range from the very low-tech (paper, marker, whiteboard), to mid-tech (simple electronic drawing tools without many bells and whistles) to very high-tech and advanced (tools built for designers and artists whose focus is creating high-fidelity graphic designs).

Simulation tools (sometimes called or created from *pseudo-code*) are one variety of high-tech prototyping tool. Their features take prototypes a few steps further by activating them for stakeholders to try out; however, the screens don't actually work. A simulation isn't working software; it's an active picture or application example that demonstrates how the functionality of software will work after it's built in the future.

These tools add value by supporting the fact that sometimes seeing is believing. If stakeholders can get a look at what's going to be built, they can provide feedback about what they'd change before changing it is too expensive. For that reason, many definition tool vendors are incorporating prototyping and simulation features into their tool suites for full coverage. The more easily you can go from creation of requirements through visualization of the solution, the faster and cheaper the development effort!

Reviewing Requirements Management Tools

Requirements management tools initially came about to support larger companies. Projects so often went over schedule and budget or came under their scope that companies demanded answers. What was going wrong?

Problem analysis identified requirements as the root cause of the delivery issues. Developers complained of changing requirements, testers identified that requirements were misunderstood (or flat-out missing), and project managers struggled to meet users' and stakeholders' demands without getting in trouble for differences between estimates and actuals.

Requirements management tools reduce these challenges by tracking all the requirements as they progress through development. Use them when you need visibility across all the requirements and need to allow project managers to better manage expectations and issues. Look for tools to offer benefits such as *in-flight* (throughout project execution) key performance indicators and requirements metrics, among other things:

- **Documenting the requirements after they're defined**
- **Tracing the requirements:** Identifying and recording which ones relate to others
- **Managing the requirements:** Tracking them through development and testing
- **Identifying changes to requirements (and analyzing to determine impacts)**
- **Controlling changes to requirements:** Facilitating discussions with stakeholders to decide whether changes are necessary and impacts are acceptable; recording agreements; and documenting adjustments to scope, schedule, and budget

Requirements management tools are best suited for you if you're a knowledgeable, senior-level BA providing repeatable processes; sound practices; and predictable results.

Low- and mid-tech options

Low-tech options for requirements management usually amount to manual tracking and management tricks, but more frequently, BAs simply track updates on the overall requirements document(s).

One particular low-tech solution is gaining in popularity, and it's great if you're working with agile or iterative projects where user stories and cards are used: Requirements are managed by taping or pinning the index cards up to a wall and putting them in visually chronological order.

You can also use a variation of this setup called a *Kanban board,* which tracks and manages work in a production flow model and shows requirements progress more clearly. A Kanban board has different columns depicting the different states or statuses of requirements during the development process (such as "In Definition," "In Development," "In Test," and "Done"). You pin the story cards to the board within the specific column corresponding to their current state and move them along to the different columns as things change.

If you prefer mid-tech options to track the information within electronic tools or spreadsheets, look for tools that provide sorting, calculating, tracing, and sharing (just note that these are manual efforts where frequent updates are necessary).

High-tech options

High-tech tools provide data entry features for getting the requirements into the tool. They offer workflow and status tracking to stay on top of which requirements are in whatever states of development or testing at whatever time, and they measure rates of change (often called *volatility* — the extent to which requirements continue to change and reach a stable state of definition) and other metrics. The high-tech options are the ones that really add the value for requirements management.

If defined requirements aren't entered and tracked in the tool, metrics can't be generated on them. Luckily, greater incentives and opportunities are on the market today for getting data into the management tools, and now that requirements definition tools have matured, business analysis professionals are experiencing the benefits of tool *convergence* (both requirements definition and requirements management functions are now available within a single tool or tool suites).

Picking the Right Tools for the Situation

The key to finding the right tool is identifying the kind of support or productivity boost that would be right for you by inventorying the situation you have now and determining what situation you need or want to have later, while being sure to avoid unnecessary tools. You also need to consider team size and budgetary constraints. Review product offerings and functionality against your true needs very carefully. Consider specifically what you need to speed your definition work, and match your wish list of features to the product options accordingly. The following sections help you evaluate which tools best fit your project's current and future state.

Always make sure you get to know a tool and its feature set or benefits before you purchase or deploy it. If possible, try out or pilot test a tool first to accomplish a real-world business need. No matter how fantastic a collaboration or analysis tool may be, what's ultimately useful must line up against what you need to do with it. Just remember: No tool — no matter how slick and cool — magically solves all your problems.

Depending on what tools you pick in the end, you may need to get approval before deploying them, so keep that on your radar. For example, if the tool you want to use is fairly simple and economical (like index cards or sticky notes), chances are you don't need to go through a whole approval process. However, if the tool requires a significant outlay of cash and/or resources, you need to make sure you're cleared for the expense. To get approval, just follow the general business analysis process: Identify your needs and requirements, define solutions, and present your case to whoever has approval power.

Inventorying the situation you have now

Review the current characteristics of your team, along with the productivity challenges you're having, and write down the following:

- ✔ What big-picture items (goals or end-products) you're communicating or collaborating on

- ✔ What you're collaborating about (topics, information, or areas) within those items

- ✔ Who's adding to the collaboration (specific people)

- ✔ What your team members are contributing (words and information, pictures or drawings, physical objects, and so on)

- ✔ What the team members are doing with the contributions of others (assessing, enhancing, planning, managing, constructing, and so on)

- ✔ Where the team members collaborate (physical location and typical atmosphere/environment)

- ✔ At what time(s) of the day and for how long each individual is active in contributing toward the goal

- ✔ What business analysis-related challenge you're experiencing (or expect to be experiencing) and what change or improvement would help facilitate or increase your (or your team's) productivity

Determining what situation you need later

After you've inventoried your current situation (refer to the preceding section), identify the business analysis and other activities your team needs to perform as you collaborate on your project. What does your situation look like after you implement a tool? Look for gaps or challenges where you think your team can use additional support to become more productive — especially if you need to perform activities while separated by time or location. Here are some considerations:

- ✔ If you could all be together in one room, what would the optimal situation look like? What activities are taking place; what's being created and how?

  - Is the team brainstorming ideas or generating plans?

  - Are you sharing or documenting knowledge and creating content?

  - Does the team need calendars and schedules? Does work get done in a specific order? Would notifications at certain points be important?

  - Will the team be developing or creating things together?

- ✔ Will everyone need to just see and talk about what the leader is doing, will everyone have a hands-on role, or will some just need to review results when the work is finished?

- ✔ Will individuals have time to think about what they contribute, or will their contributions be fast and spontaneous?

- ✔ Does everyone on the team know each other, or are relationships still being formed?

  - Will people feel comfortable contributing, or will they need to be encouraged?

  - Do people need to see each other's faces to engage effectively?

- ✔ Is the work product or collaborative output temporary for immediate use, or will it be used as input to a next step? Will team members need to go back to read and review contributions later or publish content for a longer-term? What historical information will you need to keep?

- ✔ Will people be paying active attention to the work and collaboration as it happens, or will they need to be notified or reminded about doing the next step?

- ✔ Will other people be paying attention to what's going on with the team and try to find or pull information, or will you need to proactively push information out to them?

- ✔ What do you expect to generate at the end, and what happens next with it? That is, are you creating recommendations or information for someone to act on, a deliverable asset or thing someone can touch or leverage, a final end-product for an audience, or a component of work other team members need in order to do their work?

Avoiding unnecessary tools and features

Before you discount or leap to an electronic or particularly feature-full tool, consider how specific the analysis or collaborative exchange needs to be and whether the technology you have in mind is truly the vehicle to get you there. Don't make the mistake of falling in love with features you don't need. Keep the following in mind to avoid this fate:

✔ **Don't overengineer.** If your primary collaboration requirement is to communicate with each other, keep things simple; a tool specifically for collaboration may be overkill if talking on the phone can do the job. If your needs start and end with your small team, a large high-tech tool may be completely overengineered or overcomplicated.

✔ **Don't get caught up in the flash of electronic tools.** Be sure to look past bells and whistles to evaluate whether a tool really provides the needed functionality. For instance, some general collaboration tools provide visuals but no sound; some provide sound yet lack visuals; and some offer both. If sound is critical to your need, don't get wrapped up in the amazing visual effects of options that don't offer it.

✔ **Don't settle for virtual when in-person analysis or collaboration is really required.** Think about what you need to accomplish and the kind of contact that enables you to do so. No matter what tools you use, connecting virtually still may not provide the value of an in-person event. Your collaboration topic may be best served by a real conference room and a travel budget, and without that, your results will be insufficient or ineffective.

Money, money, money: Facing budget challenges

Cash: It's the big kahuna. After all, business all boils down to money. So before you invest a considerable chunk of cash or time on a productivity tool, be sure to consider what it's really going to cost you and where the budget will come from. The initial expense or "purchase price" of your productivity tool may be the most visible financial component, but it's not the only financial component. You have to consider a few other things when thinking about what budget you have versus what budget you need:

✔ **Licensing or initial purchase of the productivity tool:** What it costs "out of the box."

✔ **Installation or distribution costs for individual users:** What putting the system in-place so it works properly costs.

- ✔ **Training costs to get people up to speed**:
  - **Cost of time for people to attend training:** Includes travel and expenses. Policies may differ among firms, so be clear on whether consultants get paid for any time they attend training.
  - **Cost of effort for people or the vendor to deliver training:** Travel and expenses and materials, books, and supplies.
- ✔ **Annual maintenance costs:** Ensuring that you get appropriate software upgrades and/or functional support from technical or customer service teams.
- ✔ **Hardware costs**: Basically, anything that may be paid for inside your company (or charged by the vendor) — such as servers, networks, backups, and security — that enables physical and technical support for your tool.
- ✔ **Opportunity costs**: The areas or opportunities that will be lost due to your implementing the tool. What will you not be able to purchase as a result of investing in this tool? What projects or specific requirements won't be worked on as a result of your team's spending time implementing the tool, developing and communicating new processes, and getting up to speed on how it works? What risks may you incur?
- ✔ **Internal support costs**: Whether someone inside the company needs to be a go-to support or help contact for the tool — both from the technical "help make it work" perspective and from the functional "help me work with it in our environment" perspective.

You may find other cost components, but overall you should look for and analyze the various cost components that contribute to the total cost of ownership over the longer term. You should be able to clearly state to others whether the project will deliver as expected or you'll need an extension, and whether the costs will end with the life of the product or project or go beyond the project lifecycle into the next project.

Preparing Team Members for Change

You've evaluated your needs, identified your options, and selected the best tool for you. Great! Now what?! Do you just go forth and implement? In some cases, perhaps (certainly if they're small tools). But the large, high-tech, enterprise-wide tools are complicated, and they need to be implemented with care for true success. You can't just buy a tool and toss it out there. People need time to plan and adjust. They need to know

✔ What the new process is (including training and additional time to get their work done)

✔ How they — and anyone else — are supposed to be working with the new tool

✔ Who they're supposed to turn to for help when they're confused or before specific details are all ironed out

✔ What benefit they're supposed to get from this new tool that's costing them energy and time

To ensure a successful tool implementation, you should focus on two key areas to help get the team on board for the change: motivation and competence (more on building these areas in Chapter 15).

The key to motivating stakeholders to accept a new tool is to explain why it's good for them. Always tie the discussion back to how this tool applies to each specific team member. When members know how and why the tool can improve their work, they become more motivated to accept and use it! Building competency with the tool requires that you provide a clear and thorough training plan, as well as support from all levels for integrating the chosen tool. Make sure you fully teach the stakeholders how to successfully use the new tool.

People don't like feeling confused and easily reject a tool that makes them feel like they're not getting it. You can avoid that by making sure you're in constant contact with users as they learn how to use the tool so you can guide them and address any concerns or problems right away. And don't forget to check in along the way to solicit their feedback; sometimes they suffer in silence. Be sure to actively seek their input on the experience.

A team with inappropriate training or without a clear process around a tool may just get aggravated and become decidedly unproductive. Although the new end-product may be the same or similar with a new tool, the actions required to finish typical work are commonly different enough to confuse even a senior analyst until she's had enough time to practice.

Whenever you bring in new tools to improve something, the situation always gets worse before it gets better. (We don't mean to scare you; it's just that to be successful, you must acknowledge the reality.) People first get excited about change, and initial expectations are high, but folks often become frustrated with the pace and reality of change (described in change management literature as the *Valley of Despair*). As long as they don't get so frustrated that they leave their new situation (an *Exodus of Talent*), figuring out the new normal, adapting, and recovering their confidence takes a little time before they get back to or achieve productive performance.

Chapter 5

Understanding What Requirements Truly Entail

The difference between a requirement and a need is at the heart of a business analysis project, but it can be a little tricky to understand. This chapter explains this difference and then explores how you can create excellent requirements.

Defining Needs

A *need* is an unsatisfied goal or objective. The concept seems simple enough, but needs can be rather hazy and subjective things that are difficult to identify or define. That's because what people say they need is often not what they really need; it's typically a solution they've identified to serve their need.

For instance, maybe someone says, "I need clothes." Perhaps he does. But why? Besides the fact that he may want new clothes, what's the reason he needs clothes? If you as a business analyst (BA) were to ask him different questions in different ways, you could find out information that would help uncover the real need (without any covering, he'd be cold and naked; clothes help keep him warm and comfortable). Aha! Having clothes isn't really his need at all; it's a good solution for keeping warm and comfy, but technically, it isn't the only option. Blankets, a space heater, and even a hot tub are all options that could potentially serve the need to be warm and comfortable.

Typically, multiple options are available for serving business needs and solving business problems. But if you have lots of options for solving problems and serving needs, how do you make sure you're giving your requestors the right solution? You must make sure you understand and truly address the real need and the real problem.

As a BA working with stakeholders and eliciting their requirements (which we discuss in Chapter 6), one of the most important things you do is ensure you identify stakeholders' real need(s) to be sure you're solving the right problem.

The business's needs and the stakeholders' needs may differ from and even conflict with one another. Therefore, identify and articulate the needs of each group separately.

When getting to the bottom of what the real needs are, you investigate *business needs* (what the business must have or achieve in order to run) and *stakeholder needs* (what a specific stakeholder or stakeholder group needs in order to support the business). Knowing the difference between these two ensures that you plan and manage your project effectively. We cover both in the following sections.

Business needs

Whether public, private, or nonprofit, a business serves a market, executes a mission, and — presuming all goes well — fulfills the vision that the leaders have set for that business. Throughout the course of operations, business leaders set goals and objectives for their enterprise, and they rally teams to work hard and deliver on them. These goals and objectives are business needs; they are the things the business must have or achieve to run, to be profitable, to serve effectively, and to deliver successfully on its mission.

Business needs defined at the highest level may include *capability needs* (statements about providing certain services, delivering a suite of products, assisting others in need, or ensuring the business's own operational effectiveness) or *improvement needs* (suggestions meant to increase efficiencies or decrease costs, effort, or time-to-market).

Articulating and defining business needs is a part of the activity called *enterprise analysis* and includes identifying and understanding the business's goals; articulating its strategic direction; and capturing any key concerns pertaining to the business's successes, challenges, risks, or problems. (For more on enterprise analysis, turn to Chapter 2.)

Successfully identifying business needs requires critical thinking, analysis, and insight. The business leaders of a company may not clearly tell you what they need, but they'll probably suggest solutions they want, complain about capabilities they don't have that'd be helpful, and talk a lot about opportunities they could go after if they only had the hottest new technologies.

Therefore, you must do a lot of interpreting. Digging into the source of leaders' wishful thinking can give you information about their business objectives and targets. When you work toward identifying why they need those things, you identify the core activities or drivers of the business. A popular business analysis acronym is *IRACIS,* or "increase revenue, avoid costs, improve service." Typically, the business needs are related to one of these targets.

To serve needs effectively, BAs must articulate

- ✔ What objectives or goals are being served or attempted in specific business area(s)

- ✔ What results or outcomes are desired

- ✔ What issues or problems are getting in the way

- ✔ What solutions are being suggested or considered for implementation or adoption in order to get the business needs met

Outcomes desired versus problems perceived to be getting in the way of business success should be paired together in the analysis when identifying business needs, as shown in Table 5-1. But that does not mean a problem and opportunity will always be expressed together. The business may express a problem without an associated opportunity or, conversely, an opportunity without an associated problem, as the third entry in Table 5-1 shows.

Table 5-1	Pairing Problems and Opportunities	
ID	**Problem**	**Opportunity**
1	Manually tracking student registrations for classes takes too long.	Automate the registration process.
2	Manually tracking instructor availability and other business rules is too cumbersome.	Automate instructor availability and additional business rules.
3		Our competitors do all their scheduling manually, and we want to be first to market.

You typically express business needs as broad statements characterizing strategic (and sometimes lofty) goals or as specific statements describing tactical objectives, such as what will be done by when. Consequently, effectively meeting business needs may require broad solutions, like a collection of organizations or operational stakeholders that participate in a variety of initiatives, subsequently designed to meet the objectives.

Stakeholder needs

Stakeholder needs are similar to business needs in that they also collect and describe information about business goals, strategies, objectives, targets, and key concerns about successes, challenges, issues, risks, and problems. Whereas business needs describe the needs of the enterprise itself, stakeholder needs describe what a specific stakeholder or stakeholder group needs in order to support the business. (They describe the needs of the stakeholder in service to his own objectives, while participating in initiatives or performing his role, but all in contribution to meeting the enterprise's business needs.)

Stakeholder needs look very much like business needs and are often mistaken for them. In many respects, stakeholder needs are business needs, which often confuses new BAs trying to understand definitions and the distinction.

Analysts must ensure that stakeholder needs

✔ **Are defined for the distinct and limited perspective of that particular stakeholder or group:** If you have a lot of stakeholders to analyze, identify those with similar roles or goals and organize them into representative groups, as shown in Figure 5-1.

Figure 5-1:
Break stakeholders into smaller groups according to roles or goals.

Stakeholders	Product Phase			
	Product Ideation	Product Development	Product Rollout	Product Maintenance
Sales Reps			✓	
Product Managers	✓	✓	✓	✓
Marketing Specialists	✓		✓	
Developers		✓	✓	
VP, Finance	✓			

Illustration by Wiley, Composition Services Graphics

✔ **Convey only the needs relevant to the project and related to the stakeholder's particular role:** That role may be either supporting the relevant business needs or interfacing with the solution being delivered.

✔ **Are separated for different stakeholders:** Keep the needs of different stakeholders separated in organizing categories. *Note:* When you're documenting needs for interaction between stakeholders, capturing the needs of both sides is frequently necessary. However, you must identify the specific needs for each side of the interaction separately to ensure that the solution ultimately meets the needs of each collaborator.

For each individual stakeholder or group you analyze, you should capture the following:

- ✔ Specific organizational or operational objectives
- ✔ Any performance targets that either support or are affected by the overarching business needs or goals
- ✔ Any lower-level goals, activities, or processes that can potentially be served by the solution in question

As you analyze, note specific issues and their root cause(s), as well as any aspirations the stakeholders may have for their own group's performance or capability-building.

Not all stakeholders are within the business you're analyzing! Some stakeholders are outside your business (such as customers, vendors, or suppliers). Their needs for the solution may be just as important as the requirements of internal stakeholders, so be sure to look at all the business analysis artifacts at your disposal (such as process diagrams, data flow diagrams, business architecture diagrams, or backlogs) to find and include them.

Defining Requirements

Needs and requirements may look like they mean the same thing, but here's the difference: The need is the objective, and the *requirement* is the decision about whether to do something to achieve that objective. A need turns into a requirement when someone recognizes that having the unmet need is unacceptable and decides he requires the need to be met.

Requirements, when first identified, are really needs, wants, suggestions, or ideas — until the right person decides otherwise. Frequently, needs, wants, suggestions, and ideas are presented as requirements statements without the provider's thinking about the needs, constraints, or implications of that decision; sometimes, he's not even in the position to decide how or why the requirement is appropriate or necessary.

Decisions are made by someone for a reason. Capture and note which someone makes which decisions about specific requirements, and when.

As you've probably realized, the word *requirement* is a very vague term in the business analysis world. As a result, the official definition of a requirement listed in the BABOK Guide (as specified by the IIBA — the International Institute of Business Analysis) follows:

1. **"A condition or capability needed by a stakeholder to solve a problem or achieve an objective."** This point reflects the pivotal decision-making we mention earlier in this section.

2. **"A condition or capability that must be met or possessed by a solution or solution component to satisfy a contract, standard, specification, or other formally imposed documents."** This part shifts the focus from the stakeholder to the solution.

3. **"A documented representation of a condition or capability as in 1 or 2."** This idea notes that the documentation about requirements is also called a requirement. That's because documentation helps analysts, different stakeholders, or *documentation consumers* (the people reading and interpreting the documentation) understand the requirements for the solution along with any components they're responsible for creating. Because creators of the solution components must adhere to the requirements while developing, the documentation itself becomes a requirement.

Requirements fall into different, layered categories as shown in Figure 5-2. The primary categories include business requirements, stakeholder requirements, solution requirements, transition requirements, and technology requirements. Solution requirements include functional and nonfunctional requirements created either by hand or with technology (which has its own technical requirements). And when complete, the solutions are put into place by way of transition requirements.

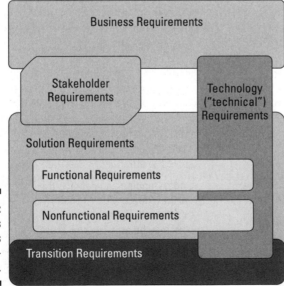

Figure 5-2: Categories or layers of requirements.

Illustration by Wiley, Composition Services Graphics

We use these requirements terms consistently throughout this book to keep confusion to minimum, but some BAs and companies use different terms. The key is being able to identify what they are, despite what they're called. You need to strategically analyze the business requirements in the top layer and then define or decompose the proceeding requirements so they clearly describe necessary capabilities for the next layers, and so on.

Going straight from a business requirement directly to a detailed technical requirement isn't possible. You must cascade through each layer or level of analysis as appropriate, cataloging and categorizing as you go.

You and your team aren't just supposed to design any solution at the end of all this cascading through the levels; you're supposed to use the requirements to design a successful solution. You must probe deeply enough to elicit all the necessary requirements (for detailed info on eliciting requirements, head to Chapter 6); otherwise, you risk missing some requirements.

You can reuse documented requirements (and needs, for that matter) at the business and stakeholder (and sometimes the solution) levels! Reused requirements can save project teams and stakeholders time and money. You should organize and save your requirements from your projects (perhaps in an enterprise repository or centralized requirements-reference place) in case you want to use them again on another project. Requirements that were once *to-be* requirements (for the future business environment) can become your *as-is* requirements (for the current business environment) and provide a new starting point for the next project.

What versus how

In business analysis, you have to differentiate between business requirements and solution requirements. These components are often referred to as *the what* and *the how*.

✔ *What* describes the business needs, problems, goals, objectives, information, and activities of concern independent of how these things are performed or managed now or potentially will be in the future.

✔ *How* describes the way business activities are performed or managed, including how and where business data is stored or how specific processes and tasks are executed. The how may or may not be automated by any technology or system.

Separating the what from the how allows you to focus and clearly understand what the business area is and what the stakeholder problems are before getting distracted by slick technologies, innovative approaches, or an avalanche of details around how their problems should be solved to effectively meet their needs.

Understanding and defining the what first (what do they need, what do they want, what must they have) is important because more than one how may be able to solve a problem.

Business stakeholders may not necessarily care how problems get solved, but they typically do care very much about what they need to do or have after their problems are solved.

Just one missing requirement can cause problems with the stakeholders and team members and can also affect the solution(s) you build. The solution may be lacking or costly, create ongoing quality or support concerns, suffer buggy or failing interfaces, put downstream systems in jeopardy, and result in systems that are (more) difficult to support, causing manual work-arounds or additional processes. These challenges can hurt user and customer satisfaction and business outcomes, which may result in decreased sales and an impact to revenue.

Business requirements

Business requirements are derived from the needs of the business; they're the things that must be in place to benefit or serve the business or enterprise as a whole. They characterize and quantify outcomes desired for the business, and document what business the business decides to be in, what products the business will offer, or what markets the business will expand into or exit.

At a project level, business requirements also include the reasons and objectives for the project, as well as the success measures and metrics that the project team will be held accountable to. All these requirements should be stated from a business perspective — that is, not specific to any one stakeholder but rather from the overall business view.

Stakeholders often offer much more than just business requirements even if that's all you're eliciting from them. They may also provide stakeholder requirements, solution ideas, solution requirements, technology suggestions, and transition needs, so your challenge is being able to successfully peel apart that onion and identify which category each statement really belongs to. Distinguishing between an idea or suggestion and a truly decided-upon requirement that the team or solution will be held to support is especially important.

This overload is the primary source for *scope creep* (when projects inch out of their previously determined boundaries). Stakeholders frequently see opportunity in every new development effort and may load up on "requirements" that they just "must have," though those opportunities may fall outside the scope of the project objectives. (Chapter 10 has info on defining and managing the scope of requirements for a project.) You may need to capture all these requirements but then defer their consideration to a later time.

Stakeholder requirements

Requirements that describe the needs or problems of the stakeholders in achieving or supporting their goals — whether related to organizational or operational concerns — are *stakeholder requirements*.

Just as stakeholder needs and business needs look alike (as noted in the earlier section "Stakeholder needs"), stakeholder requirements look an awful lot like business requirements. Stakeholder requirements define decisions about business needs, goals, and objectives — just as business requirements do — but from the perspective of the stakeholders and their role in the business.

Stakeholder requirements are often just called business requirements because they are business requirements for a particular stakeholder. However, calling them business requirements may lead you to fail to isolate the true business requirements for the enterprise, which may result in your not identifying critical project or solution objectives in the process.

In Figure 5-2 earlier in the chapter, you can see that stakeholder requirements, being the layer of requirements between the business and solution requirements, relate to both contexts. On one hand, stakeholder requirements define what functions the stakeholder performs (or will perform in the future) and what he's responsible for. On the other hand, stakeholder requirements are also related to the solution: After the problem and potential solution become clear, they define each stakeholder's potential interaction(s) with a solution, including the solution objectives, success, and acceptance criteria from the perspective of the stakeholder.

Using stakeholder analysis to identify stakeholder requirements

Prior to or during the elicitation and identification of stakeholder requirements, you perform *stakeholder analysis* in order to identify the stakeholders and understand their different characteristics. Information captured during stakeholder analysis may include the organizational positioning of a stakeholder and his level of influence and attitude (either within the business in general or with respect to the solution); his readiness for change; and his interest in the outcome of the project and solution. (Check out Chapters 3 and 11 for more on stakeholder analysis.)

Stakeholder analysis information, together with the stakeholder requirements, provides a starting point for designing or modifying the solution, especially any automation aspects of the solution. Get stakeholders to clarify which of their requirements are, in fact, suggestions and which conditions or capabilities are so important that their needs wouldn't possibly be met without them; stakeholders must identify what is truly required for a successful solution.

The information gathered during the stakeholder analysis is also often called stakeholder requirements. In fact, the word *requirements* becomes the catch-all term for any information gathered during the business analysis process, which is why working on requirements is challenging and can trip up even the best of analysts.

When requirements collide: Addressing conflict between stakeholder requirements

Different stakeholders can provide different objectives and success or acceptance criteria for the same solution! As a result, stakeholders may identify individual requirements that unintentionally conflict when viewed in light of the overarching business objectives. Stakeholders have individual goals and objectives, but they still must collaborate to meet common business goals and drive the business. They sometimes lose sight of this fact, and it's your job to remind them.

Sometimes what's best for the business overall may not be best for stakeholders individually, so you must influence stakeholders' understanding so they can come to consensus on requirements (which we discuss in Chapter 3). Solving these conflicts provides opportunities for innovation, improvement, and business benefit.

You create solutions from the requirements of many people, which means you may sometimes have to consider trade-offs and evaluate which stakeholder gets the most benefit or suffers the most risk. To do this task, you and your team need to understand all the important factors while defining the business/stakeholder needs but before deciding which of these needs merit being bumped up to a requirement. Otherwise, several consequences may occur:

- ✔ Stakeholders may feel as though they didn't have a say in the plans or priorities; if they feel you weren't listening, going forward, they may raise concerns later in the process than is helpful and may not buy in to important decisions.

- ✔ If stakeholders aren't ready for impacts in their domain, they may end up lacking features or funding they need to transition.

- ✔ Team members may feel frustrated and overloaded at having to accommodate new requirements as they pop up, leading to missed deliverables, deadline or staffing challenges, and lack of time to plan or manage communications.

Solution requirements

Solution requirements specify the conditions and capabilities a solution has to have in order to meet the need or solve the problem and provide clarity around delivery needs. They don't define how the solution will solve the problem technically or specifically; that happens later. Solution requirements must meet or support the driving project and business objectives, in addition to meeting stakeholder objectives.

When developing solutions or solution concepts, stakeholders commonly focus first on identifying and writing software requirements and worry about the rest of the requirements later. But doing that without really knowing which features or functions will be most valuable in meeting the business and stakeholder requirements means your team may end up building some cool stuff without actually solving any important problem. You can't really be sure what capabilities will be truly valuable until the overarching solution vision is clear.

People get excited by technology or by finding great opportunities to improve. At this stage, beginning to brainstorm approaches or evaluate how something may be or designed is very easy. Don't let that happen! Instead, brainstorm about what the solution has to achieve for stakeholders before everyone gets caught up in the details of how to build it.

Using a vision statement to define the solution

A *vision statement* articulates and defines the holistic need for the solution. It's the most important of all the solution requirements. The vision specifies which conditions and capabilities are critically required for the solution to effectively meet needs and deliver value.

Developing a clear vision enables you and the stakeholders to focus on identifying requirements for what stakeholders need first, without inadvertently going too far down a single solution option path. Because many options are often available for solving a problem, you want to be sure to focus discussions on solution outcomes, results, and what-nexts and gain agreement first on what the solution has to support or enable. Without agreement on the overall vision, the requirements will end up just being a collection of stuff delivered without a solution delivered.

Breaking your solution requirements into categories

After you've got a vision, you can venture into breaking the solution requirements down into two different categories: functional requirements and nonfunctional requirements. Here, we describe them all briefly. For a more in-depth discussion, visit Chapter 12.

- **Functional requirements:** *Functional requirements* define the specific behaviors, responses, information, rules, or operations of a solution. They outline

  - What functions or functionality the solution will support

  - What specific stakeholders will do or experience while being a part of or using the solution

  - What information or data will be managed

  - Under what circumstances the behaviors and responses happen (or not) in order to ensure the required results and outcome

Although functional requirements are usually specified in the context of software and technical system capabilities, manual solutions also have functional requirements.

✔ **Nonfunctional requirements:** *Nonfunctional requirements* specify the manner or the environment in which a solution is intended to operate. They describe the qualities a solution must possess and any supplemental expectations or conditions it must meet support. They define standards for

- **Usability:** How easy the solution must be to understand or figure out

- **Reliability:** To what extent users can rely on the solution to be accessible and work when needed

- **Performance:** How quickly and efficiently the solution works and how it responds to commands and requests for action

- **Security:** The level of protection the system and its data are expected to have in place

- **Design:** The visual elements expected from the solution

- **Accessibility:** The support that must be provided for users with disabilities, including hearing or vision loss, typically in compliance with relevant regulations such as the Americans with Disabilities Act of 1990

- **Documentation:** The type and extent of written documentation expected or needed

- **Information capacity:** Requirements for the amount of data or media to be stored, including the expected growth of the information over time

- **Information architecture:** Any needs for the arrangement or organization of the information in the solution

- **Anything else:** Whatever else the stakeholders decide is required of the solution

No matter what kind of solution requirements are identified and defined, those you elect to implement should be validated as capabilities that stakeholders really need and (as a result) decide must be included in the solution — either because including them is strategically, functionally, or technologically smart.

Transition requirements

Transition requirements define any and all temporary capabilities, conditions, or activities that are necessary for moving solutions out of development and into real-world business use. Here, we describe them briefly. For a more in-depth discussion, visit Chapter 15. They do the following:

- Describe what has to be done with people, process, and technology before you can get from the as-is into the to-be.

- Cover awareness-building, education, and training for the new way employees must work, accounting for, and outlining the differences from before to now.

- Define any shifting, movement, enhancement, or change to data and information out of their original structures or locations into their new data homes.

Technology requirements

After the solution requirements are understood, a team has enough information to propose the best way for solving a problem, which frequently includes technology. Enter technology requirements.

Technology requirements facilitate communications between the analyst and the *technology engineers* (system architects, programmers, and designers). In fact, sometimes technology architects or engineers are the analysts for technology requirements. Whoever writes the technology requirements has to make sure that they describe the specific characteristics of all the data and processes that will be implemented in the solution, including what the data should look like, how the processes should be done, and how the screens should behave. All the solution requirements previously specified get translated at this level from what the business decides it wants into how the solution will work and be built.

Like stakeholder requirements, technology requirements have two perspectives or contexts: the business context and the solution context. In the following sections, we focus on the solution context because that is mostly what you're concerned with as a BA.

Technology (technical) requirements for the solution

From the solution context, technology requirements are also known as *technical requirements,* and they specify the design and architecture of the specific technical components needed for the solution to be developed, implemented, and operated. They address how the solution will deliver the capabilities, be programmed or coded, and store and display the data.

You shouldn't create technical requirements until after the stakeholder and solution requirements are understood because which solution option is appropriate fully depends on what capabilities the stakeholders need from the solution. Not every technical "how" option will provide the same capabilities, so selecting the one that provides the capabilities that are just right for solving the business problem(s) is the key. Those designing technical requirements must balance cool, slick technology against stakeholder and business requirements.

That said, you don't have to do all the requirements for a solution prior to doing any technical work. Although teams can choose to define all stakeholder and solution requirements first and then do the functional/nonfunctional and technical requirements (a methodology known as *waterfall*), they can alternatively work in a more *agile* or iterative fashion where they take one or a few abstract requirements quickly down to technical detail and then go back and do some more. (Refer to Chapter 12 for more on development methodologies.)

Technology requirements for the business

Sometimes, technology needs, problems/opportunities, standards, constraints, and requirements begin to take on a level of importance or significance above that of the technical requirements for any one specific solution; at that point, they grow into serving solutions broadly as a category or layer of requirements on their own.

No matter what method you use for development and delivery, technical requirements get defined and implemented in support of many solutions over time in a business, enabling sets of stakeholders and serving many business requirements. As a company implements and grows its technology *stack* (collection of technology-enabled solutions), technology and even the technology industry begin to have needs as a stakeholder on their own.

Making Your Requirements Excellent

Your unique responsibility as a BA is to write and communicate excellent requirements. This job is important because requirements consumers depend on the requirements in order to effectively design and construct solution components.

Excellent requirements leave no room for interpretation, create no cause for confusion, and omit no critical detail. They ensure that any consumer of the requirements information (such as developers, software or process engineers, database administrators, interface designers, architects, product managers, and sponsors) can understand what's been requested. Excellent requirements possess seven different characteristics, which we cover in the following sections.

Requirements that generate more questions than they provide answers aren't excellent requirements; lacking that clarity, the team may find delivering the appropriate solution much more difficult and frustrating.

Complete

A *complete* requirement thoroughly describes the user task and all the information required to support that task. To create complete requirements, push stakeholders to focus on describing the goal to be accomplished and the requirements for achieving that goal, as opposed to talking about the system functionality. Focusing on system requirements often creates gaps because stakeholders frequently think of only the specific tasks that pertain to them. They miss critical interactions with or dependencies on others around the goal or outcome, and those elements are typically important for the overall solution. Here are two contrasting examples of completeness:

- **Non-excellent/incomplete:** "Accounting needs to be able to process employee expense accounts."

- **Excellent/complete:** "Accounting supervisors need to be able to approve expense accounts submitted from employees."

Correct

A *correct* requirement appropriately meets the goals of the project and accurately describes the user's expectations of the functionality being specified.

You must challenge and eliminate assumptions that occur when stakeholders who are very familiar with their business areas internalize different business rules or scenarios and then omit those critical details from their requirements. Here are two examples of varying correctness:

- **Non-excellent/incorrect:** "An employee may change his or her last name after a change in marital status."

- **Excellent/correct:** "An employee may change his or her last name after submitting appropriate legal proof of name change."

Unambiguous

An *unambiguous* requirement is crystal clear. Based on the requirement you wrote, all readers should arrive at a single, consistent interpretation. Misinterpreted ambiguous requirements can result in the wrong system being developed, a situation that may not be found during testing if the tester is working under an incorrect interpretation of the requirements. Here are two examples of clear/unclear requirements:

✔ **Non-excellent/ambiguous:** "Overtime is not permitted."

✔ **Excellent/unambiguous:** "Any consultant's time sheet that's submitted with an excess of 40 hours worked will be denied for payment and returned to the consultant for revision."

Verifiable

Excellent requirements need to be testable in order to verify that what you get when the solution is completed is what you wanted in the first place.

Requirements that aren't verifiable may be descriptive enough to be subjectively assessed, but they aren't provable, which can complicate ensuring someone really got what was needed. Here are two contrasting examples of verifiability:

✔ **Non-excellent/unverifiable:** "Order fulfillment should be able to pack most orders within 5 minutes."

✔ **Excellent/verifiable:** "Order fulfillment must be able to pack 90 percent of orders within 5 minutes after receipt of the packing slip."

Necessary

Requirements need to clearly support a project goal or objective; they should not be on someone's personal wish list, and they shouldn't be requirements that anyone would review and declare to be scope creep. Every project operates under time and budget constraints; if a requirement isn't necessary, it can be deprioritized. Here are two examples of levels of necessity:

✔ **Non-excellent/unnecessary:** "Accounting systems must have current, up-to-the-minute exchange rates available."

✔ **Excellent/necessary:** "Accounting systems must have their exchange rates updated once daily."

Feasible

Make sure that all requirements are technologically and realistically possible for a reasonable cost. To do so, bring in the technical team and discuss the requirements and potential solution options. Here are two examples highlighting feasibility:

✔ **Non-excellent/not feasible:** "The web system's intrusion detection functionality must capture the reason for any intrusion attempt."

✔ **Excellent/feasible:** "The web system's intrusion detection functionality must capture the date, time, and IP address of any potential intrusion connection, as defined by intrusion-suspect criteria factors."

Prioritized

After you decide that everything on the list is necessary, requirements must then be prioritized — just in case completing all of them right now still isn't possible. Rank requirements from the business perspective, the technical perspective, or both. Facilitating these two perspectives involves some give and take:

✔ **From a business perspective, prioritize requirements according to their value, level of risk, or expected frequency of use in the business.** Stakeholders can characterize what they need by using declarative statements they must have X, X should be present, or X would be nice to have. Also identify requirements that may be considered a *delighter,* or something stakeholders may find unexpected but exciting and value-adding. (This concept is sometimes important in commercial situations.)

✔ **From the technical perspective, the technical team may need to implement requirements in order of technical importance or simplicity rather than by business importance.** Requirements for compliance with governmental regulations, operating system upgrades, and other drivers may not have been initiated by the business but are still important to the business. Make sure the business understands why you're prioritizing these items.

 Excellent requirements are not just textual statements. As we discuss throughout the book, requirements can be communicated in many forms: textual statements, diagrams, pictures, and so on. The characteristics of an excellent requirement apply to any form of communicating requirements.

Focusing on the Four Core Components

For each requirement, you have many different consumers, and you don't want to overload any of them with requirements that they don't need to worry about; otherwise, they may miss the things that are important for them. For this reason, requirements are broken down into four major *core components:* data, processes, external agents/actors, and business rules, which we discuss in the following sections.

Organizing and presenting the requirements according to the core component they describe helps the consumers focus their knowledge-building and requirements assessment in support of the work they need to do. They won't need to sort through and interpret or eliminate irrelevant requirements; they can instead review and understand requirements directly related to the portion of the solution that they are responsible for building.

Additionally, organizing requirements by their core components helps you because you can look holistically at one core component and then cross-check across the other core components to seek out inconsistencies and gaps and ultimately identify missing requirements.

Data

Data is information that frequently gets stored. Whether it's big data (such as volumes and volumes of multimedia or real-time information) or small everyday data (such as invoices, billing, sale projections, and personnel records), requirements for business data define what each piece of data is, what it's for, what it means, how it's represented, and what relationship it has to other pieces of data.

You typically store information in a database with both a physical and a logical design. The database is a physical place with structures (tables and columns) that capture and organize all its data. Physical database designs represent the technical requirements for how the business data will be stored, and these are frequently designed by the database administrators or data engineers. The *logical* design reflects what the solution's functional data requirements are to support the business needs. It's called logical because it shows logically how the business thinks about the data and its interconnected relationships from the business perspective. The BA frequently defines logical representations of data requirements after the information is elicited from the business stakeholders.

Defining business data from the logical perspective presents three major concerns: the entities, their attributes, and the relationships between them. We address those in the following sections.

The business may want to store a lot of valuable information, but when it comes to the question of storage and whether the business would pay to keep track of it, you need to push your business stakeholders to think about their data requirements carefully, remembering that data stored must be maintained, managed, tracked, validated, and retrieved. Make sure you walk your stakeholders through the financial impact their data requirements will have.

Entities

Entities are the biggest pieces of business data, and they represent major information elements. An entity is a uniquely identifiable person, thing, or concept that the business cares about and wants to store information for. Entity data is stored within tables, but as a requirement, an entity is a named noun, described by a textual definition.

Attributes

Named with nouns or noun phrases, *attributes* capture the many details known about an entity. They are stored as columns within a table and are pieces of information typically included on screens, web pages, and reports. The most important kinds of attributes collect information about the business data entities. To make it obvious which attributes describe data fields for which entity, business analysts commonly prefix attributes with their entity name in capitals. Some examples are EMPLOYEE.first-name, EMPLOYEE.last-name, and BUSINESS-UNIT.name.

Beyond the business information, you must also be concerned with attributes of the attributes. These characteristics describe the meta data about an entity and its attributes. *Meta data* is essentially data about the data. Attributes from a business perspective store business information about the entities, but attributes from a requirements perspective store information about the physical characteristics of each data field within the table. Clearly identifying what these characteristics are is critical for the data requirements and for ensuring the appropriate behavior of the solution. These sub-attributes include uniqueness and cardinality:

- ✔ **Uniqueness:** The first question to be answered about an attribute is whether it's unique for every occurrence. For example, if the attribute PERSON.first-name is specified as a unique attribute, one and only one occurrence of that entity can have that value. If your personal information is captured within the solution, then no other person occurring in the database can have the same first name as you — ever.

- ✔ **Cardinality:** The second and third questions deal with the attribute's *cardinality* (whether an attribute may or must have zero, one, or multiple values). First, you must determine whether the attribute is a mandatory field: Must data for this attribute be captured, or can the attribute value be left blank? If the attribute is optional, no data needs to be captured — blanks are okay. If the attribute is mandatory, something must be entered or an error will occur. In the first name example, if first name is mandatory, you must enter a name of some sort. You can't enter anyone into the database and not know and record what his first name is.

  The third question is about repetition. If an attribute has or is allowed repetition, then the business expects to collect multiple valid values for that attribute. You must consider whether the business is describing a *single-value field* — where the entity has one and only one of these things — or whether the entity the attribute describes may have many (or a collection) of these attributes. Repetitive attributes are frequently used to allow business stakeholders to collect different types of the same attributes or the same attributes across different points in time. An example of a repetitive attribute is PERSON.address. Think about how many addresses a person may have now: a home address, a work address, a shipping address they prefer for deliveries, a billing address, and maybe even a vacation address. And over time, he may rack up several of each of these as he moves from place to place.

Relationships

The last major concern in data requirements is the data's relationship to other pieces of data in a database. Relationships are defined by using *keys,* or relationship identifiers, that connect data tables together. They're also attributes, but they're special attributes in that they provide unique identifiers for individual data elements and denote relationships an entity has to other entities or attributes.

Data relationships also have cardinality defined. You must define whether a relationship must exist (for example, if salary data is captured, it must be related to an employee) or is optional (a person may or may not have a dependent), and whether any relationship that exists is expected to be repetitive between the related entities (a person may have a relationship to more than one dependent).

Process (use cases)

A *process* is something a person or thing does that gets stuff done. It's the collection of individual steps, activities, or other processes that together transform data and achieve an end goal (for example, "pay vendor invoice" or "find a local doctor"). Processes and *use cases* (written accounts of the sequence of steps performed by a user of an application to accomplish a complete business transaction) may be implemented as programs, modules, screens, or reports and can be manual (people perform each individual step) or electronic (systems perform each step). More and more, processes have elements of both, where a person does some part of the process and systems or technology does other parts, such as "balance checking account." (Read more on use cases in Chapter 13.)

Process requirements can be documented and represented in many forms. Use cases are a popular technique for process definition, but other techniques such as user stories, process flow diagrams, or workflow models are equally, if not more, useful depending on the need or documentation audience. (See Chapter 13 for guidance on choosing requirements techniques.)

Whichever techniques you use for requirements, the processes and use cases identified in those requirements are named with a verb phrase: verb and noun, where the verb is the transformation activity being performed, and the noun is the thing or piece of data being transformed. In technology-based processes, the documentation assures that modules and methods talking to the computer can access the right data, perform the right calculations, print reports, display screens, or correctly transmit information needed. In manual processes, documentation gives the people who will be performing those activities an idea about what needs to be done, what steps to take, and what data to access or provide. It also helps with actor identification, data calculations, and error or business rule checking.

External agents and actors

An *external agent* is the first person, organization, or system identified in requirements. Typically identified during the very early scoping part of a project, external agents are those with which the business area interacts. External agents either provide or are given information within the scope of the project or solution.

Actors, typically identified later in the process, are defined at the solution level. *Actors* are people, systems, or devices that directly interact with a system or solution, but actors are always external to the system. In the requirements, actors are named for their roles or with a generic title of the responsibility being represented (no actual names or specific people).

Actors become significantly more important in business analysis at the point where solution requirements are getting specific and more detailed at the functional and nonfunctional levels so that technical options and requirements can be effectively identified. Actor information, reviewed in context with their specific stakeholder and solution requirements, is critical to identifying and building the specific interfaces needed by the actors, as well as defining any security access requirements.

Actors interact with systems or solutions through an interface of some kind. Technical interfaces have different forms of implementation, and depending on the complexity of the interface, the requirements needed in order to effectively design and develop it vary. Systems or devices always interact with solutions by using electronic interfaces; however, our human friends may have more diverse interface requirements.

Core component requirements related to actors and agents include references to processes they perform, data they transform, and the business rules that govern or constrain their actions. Actor requirements are typically functional requirements and should outline information about the following:

✔ The screens and reports they need to see or use

✔ Data of concern

✔ Validation requirements for their data, specifying what is or isn't acceptable based on their role or any events

✔ Instructions needed by the actors for how to use the system (usability) or guide them in changing what they'll do after the solution is implemented (transition requirements)

If you find yourself immersed in interaction or usability design concerns, turn to the experts! Design engineers, product designers, and human factors engineers all have a specialty in psychological science and/or human-computer interaction and therefore can be terrific advisors or advocates for good interaction design (and experts on what not to do).

Business rules

Whether implemented in a technology solution or not, *business rules* define the way that a business works. They provide a model for how a business runs and manages its enterprise; describe the governance framework for the processes, data, and actors within the business; and define the business logic that ties together the data, processes, and agents/actors.

Business rules are the defined control or constraint conditions under which an actor may (or may not) perform or complete processes or actions and/or successfully view or transform data. Overall, business rules provide for different outcomes or results. Positive business rules give permission or allow something to happen, such as "employee is given one additional vacation day credit after 2 years of employment," while negative rules restrict actions or data values, as in "check number must be greater than 99 and less than 9,999,999."

The solution should not allow business leaders, processes, policies, or data to be undermined or compromised by allowing actions or data changes contrary to business operating procedures, regulatory policies, state or federal laws, or any other relevant stakeholder rule.

Facing the special challenges of discovering business rules

Writing excellent requirements, as explained earlier in the chapter, gets most challenging when you're defining business rules because business stakeholders frequently don't realize the circumstances under which they make decisions or allowances. In fact, stakeholders may not even recognize that certainly policies exist if they haven't consciously thought about them.

Identifying and isolating the decision factors in the business rules that govern the work or the data is considered a bit of an art. A whole segment of the business analysis industry — including many specialists and technology solutions — devotes itself solely to the art of identifying and managing business rules, decision models, and decision automation.

Barring those tools, you as a BA must be able to recognize cases where a business rule exists and at least write down its description or outcome at a high level. Then work with your stakeholders to figure out all the exceptions to that rule — because those exceptions usually turn out to be the primary business factors and decision criteria. Work can be done or situations resolved in plenty of different ways, but in a business environment, the decision about whether or how something will be done depends on different decision criteria or factors. Evaluation factors such as data values, security rights, order of events, or timing of actions can all play a part in determining whether something should or will be allowed to occur within a system or solution.

For instance, a business rule may be "benefits enrollment is allowed only 90 days after hire date or during the open enrollment period." But to identify the outcomes and exceptions, you really need to dig beneath the surface and ask the stakeholders things like "What if the employee is a rehire working here for a second time? Which hire date gets used in the evaluation of this rule; does the rule mean 90 days after the latest hire date? What happens on day 91?"

Considering cardinality for business rules

Business rules also have cardinality (described in the earlier section "Attributes"). The business must decide whether rules are optional or mandatory.

Optional rules allow actors to perform the action or transform the data despite a suggestion to the contrary. They show themselves through warnings or what we like to call *ask-the-user-first prompts.* You've probably seen one of these while using your own software solutions — after requesting an action or trying to update information that goes against what the system is supposed to do, you may have been asked something along the lines of "Are you sure?" or "You're not supposed to do that; do you want to do it anyway?"

If the actor isn't a human who can immediately respond to warnings but rather is another system, warnings or optional rules either will be suppressed and not seen or will be documented on a report or *exception log* that tracks the success or failure of the interface transactions. There, you see a list of messages raising concerns about the data transmissions or changes, and suggesting that the specific transactions be reviewed or issues resolved.

Mandatory rules create errors for the actor, who experiences a block or pause in the workflow such as a message or window that stops the activity until the actor responds to the error and resolves the issue. A familiar rules-based error is "wrong password, try again" (the accompanying mandatory rule may be "user must provide a valid username and password for access").

In system interfaces or *batch jobs* (automated, unattended data transformations or information transfers), errors may result in data not being processed or transmitted at all. In that case, errors are commonly recorded and reported through the exception/error log for later review and resolution.

Chapter 6

Hunting for the Right Information, Part 1: The Process

- -

In This Chapter

▶ Asking the right people the right questions

▶ Previewing elicitation approaches

▶ Making sure your language helps rather than hinders

▶ Organizing your information to make a plan

- -

So the time has come to sit down with everyone involved in the project and figure out what each person's problems are so you can eventually help solve them — well, *some* of them, anyway. (You can leave the rest to their therapists and mothers-in-law.) Easy, right? Not so fast.

Even though the project's stakeholders may tell you otherwise, identifying a company's problem and corresponding requirements isn't as easy as just asking people what they think is wrong and how to correct it and then simply implementing their suggestions. After all, doctors don't remove your gallbladder just because you tell them you think the gallbladder is causing your stomachache, so why should you put a solution in place for a business without doing your own thorough and specialized investigation? Even though you're not performing brain surgery (or the aforementioned psychotherapy) here, following certain techniques is just as important to the success of your project.

The information in this chapter explains the process you use to elicit the information you need to get to the root of the problem. For the tools you use to perform these tasks, head to Chapter 7.

Elicit, Don't Gather: Developing the Right Questions

To get your stakeholders to reveal the real issues, you have to do a bit of hunting. See, stakeholders aren't just sitting like ducks in a row around the conference table with all the problems and answers outlined for you on a nice, neat, big master list. Chances are that each person has a different perspective of what's wrong and how to fix it. Or maybe they're just telling you (or their boss) what they think you want to hear. Or perhaps they don't even know what the real problem is or how to fix it.

To be successful in your analysis, you must go beyond just gathering up whatever information the stakeholders present to you and elicit requirements instead. (For the basics on requirements, flip to Chapter 5.) If requirements were simply lying around to be picked up like ticker tape on the floor of the New York Stock Exchange, you wouldn't need business analysis at all!

Maneuvering about the human mind takes skill, finesse, and cleverness. *Eliciting* requirements is all about knowing how to design and ask a question, topics we explain in the following sections. (For more on communicating effectively with different stakeholders, turn to Chapter 3.)

Put the time in early! Develop questions prior to the elicitation session to make the most of it and drive out the information you need.

Identifying the type of question you want to ask

The first step in developing the greatest questions ever (or ones that really get to the problem or opportunity anyway) is to figure out which type of question — "what," "how," "why," "when," or "where" — you want to ask based on the information you need to obtain.

To determine which kind of question best suits your purposes, consider what you already know, what you don't know, and what information you need to get started. In the following sections, we tell you which questions elicit which kind of information and give examples of these questions in action.

You can find more sample questions by using templates, interview worksheets, brainstorming sessions, and other tools.

"What" questions

The answers to "what" questions help you build a general, big-picture framework so you can start filling in details with the other types of questions later. The answers to "what" questions provide information on the scope of the problem or a description of the problem. They get to the basics of the basics — the heart of the matter, the bottom line.

"What" questions are questions such as the following:

- ✔ **"What is the problem you're attempting to solve?"** Usually, businesses undertake business analysis projects to solve business problems. By understanding the problem a business is facing, you can best guide the follow-up questions to glean what the business really needs. Suppose you ask this question and get the answer "I can't enter detailed notes about my customer contact." With that info, you now know to follow-up with questions such as "What are the types of customer contact? What types of customer(s)? What types of customer contact call for notes?"

- ✔ **"What is the opportunity you're trying to take advantage of?"** Sometimes the company doesn't actually have a problem; it just wants to take advantage of an opportunity. For example, Apple didn't create the iPod because people were sitting around listening to their portable CD players and saying, "Man, it's a problem that I can only listen to 12 songs at a time on my portable music device." No, Apple designed the iPod to hold more than 1,000 songs in order to take advantage of an opportunity the company saw.

  Apple's answer to this "what" question probably would've been something like "We want to take advantage of a shift in the music industry to connect a music device onto a portable hard drive. Users can then carry around their entire music library with them." With that info, you'd then have been able to follow up with "What is the goal of the project? What indicates success? What revenue opportunities do we have?"

- ✔ **"What is the information/data you need to record and store?"** Businesses live on information, so they have to understand the data they need. Asking "What information do you need in order to make decisions in your daily operations?" leads to follow-up questions such as "What does *order history* mean? What does *customer profile* mean?"

"Who" questions

If you need to know the people involved in any given aspect of the project you're analyzing, ask (you guessed it) a "who" question. The answers to "who" questions help you understand not only the people but also the systems within the scope of the project. You really get a sense of who's turning the cogs and how they all relate to each other. And the relationships that "who" questions uncover can prove to be some of the most revealing information of all.

"Who" questions are questions such as these:

- ✔ **"Who will be creating the information?"** Answers to this question can lead you to discover stakeholders who may not have been identified in the beginning. Follow-up questions may be "Why is she the employee who creates this information?" and "Who does she collaborate with to create it?"

- ✔ **"Who will be using the information?"** Just knowing who creates the information is only one piece. Knowing who receives the information also helps you understand how many people are involved and how information should be communicated in the future. This question can lead to follow-up questions such as "Who are the people in that organization?", "What are their skill levels?", "Who do they interact with?", and "How is the information passed from the creator to the user?"

- ✔ **"Who is impacted by the solution?"** When you understand the people impacted by your solution, you're in a much better position to understand the direction and effort you need to put into the solution. If your answer is "toddlers" (meaning that you're building software designed for young kids, not that you consider your users childish), you're going to approach the solution differently than if the software is for adults and has to interface with Microsoft Office.

Don't think the who is important? Asking "who" questions can lead to your finding people affected by the solution whom you may not have included in your project scope. On one project Paul worked on, the sales department had initiated a project to have call center agents (rather than the more-expensive sales force) pre-qualify sales leads. Great idea from a cost perspective, but no one told the call center folks, so they were unprepared. After they were informed, the project had to increase its scope and budget to account for training the agents on their new responsibilities. If "who" questions had been more thoroughly explored, the team wouldn't have missed identifying, looping in, and training the call center as an important part of the project.

"Why" questions

If you want to understand the reason behind the project (or maintenance request), ask a "why" question. On the surface, this question type gets you to the motivation behind the request. But it can also unearth deeply hidden information because it requires stakeholders to really be conscious of their operations. Think about it; doesn't everyone fall into a sort of autopilot-driven routine at work? The "why" questions flip that switch back into manual mode and force stakeholders to think about what they're doing, which is super important for your analysis. These queries are great questions to lead you to the motivation or the reason the company is spending money pursuing this opportunity.

Here are some examples of "why" questions:

- ✔ **"Why is the company pursuing this opportunity over another?"**
- ✔ **"Why did the company decide on purchasing that software over other available options?"**
- ✔ **"Why are we rolling out a requirements management tool right now?"**

    What you may really mean by this question is "Why are we buying a requirements management tool when we haven't even defined our internal processes yet?" but phrasing it the second way may be politically volatile. The former version addresses the same issue in a more neutral way.

- ✔ **"Why is the ROI (return on investment) 2 percent over 10 years for this project?"**
- ✔ **"Why are we furloughing people with the highest intellectual capital in the company?"**
- ✔ **"Why isn't the company changing to keep up with the times?"**

"Why" questions don't always produce direct answers right away; you may get responses like "because that's the way we've always done it" and the business analysis version of the parental standby "because I'm the parent, that's why!" In these cases, figure out what the stakeholders don't understand or why they don't want to share. Rephrase the question ("Why has it always been done that way?" or "Who first did it that way?" for example) and go find the answer together with them.

"Why" questions can be tricky. They can have a negative impact if they're not asked the right way. They can easily put someone on the defensive. If you feel leading the questions with "why" will be problematic, start the questions with "What was the reasoning behind . . . ." This approach gets you to the answers you need, without making someone try to defend his or her rationale.

"Where" questions

If you need to understand where something is happening, ask a "where?" question. "Where" questions help you understand data sources ("Where is the data kept? Where do you get the data? Stakeholders, where does the data come from?") and can also help with planning ("Where are those users located?")

Some examples of where questions include the following:

- ✔ **"Where is the data coming from?"** Maybe it comes from users giving input or is pulled from another system or an outside source. Knowing the source of the information can help you plan interfaces or look for alternate sources of data. It can also reveal duplicate sources of data within your organization.

✔ **"At what point is the process most inefficient?"** This question may seem like a "what" question, but it's actually a "where" question because it enables you to pinpoint the location of bottlenecks and other inefficiencies.

Sometimes, you have to be crafty, especially if you're asking questions whose answers may put people on the defensive, just like "why" questions. When you experience this situation, think about different ways to ask the question, such as "Where is the bottleneck?" or "Where do people have the most problems?" The latter questions are not-so-obvious ways of getting the same information from your stakeholders.

✔ **"Where are the stakeholders themselves located?"** or **"Where are the people I'm eliciting requirements from located?"** Knowing the answers to these questions helps you plan your elicitation sessions. For instance, knowing your stakeholders are located halfway around the world alerts you that you can't just plan to stop into their offices and ask them questions; you may have to rely on phones, video conferencing, and other technology.

Knowing the proximity of resources and stakeholders is a vital piece of the "how long is this project going to take" equation because this knowledge helps you create an effective and efficient approach for project elicitation. For example, if many of the resources you need are offsite, you know to add time in for that situation when planning your project. And as the project's timeline and resource needs increase, so does the budget.

"When" questions

If you want to know the time aspect of something, ask a "when?" question. The "when" question gives you an idea of, well, when the problem or the trigger for a process occurs. The answers to "when" questions also give you more clues about how all the different stakeholders and tasks are related — key information for your overall understanding of the project.

Some examples of "when" questions are

✔ **"When do you experience the problem?"** Automotive service technicians often ask questions like "When do you experience the steering wheel shaking — just when you brake, or all the time?" and "When does the car refuse to start — in the morning, after a rainstorm, or all the time?" They're trying to narrow down the situations in which a problem occurs by asking leading questions.

The process is the same in business analysis. You identify possible triggers while ruling things out. For example, if you're working with a healthcare provider who's experiencing problems with timely billing of patients, you may ask, "When does the patient hand over the insurance card?" The answer to the question can help you determine when the doctor's office has the patient information, whether the doctor can see the patient, and when the office can bill for the service.

✔ **"When do you perform this process?"** This question helps determine the level of effort and priority associated with the request. For instance, if the process is performed hundreds of times per day, that process may be higher on the priority list than a process performed once per decade. (Sometimes, users may even say they can't remember the last time they performed the process!)

✔ **"When does the process begin?"** This question helps you understand not only the triggers for a process but also the users' understanding and recognition of the process. Asking users when the process for pumping gas starts helps you understand what they consider "pumping gas." Does the process start when they pull into the gas station? Pull up to the pump? Get out of the car and swipe their credit card?

"How" questions

The "how" question primes the pump for getting down to a solution. The answer to a "how" question helps you understand the current way in which a task or activity is done or the impact a change has to a business area. It's another layer of detail in your big picture.

Examples include the following:

✔ **"How does this problem affect the way you work?"** This information helps you understand the impacts to the business area. Knowing these effects, you can plan your solution and analysis phases and strategy (more on this in Chapter 11). As you uncover some of the "hows" in the process, you may also identify some stakeholders.

✔ **"How will these changes affect your business area?"** This question gets to the core of transition requirements (see Chapter 15). After you know how the specific change affects the stakeholders, you can plan for solutions to help ease the transition and change and account for training, migration, and preparing for the new solution.

Identifying appropriate sources of information

The type of question you ask determines your source, so after you have your type of question figured out, you know who to go after! At this stage in the game, you may not have actual names of stakeholders; you may only be able to identify your sources by titles or positions. Review the company's organization chart and ask questions about any positions that are unclear. Then go through the chart and pair questions with the positions and titles.

You generally direct "why" questions to the higher-ups in an organization, while the lower-level employees doing the day-to-day work are a fit for "what" and "how" questions. This approach makes sense if you think about each person's position within the organization. Employees in managerial roles typically understand more of the strategy — the why — behind performing a particular procedure and are more likely to understand interactions with other processes or departments. CEOs, directors, and managers can all put the operations within a great mission-driven context for you, as well as tell you how everything should run (or at least how they think it runs). The people actually performing the job can (usually) tell you exactly what they do and provide you with the step-by-step instructions or procedures that outline how to do it. That is, the line staff can tell you what really happens in those trenches.

The sample organization chart in Figure 6-1 illustrates this division. For example, if you want to understand how the sorters perform the sorting process, who should you ask? The sorters. Why? Because they do the job day in and day out. True, the line manager may once have been a sorter and probably still knows how the process works, but she now has more management responsibilities. The farther you go up the *org chart* (business lingo for organization chart), the farther away from the day-to-day operations of the business process you get. If you need an answer to the question "What are our sales quotas for all regions in the United States?", however, you ask a higher-level manager. The sorter, though able to figure out work-arounds and alternative ways to accomplish the process, may not be aware of this information.

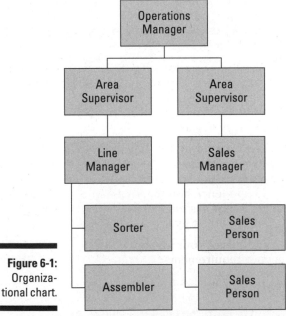

Figure 6-1:
Organizational chart.

Illustration by Wiley, Composition Services Graphics

Every day a manager is out of the hands-on operations of her business, the more she loses the knowledge of the how a procedure is done. We like to say these managers start losing their "SME-ness" (or subject matter expertise) each day they aren't performing the subject matter, so keep that in mind when pairing sources with questions.

Here's another example: Suppose the business has received complaints about shipment deliveries. According to Figure 6-1, you'd ask the operations manager and possibly the area supervisors questions like "Why is this a problem for the company?", "What are the current profit margins?", and "What is the impact to future sales and customer service metrics if we don't fix this?" Then maybe you'd ask the line manager and sales manager "Who was assigned to the specific deliveries in question? How were they trained?" Then you'd ask the sorters, salespeople, and assemblers questions that reveal the nuts and bolts: "What are the processes we perform to sell a product, take an order, assemble it, and deliver it?" and "How can those processes be improved?"

Choosing an Approach

Not only do you need to identify your sources within an organization, but you also need to choose an approach with which to elicit information. You can use 11 major elicitation techniques to draw information from your stakeholders (we go into more detail in Chapter 7):

- ✔ **Document analysis:** Look through existing documentation to figure out questions you want to ask stakeholders during your elicitation sessions.

- ✔ **Observation:** Watch business users perform their tasks to get firsthand insight into a company's true operations. Observation is an excellent technique to use when you want to automate a manual process, for instance. It's also a great way to establish rapport with your business users by performing the processes yourself.

One of the best ways to understand how the business does its work is by doing the work right next to the business. However, this approach does have its limitations in certain industries and tasks. For instance, you may be able to learn by experience how an administrator resets someone's password on a computer system, but you most likely won't get to learn how to land a 747 jumbo jet by actually landing it.

- ✔ **Interviews:** Ask probing questions of your interviewee to understand answers that will become your requirements.

- ✔ **Surveys:** Use these items to track metrics and elicit requirements from a large number of stakeholders located in a lot of different areas around the world.

- ✔ **Requirements workshops:** Use this technique, sometimes called *facilitated work sessions* or *Joint Application Development* (JAD) sessions, to bring project team members together in highly structured, focused meetings led by an independent facilitator (possibly a business analyst [BA] or project manager [PM] not closely related to the area) to develop high-quality requirements.

- ✔ **Brainstorming:** Get team members (and stakeholders) together to develop creative ideas to approach a specific problem or attack an opportunity from a different perspective. Allow ideas to flow creatively with the hope that an out-of-the-box solution arises.

- ✔ **Focus groups:** Pull together a randomly chosen group of individuals that meet a particular demographic to discuss a particular product or service. Focus groups are used mainly by retail businesses.

- ✔ **Interface analysis:** Examine documentation and discuss with technical stakeholders the interfaces among systems, people, and hardware to understand *system impacts* (how the data/process interacts with your system and another system).

- ✔ **Prototyping:** This method is ideal when you're working on a computer-based solution. Develop a model of the computer screen being developed as a solution so users have a picture of what the solution will look like.

  When creating prototypes with the business users, bring in the technical team. The technical folks can not only help with design suggestions but can also help guide you so you don't create a solution that can't be implemented. The result is that the business users don't get something in the end that they didn't see in the prototype.

- ✔ **Reverse engineering:** Take apart a product to see how it's built. With software, this approach may mean looking into the code to find out how it sets values and enforces business rules. For example, when you look at how a formula calculates a value in Microsoft Excel, you're reverse engineering.

- ✔ **Competitive analysis:** Look at the competitor's products to see what the minimum features your company has to offer in order for your product to be successful.

We explain all of these approaches in great detail in Chapter 7, but for now, knowing which technique works best based simply on the number of stakeholders goes a long way in helping you get started.

To choose an approach, figure out how many stakeholders you need to elicit information from on the project and then match that number up with the elicitation technique. You may find Table 6-1 helpful in deciding. (Keep in mind that the pairings in this table aren't hard and fast. Use them as a starting point for selecting your elicitation techniques.)

Table 6-1	Elicitation Approaches by Number of Stakeholders			
Approach	*Self*	*1–2 Stakeholders*	*5–7 Stakeholders*	*10+ Stakeholders*
Document analysis	X			
Observation		X		
Interviews		X		
Surveys				X
Requirements workshops			X	X
Brainstorming			X	
Focus groups			X	
Interface analysis	X			
Prototyping		X	X	
Reverse engineering	X			
Competitive analysis	X			

As your business analysis skills evolve, you'll probably find one technique you prefer over others. That's fine. But remember that you can fall back on other techniques if you find you're just not getting the information you need from your stakeholders.

Using Clear, Consistent Language

Forget everything your creative-writing teacher taught you in middle school; being predictable and repetitive when you're eliciting information is good in the world of business analysis! When eliciting, use the clearest communication you can. Make your sentences concise and complete. Avoid long sentences that keep going on and on and on and don't end and have multiple clauses that keep linking together and leading to a difficult way of interpreting the sentence (sort of like this sentence). The next sections highlight the key components of clear business communication and explain how you can frame your questions in a way that gets you the information you seek.

Choosing terms consistently

Stay away from using unnecessarily creative words and mixing up terms just for the sake of keeping your readers engaged. Pick a term and stick with it for maximum clarity in your communication. For example, don't mix terms such as *customer, account,* and *client* interchangeably to describe the same type of person. Instead, you may choose to use only *customer;* if you need to differentiate among different segments of the customer pool, you can describe them with different statuses such as *current, potential, preferred,* and so on.

To you, choosing one term among many that are similar may seem like mere (and innocent) semantics, but your job is to understand the company's culture and respect what its words and definitions mean. Inconsistently using terminology can confuse your audience and lead to things like incorrect security access to the solution (that is, you may end up giving the wrong people access to features they weren't supposed to access).

Using language that's consistent with the company's language

Each company you work with has its own terminology. For instance, Disney calls all its customers "guests" and its employees "cast members," and it uses this terminology in every communication and interaction. Adopting the company's language is important; doing so not only lets you avoid confusion but also reiterates that you're aware of and understand what makes this company unique, a key trait in someone targeted to devise solutions.

Here are some suggestions for making sure your language is consistent with a company's:

- ✔ **When encountering new terms, ask for the definition.** Understand what the company means when it uses a word like *customer, client,* or *guest.*
- ✔ **Each time you find a term you don't understand, ask for clarification.**
- ✔ **If you find a term very close to one already defined, ask your stakeholders if the new term is the same as the previously defined term.** If so, ask them to select one to use as the preferred term.
- ✔ **Create a glossary for yourself and for the project team.** Record all terms and company lingo so you can refer to them throughout the project.

Unless you've been working with a company for a long time, avoid making assumptions about terms (or anything in general, for that matter). Make sure you clearly define all language before using it. The clearer you are and the more you let stakeholders explain, the less chance you have for miscommunication. Don't be afraid to ask a question that might seem to have an obvious answer. If unsure, just ask.

Framing questions that clearly reveal core needs

We're sorry to say that even if you already understand the people you need to interact with, their level within the company, and the elicitation techniques you plan to use to draw out the information, you're still not quite ready to jump in. To get the real truth out of your stakeholders, you have to properly *frame the questions,* or ask your questions in such a way as to drill down to the real business or stakeholder need rather than just the suggested solution.

Frame your questions correctly, and you may even find a completely different problem than the one the stakeholders suggested. Imagine, for example, that a stakeholder states this requirement: "Open the address field on screen 1.6." Asking a question about what problem led to that request may reveal that the stakeholders need to track comments around customer contacts and saw an unused address field that would work perfectly for their solution. What they didn't know was that using the address field for something other than an address would lead to non-address data residing in an address field, which may cause a system failure due to dirty data.

So how do you frame a question properly? So glad you asked.

- **Ask open-ended questions.** *Open-ended questions* are questions that stakeholders can't answer with a simple yes or no. For example, ask "What are the problems you experience?" rather than "Do you experience slow response times?"

- **Figure out what the stakeholder is asking for.** A great place to start is with asking "Why does this stakeholder need this solution?" or "What is driving this request?" Your goal here is to uncover the real problem rather than just put in a solution, because putting in the solution doesn't get to the root cause. If you fix the wrong problem, the business may end up blaming you, the BA, for not fixing the problem even though you did exactly what the business asked you to do. For example, asking "Why are you looking to open the address field on screen 1.6?" helps you understand why the stakeholders are approaching a solution to a problem so you can understand the real problem. In this case, the original requirement presented to you — "Open the address field on screen 1.6." — was really a solution to an underlying problem.

✔ **Think about answers that may elicit a follow-up response.** Elicitation is not all about asking questions. It is about listening, too. Be careful not to jump ahead to other questions on the assumption that you know where the answer will take you. Listen to the answer to a question and ask clarifying questions to make sure you understand the answer fully.

✔ **Make your questions relevant to the business.** Although you don't have to be a domain expert to be an excellent business analysis professional, you do need to do your homework. Make sure your questions apply to the project and business area you are working with. "What business problem is the business attempting to solve?" "What would an ideal solution look like?"

Planning Your Elicitation Sessions

After you've designed all your questions as we discuss earlier in this chapter, it's time to arrange it all into a master plan to take over the world, muahahahahaha! Oh wait, that's a different book. Sorry. Seriously, though, you're ready to lay everything out so you can move forward and get the information you need. The plan is also vital for keeping everyone on the same page and keeping your session — and therefore, the project — on track.

Elicitation occurs throughout the project, in different phases and from different people. In fact, it occurs anytime you capture project information. The key of any elicitation session is to note what info you need to capture, whom you need to capture it from, and when you can capture (a meeting schedule).

Planning your elicitation sessions isn't an exact science; it's really more of an art. However, we have a rough checklist for you to follow as you lay everything out and capture the project information:

1. **Determine how many systems you're interfacing with.**

   Knowing how many systems are involved helps you identify the stakeholders you need to elicit information from in order to understand interfaces, data, processes, and business rules.

2. **Detail the number of stakeholders you're eliciting from.**

   By knowing the number, you can determine which elicitation techniques work best.

3. **Figure out where the stakeholders are.**

Eliciting from people who work in the same office as you do is different from eliciting from people in another state (or even halfway across the world). You may choose similar elicitation techniques for each group, but the meeting tools you choose may be different. For instance, you can still have a facilitated workshop, but instead of physically gathering stakeholders together in one meeting, you may have to use an online meeting tool.

4. Outline your stakeholders' personalities.

Are they visual people? Auditory people? Kinesthetic people? Everyone has a primary learning and interaction style. Knowing your stakeholders' preferred style puts you in a better position to tailor your message to your audience.

5. Specify the time frame you have for elicitation, according to the company.

You may need to collect all the requirements in a short period of time. This constraint means you may need to develop and elicit the requirements in a highly-intensive JAD session (explained in the earlier section "Choosing an Approach").

6. Explain the scope of the project.

After the project is underway, it should have a clearly defined project scope indicating the boundaries of your project and the objectives to be delivered by the project (much more on this in Chapter 10). You don't want to go outside the boundaries of the scope. Admittedly, moving beyond the project scope helps you understand more about what goes on outside the boundaries of the project at hand, but you only have a limited time with which to focus on the scope of the project.

7. Break down which questions go with which stakeholder.

Refer to the earlier section "Identifying the type of question you want to ask" to determine which questions you ask of each stakeholder.

8. Write out your stakeholders' schedules and find the time that works best for them; then book your session.

Remember to address not only stakeholders' schedules but also their time zones and when their days start and end. Schedule at a time when stakeholders are going to be at their best. Knowing a particular stakeholder is a "don't talk to me before I've had my morning coffee" kind of person is a great piece of information to have; you don't ever want to schedule her for a session first thing in the morning, or you may suffer the wrath of an improperly caffeinated stakeholder!

When you book your sessions, make sure everyone understands where the session is going to take place and what the objective is.

9. **If you're using applications and tools for elicitation, make sure you** *pre-trip* **— or test out — the tool prior to the actual elicitation session.**

   You want to do everything you can to avoid technical problems during the actual elicitation session.

10. **Conduct your elicitation session.**

    Show time: Now you get your hands — er, and also eyes and ears — dirty! Be ready to improvise in your elicitation sessions. Do not go down your list of questions one by one. Your questions are just a starting point; let the conversation flow naturally. You can't possibly come up with all the questions you need to ask, and some will come out of the sessions, so go with the flow. Your stakeholder may have lots of good information you didn't plan for.

Don't be overly concerned if all your initial questions aren't answered. You can always schedule another session to clarify, and some of the information the stakeholders offer may answer some of the future questions you have (and you don't even have to time-travel).

Chapter 7

Hunting for the Right Information, Part 2: The Techniques

In This Chapter

▶ Uncovering information by using different elicitation techniques

▶ Figuring out which techniques work best given your audience

▶ Determining which elicitation techniques work better for different requirements

Although every BA has his favorite primary elicitation method, all BAs should be comfortable with and adept at all the methods in this chapter. Chances are you'll need to use more than one technique every time you elicit requirements. Which one(s) you use depends on the size of the group, the company culture, and the types of requirements you need to elicit. Pick the right approaches for the given conditions, and you will successfully glean the info you need to move forward.

In this chapter, we detail all 11 techniques, telling you when each technique is most appropriate, how to use it, and more. This information not only forms the foundation of your info-extraction business, but it also is tremendously helpful in the requirements-planning phase (see the details of this phase in Chapter 11).

Starting with Document Analysis

Document analysis is probably your first stop in elicitation. Here, you peruse company documents to glean information about the current environment. Why go off and try and create something new without understanding what the company's operations are all about? You don't go into a job interview without understanding the prerequisites and skills needed for the job. You don't shop for a car without understanding the available options and warranty information. Similarly, you don't want to start eliciting requirements from stakeholders without understanding more about their current environment. The following sections show you why document analysis is a useful technique and give you a look at the wide variety of documents you may have to work with.

Understanding the benefits of document analysis

Analyzing existing documentation gives you a good sense of the project; the business processes you're supporting; and the rules, data, and stakeholders involved. You can get a good return on your investment for your time spent using this technique.

Gathering up and reviewing existing documentation also gives you clues as to who needs to be interviewed, data that needs to be captured, business rules that need to be enforced, processes that need to be followed, and that sort of thing. For instance, suppose you're assigned to a project to create or update some marketing reports. You start by gathering the reports that are currently in production. Here are some things you may notice:

- ✔ **The fact that the report can be run for salespeople, sales managers, and division managers:** That information tells you that these people need to be included in your elicitation sessions so you can understand their needs.

- ✔ **What data the company is currently capturing:** That info is important because this data is the information the stakeholders need in order to make decisions.

- ✔ **Info that helps you understand the business rules the company enforces:** *Business rules* are guidelines, such as calculations and security clearance levels, that define and shape a company's business operations and procedures. Consider these rules when defining and designing the solution for your project.

You can pull all of this stuff out of the existing reports to create a starting point for developing the right elicitation questions, which helps you create the new report.

To perform document analysis, follow these steps:

1. **Gather documentation that has already been created on the business area, systems, and so on, and that is in scope for the project.**

    This documentation may be all over the place — on document collaboration tools, such as Microsoft SharePoint, in servers, and in binders on people's desks. If you don't know whether the documentation exists, ask people involved with those systems whether you can find existing documentation.

2. **Read the documents and take notes.**

   Include in your notes things such as unclear information, glossary terms you need to define, processes that are executed, data involved, and systems and people that interface with the areas under study.

3. **Develop in-depth questions for the project team, based on your findings.**

   Examples of such questions include "Do you still pull data from System ABC?", "Are the stakeholders still located in California?", and "Does System X still contain the validation routines?" These are the kinds of in-depth questions this approach generates.

Perusing examples of documents you can review

Documents can be many things in many formats, from actual printed documents to printouts of screenshots to websites and blogs containing company and department information. In the following sections, we explain some of the various kinds of documentation you can review.

If a stakeholder pulls a dusty binder off a shelf to get you the documentation you're after, you may be working with an out-of-date document. (You can also inspect the document for a publication date to be sure.) But old doesn't necessarily mean worthless. Even if a document is a bit long in the tooth, you can still use it to as historical data and check to see whether the processes and data it mentions are still valid.

Reports, letters, and brochures

Pick up all reports, letters, or brochures you can get your hands on! Any of these artifacts is a gold mine for understanding how a company implements its processes and enforces policies. Each document holds its own special secrets:

- ✔ **Reports:** Aside from the actual data contained within it, a report tells you a lot about the audience for the report and the decisions the business makes based on the information. It also shows you how the data is sorted and whether it can be re-sorted.

- ✔ **Letters:** If you need to understand the various questions a company handles and how it responds to them, look at the letters it produces.

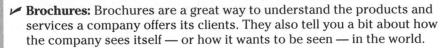

Look into the customer service area of a company, for example. Chances are that it has lots of standard letter templates (called *boilerplate* after an old printing term) it uses to interact with customers.

✔ **Brochures:** Brochures are a great way to understand the products and services a company offers its clients. They also tell you a bit about how the company sees itself — or how it wants to be seen — in the world.

When you think of brochures, don't think only of printed documents. Brochures can also exist electronically on websites.

Websites

A company's website can give you an invaluable look inside the organization. Not only do websites typically give you information about location, contact methods, and maybe even merchandise return and service call processes, but they can also tell you a lot about the company's culture, values, and mission. Spend a lot of time perusing the pages and taking notes: Is the website large or small? Is it text-based or photo-based? Does it seem to make a lot of information available to users, or does it encourage clients to contact the company for more info? What kind of image is the company presenting with its website?

Screen layouts

You can learn a lot about a company by simply looking at how its program screens are laid out when it performs business operations; truly, screens display lots of data you can use in your analysis. What data do its processes need? Look on the screen. What fields is the user required to fill out? Note those as mandatory fields. How about the labels on the screen? Are they built dynamically (such as to recognize a returning/logged-in user: "Welcome, Paul")? That's data. You need to understand where that data is coming from and how the screen builds it dynamically. Also, think about how the screen functions. What happens when buttons are pressed, or how do buttons get enabled? (Think about accepting software terms and conditions — you can't even enable the software button until you click the "agree to the terms" button.)

Screen artifacts can tell you a lot of information, and knowing the current setup — green screens versus GUIs (graphical user interfaces) — can tell you a lot. Be careful, though, of talking too much about the style of the screen too early. You need to understand the data, processes, and people who require access; then you can create a solution, which may be to continue to use the green screen or go over to a graphical interface.

In addition to live desktops, you can find screen layouts in tools used to create diagrams, like Microsoft Visio, in simulations, and even hand-drawn on paper or a whiteboard. In the early days of information technology (IT), screen layouts were even drawn on cocktail napkins!

Here are a couple of ways to document the key on-screen elements:

- ✔ To document a screen layout, take a screen shot of it by pressing the correct keypad sequence for Print Screen and then save the file.

- ✔ To save a whiteboard drawing of a screen layout, take a picture of the whiteboard; you can even use a smartphone!

Forms

Forms are very similar to screen layouts, only they're on paper. If a domain SME (subject matter expert) states that he fills out a form in the operations, ask for a copy of the form; your data elements are right there! Some forms even have boxes showing you how many characters you're able to capture, so you have a starting point for capturing data field lengths. The forms may indicate which fields need to be completed and which don't. (For info on SMEs, head to Chapter 3.)

User procedure manuals

Business rules — such as how users of a system are supposed to perform a task — are probably contained in the user procedure manuals. By reading these manuals, you can understand how the user *should* complete a procedure (compare that to observation, which we cover later in the chapter, where you find out how they really do it). For instance, if a procedure manual states that employees, users of the system, may not enroll in the company 401k plan until they have been employed with the company for at least six months, you know that any solution has to enforce this restriction. (Remember: The "user" can be an end customer of the company or the employees of the company, depending on what system you are dealing with.)

Looking through user manuals doesn't highlight only business rules. Business rules require data in order to perform their calculations or enforce their policies, so remember to gather and analyze the data, too. For example, a business rule may be "If you order more than $85 of merchandise, you receive free shipping" — a rule that enforces a company's free-shipping policy. "Handling equals 15 percent of net purchase amount" is a business rule governing how much a company charges for handling.

System documentation (including requirements documents)

System documentation, along with system architecture and interface documents, provides a lot of information about how everything works together. This data is especially relevant when it comes to your solution design (refer to Chapter 10) because you can easily keep track of which systems your solutions are linked to and then understand the impacts of making changes based on stakeholder requests. The information you get early on in the project helps you as you move through the project and put different solution options on the table.

Whether you ask stakeholders for the location of current system documentation or you go off and find it yourself on SharePoint, servers, or in the documentation library, you can discover that an awful lot of information already exists about current projects. Here are some documents containing information for review that you should keep an eye out for on your search:

- ✓ **Business requirements document (BRD):** This record provides information on what the business needed for the particular system in which the BRD was created.

- ✓ **Interface agreements:** These documents list the data fields contained in an interface with another system. They also may indicate the valid values used in the interface (for example, the interface may not use all the data fields available).

- ✓ **Scope diagrams:** These diagrams show which parties and systems are involved in a particular project.

- ✓ **System architecture:** Use these documents to see how various components of a solution link together to form a complete business system.

- ✓ **Functional requirements document (FRD):** Also known as a *functional requirements specification* (FRS), the FRD shows how the business problem was solved.

- ✓ **User interface specification:** This document shows the screens within the system, including expected actions when users mouse over a field, click on a button, and make selections within a screen.

Looking Out for Observation

Observation is observing the business doing, well, the business. (Pretty technical, huh?) One goal of observation is to understand how the process is performed, but you can also use this technique to see the business area's processes, workflow, environmental constraints, and business rules. The bonus? Observation is fairly simple to do and yields a lot of great information that's tough to get in other ways. In the following sections, we help you decide whether observation is right for your elicitation and break down how to put this approach to work.

Knowing when to use observation

Observation is an ideal elicitation technique in the following situations:

- ✓ **You're automating a manual process.** Observation allows you to understand how the process is performed manually today so you can come up with an automated solution for tomorrow.

Be careful that when you create the solution you don't just "pave the cow path." By that, we mean that you don't want to simply put technology on top of a bad process. Doing so only enables businesspeople to perform a bad process even faster. For more information on solutions, head to Chapter 10.

✔ **You're unfamiliar with the business area.** By observing, you get to learn and become familiar with the business processes, rules, and data.

✔ **You want to identify exceptions in the user's process.** Users can describe a process in an interview pretty easily (refer to the later section "Conducting Interviews"), but they typically describe the happy path — that is, what happens *most* of the time if no errors crop up in the process. For instance, if you're commuting home from work, you normally get in your car and drive home. But what if you get a flat tire? What if your spouse texts you to pick up milk on the way home? What if you run into a ten-mile backup? Observation can help you catch exceptions you'll need to develop solutions for.

✔ **You need to capture process metrics.** Perhaps the business has no idea how long a process takes. By observing it and timing it, you gain a much better understanding

✔ **You want to identify process constraints.** You may think rolling out laptops to the mobile sales force is a great idea, but then you observe the salespeople's process and see they have very little time to spend logging on to the laptop between customer visits. Hence, your solution may be a mobile phone app they can more easily access instead.

Choosing your observation method and completing the process

Even though observation is pretty simple, you can choose from three different approaches to observing a business user in action:

✔ **Pure observation without interaction:** In this model, you simply show up, remain quiet, and watch the person work.

✔ **Observation with interaction:** Here, you do get to interact with the person who performs the job. He can talk to you and you to him as he goes about performing the process you're observing. This method is a great way to not only ask questions that lead to understanding the process but also to establish rapport with your stakeholders.

✔ **Performing the task yourself:** This method is where you get to perform the job yourself a la the television program *Dirty Jobs*. With this approach, you establish even more credibility than when you observe with interaction; as an added benefit, you often stumble upon answers to unanswered questions.

Here's a perfect illustration of how valuable performing can be: Paul had a chance to work in a UPS air gateway and sort packages during the big Christmas rush. Before he jumped in to work, he noticed that almost all the sorters were wearing gloves. However, he declined a pair, assuming they were meant to keep the workers' hands warm; after all, it was December, and the doors to the tarmac were left open. What he didn't realize was that the gloves had tiny rubber dots on them to assist with the package-gripping activities. After two days of sorting packages bare-handed for hours on end, his hands didn't work very well. Before performing the process himself, Paul never would've thought to ask a question about the gloves, but by experiencing the task first-hand (no pun intended), he gained valuable insight.

Observation can not only be used to find out how things work, but it can also be used to confirm other forms of elicitation. By observing, you can see for yourself just how the process is performed in real life. Because this technique can provide so much information, you should strive to integrate different observation techniques into your elicitation to thoroughly capture your information.

Ready to get started with observation? Here's how you do it:

1. **Figure out when you want to observe.**

   Find out from your stakeholders when the best time to observe this process is. Does the process happen only at a certain time each day? Are there peak times to watch the process? If, for instance, you're observing the process of traffic management around Los Angeles, watching during rush hour shows you a much different experience than observing Saturday at 3:30 a.m.

2. **Get permission to observe.**

   Seek permission from the management team before you set up and start watching people. Showing up unannounced can make those you're observing uncomfortable.

   Try to put the folks you're observing at ease. Let them know you aren't there as a threat but rather to understand their jobs so you can make it easier for them (or whatever the actual reason is). Make sure they know that you want to hear any suggestions they have about the process you're studying that will make their jobs easier.

3. **Observe (or better yet, do the job yourself) and make notes.**

   Pay attention to these things:

   • **Process:** Note the entire sequence of events that occur, in order, being sure to include quantifiable information (such as how many widgets get pulled from the assembly line because of defects during the given time period or how often the line has to be stopped or slowed because of a glitch).

- **Business rules:** What rules are highlighted during observation. Sticking with the assembly-line example, the business rule would specify how a defect is defined.

- **External agents:** The *external agents* are the people performing the work. Note who is responsible for each part of the process.

- **Data:** The data is the information used during the process. What information is needed to perform the process, and what data is updated as a result of the process?

4. **After the observation period, use the notes you took in Step 3 to record all your observations.**

    These observations will lead to your understanding of the process and to additional questions surrounding the process. Also keep in mind that something that may seem insignificant in the process (like wearing gloves when sorting packages) can actually turn out to be pretty important.

When observing others, you need to realize that people will try hard to not make mistakes or will tend to follow the process as defined — behavior that doesn't always reflect reality. Suggest to the person you are observing to act as though you are not there.

Conducting Interviews

Interviews are probably the most-used elicitation technique for a couple of reasons: They're so easy to do (the BA asks a question, the stakeholder responds), and they can be done any time the BA and a stakeholder get together, whether in person, over the phone, or via e-mail. The following sections walk you through the interview process.

Preparing for the interview

When preparing for an elicitation interview, think through topics such as the goal of the interview, who your interviewee is and why this matters to him, what type of questions you're asking him, and what time works best to interview this stakeholder. (Check out Chapter 6 to understand which questions you should direct towards which stakeholders.)

Rather than leave scheduling up in the air or fit it in when you can, set up the interview as a meeting, even if it's a phone call. You want your stakeholders to be able to see it on their calendars to both remind them of the appointment and add legitimacy to the interview. Formal scheduling lets them know you're taking it seriously and that it's an important part of the process.

Finally, make sure you develop your questions in advance. Although you can let the interview flow along its natural course, you want to have some questions to start with and to go back to, to ensure you're on track and reaching the goal of the interview.

Interviewing the stakeholder

If your interviewee isn't familiar with the project, you may have to give him your *elevator speech,* a short summary of the project that quickly and simply defines what you're working on and its value proposition, before you start asking questions. (It's called an elevator speech because it's supposed to be succinct enough that you can deliver it to someone as you're riding in an elevator.) Here are some tips to keep in mind during an interview:

- ✔ **Ask *open-ended questions* (questions that can't be answered by yes or no).** Your goal is to keep the stakeholder talking. Like in a job interview, the interviewee should be doing about 80 percent of the talking.

- ✔ **Paraphrase what you hear.** This tactic ensures that you not only understand what the stakeholder is saying but also are interested in his situation.

- ✔ **Make the session about the stakeholder.** Focus on his needs and his problems. Stay away from project-related language as much as possible. The point is that you don't want to force him to think in terms of what he wants for the project but rather to get him to talk about what his problems are in his business area.

- ✔ **Treat the interview like a meeting.** If you scheduled 30 minutes, stick to 30 minutes (or less), and use an agenda (remember those questions you prepared ahead of time?). This approach helps keep both of you from straying too far from the topic. At the end, review any action items you recorded during the interview to ensure you both understand what follow-up items need to be addressed.

Stakeholders are people, too. Just because you're conducting a business interview doesn't mean you can't make small talk with your interviewee. Establishing a common connection increases your rapport with that stakeholder. Remember: If you are doing more listening and less talking, you are doing a great job.

Documenting the interview

For maximum results, write up a summary immediately after the interview (because if you're anything like us, you tend to lose information rapidly as more time elapses from the interview event). Write down the subjects you discussed, the decisions you made, and the action items each of you is responsible for and get the summary to the interviewee.

This documentation doesn't have to be a formal document. Paul uses outlines (in e-mail and in Microsoft Word), a *mind-map* (a technique to visually outline information discussed briefly in Chapter 4), and even Visio drawings as post-interview documentation. (Note, though, that not all stakeholders are familiar with the mind-map technique.) The important thing is getting the information from the interview in front of the stakeholder in the most efficient and effective way.

After you've compiled and sent the document, have the stakeholder confirm your interview summary. Not only does this move keep the stakeholder involved at this stage, but it also shows that you took the interview seriously and are looking for accuracy (and the stakeholder's confirmation of that accuracy). This part of the process gives your stakeholder a chance to correct anything in your summary that is incorrect or to clear up any questions you have. Plus, seeing the information again may trigger additional insight or help the stakeholder remember something he didn't bring up the first time. It's a way to get him to think about his involvement with the project without having to schedule a follow-up interview.

Having the stakeholder confirm the interview summary not only ensures you captured the information correctly but also helps prevent errors. For example, the stakeholder may have misspoken about something; even though you captured his information correctly, the recorded info is still wrong. When the stakeholder sees the summary, he realizes it's incorrect and makes the correction.

Distributing Surveys

Most of the time, you can't fly all around the world to fabulous international destinations to interview all your stakeholders (darn!). So how do you gather information from 4,000 users worldwide? Create a survey (some call it a questionnaire). How do you get them all to respond to the survey? That's a tougher answer — read on.

Dressing for the occasion: Types of surveys

Surveys come in two different question type varieties: closed and open-ended. Which type you use depends on the situation:

✔ **Closed:** Using closed questions is perfect when the responses to a question are known and finite. This type is a Yes/No question, pick a choice from a list, or pick all that apply from a list. Closed survey question results are easier to analyze than open-ended results because you can add up the like answers and compare and contrast the totals of each response to determine the requirements for your project.

✔ **Open-ended:** This question type allows for free responses. This type of question is perfect when the responses to the question are not known or the range of responses is large. The responses are more difficult to analyze, but they give you information from respondents in the respondents' own words. More information may result from this type of question than from closed questions, which allow only for responses that you include.

Feel free to combine the types of questions in one survey. You don't have to have a survey of only closed questions and another for open-ended. Regardless of the question type, think through what the goal of asking the question is and determine the best question type to use.

Maximizing the chances of getting a response

Be honest: When a website you're surfing asks you to take a short feedback survey, you usually just close out the window, right? Yet despite the fact that people often ignore survey requests, surveys are a great elicitation technique. Why? Because when done properly, surveys can generate a huge amount of data from a large number of stakeholders. Here are some pointers to help you create a survey that results in a high participation rate:

✔ **Make the respondents want to participate.** Money works, but you don't always have the luxury to offer cash to pay people to complete your survey. If you can't offer cash (and who can inside a company?), see whether you can offer the project team that gets the most responses a company-branded shirt, a pizza lunch, or whatever other tangible reward works in the organization's culture. The point is to figure out what motivator you can offer as the proverbial carrot. If all else fails, you just have to pull the "You have to fill it out because it's part of the job." card.

✔ **Be honest about survey length.** Don't say it's a 30-second survey if you know it'll take at least 8 to 10 minutes. Also, don't say it has 5 questions when each question has so many subquestions that it's more like a 60-question survey.

✔ **Use closed-ended questions.** Rather than ask for long responses, give yes/no options or a rating scale. This setup is easy for both you and the participant. Surveys yield a lot of data, and you don't necessarily have time to read all open-ended responses.

✔ **Weed out participants that don't fit your demographic upfront.** For instance, if you only want people to respond who have dined in a particular restaurant within the last 30 days, ask that question first and then end the survey for anyone who hasn't dined in.

Compiling and using the data

After you receive the data, you need to pull it all together. Look for trends in the data and for places where you can exploit opportunities. Examine the data to see what calls out to you as the BA. For information on how to develop the requirements based on the survey results, head to Chapter 12.

Getting to Know Requirements Workshops

Requirements workshops, also known as *JAD sessions, facilitated workshops,* or *work sessions,* are well-structured, intensive workshops in which an independent facilitator (that would be you) leads participants to develop high-quality work requirements (or *products*). The requirements workshop is one of the best techniques to use if you want high-quality requirements in a short amount of time. You can use these workshops at any stage in the project whenever you need to pull in a lot of brainpower from the project team.

ANECDOTE

A little flexibility here, people!

Funny story. Paul worked in a company that had a defined elicitation process of creating requirements in structured work sessions. It was so ingrained in the company's culture that some people were thrown off when Paul tried to understand business needs by sitting in stakeholders' cubes and asking them questions in a one-on-one session. They couldn't figure out why his questions couldn't wait for the work session the next day! In situations like this one, you may have to educate your stakeholders about the value of different ways of elicitation.

The products a requirements workshop produces are high quality because many people participate in the session, and the solution comes from the synergy created by everyone working together. (*Synergy* is the idea that the sum of everyone's contribution is greater than any individual part.) Different people bring different suggestions to the table and ask different questions as they come up with solutions. Whether you're a seasoned pro at facilitating groups and just need to brush up, or someone who is terrified at just the thought of running these sessions, this section of the book is here to help.

Identifying participants

Requirements workshops can range from one to many hours. You may need multiple sessions over a period of a few days. Because these workshops generally require a significant amount of time, considering who should attend is important. The attendees fall into three categories:

- **Required attendees:** These folks are the people who the meeting can't go on without. If these people don't show up, the meeting can't be successful, and you end up with a lot of out-of-meeting tasks.

- **Optional attendees:** The meeting can still go on and be successful without these people. However, having them in the session can be helpful because they may bring valuable insight and opinions.

- **Other people:** These attendees may be new team members who have just joined the team and are there to listen to how the topic being discussed works. Perhaps you're cross-training them or interfacing with them from another business domain.

Scheduling a workshop

When you schedule, you have to look at several factors — the availability of your required attendees, their location, and the length of time you need them. When, where, and for how long you have a workshop depends on knowing this information. Some questions to ask to get the answers include the following:

- **Who are the required attendees, and what is their availability?**

- **Where are the attendees located?** Are they all in the same building? Different locations? Different time zones? The answers to these questions determine whether you have an in-person or virtual workshop. If attendees are in multiple time zones all over the world, for example, you need to hold a virtual meeting.

> ✔ **How long do I make the workshop?** This determination depends on how much information you have to cover and on the limitations of stakeholder engagement. If you're physically in a meeting room together, you can easily monitor the engagement level of the attendees. If you're holding an online or phone conference, expect that people more easily multitask and may not stay 100 percent engaged. To combat that tendency, keep virtual meeting durations short (one hour or less) so people don't feel the meeting is taking away from their day; consider using a collaboration tool discussed in Chapter 4.

When planning your workshop, look at people's calendars and make sure they're available to attend. State which if any attendees are required. If those people don't show for the meeting, cancel it; having the meeting without them is a waste of time because you'll only have to have a second meeting when they do attend. If it becomes common that required attendees do not attend meetings, consider two things. First, ask yourself whether you have the right people identified. Second, determine whether the need to reschedule meetings is putting the project at risk. If the project is at risk, make sure to share that exposure with the team.

Managing the session

Properly managing a requirements workshop is essential. Info and ideas constantly fly back and forth during workshops, and if you don't capture them, they disappear. Plus, if you don't keep the conversation focused on the goal of the session and on the right track, you may not accomplish the elicitation needed for the project. The following sections show you how to keep things moving forward.

Using parking lots

A *parking lot* is a list of topics or concerns people bring up in the meeting that you don't want to address at that moment. Simply add the items as they come up to the parking lot list. This technique has so many advantages it's not even funny; here are two of the key ones:

> ✔ **It shows your concern for the stakeholder's issue.** Most people have a hard time dropping a point when they're afraid that it'll be forgotten. By adding it to the parking lot, you allay this fear, enabling the person to move on and not get stuck.

> ✔ **It keeps you on track.** The concern the stakeholder brings up may be covered later in the agenda, so tabling the point lets you stay on your agenda and not get derailed at that moment.

At the end of the meeting, make sure you set aside some time (usually about 5 minutes for a 1-hour meeting) to review the parking lot. At this point, you cover the information, assign it as an action item, or determine whether you need to schedule another meeting to discuss the topic. Before you get to the last option, though, see whether you can assign the concern to a group that can meet separately and provide a resolution.

Experiment with using different supplies, such as whiteboards and flip charts, to create your parking lot. You can even find flip chart paper that has adhesive on the back so you can hang everyone's ideas all around the room! And be prepared: The more organized the session, the more people will take it seriously.

Keeping things moving

As a BA, you act as a liaison among multiple groups, facilitating the sharing of information and ideas. Think of yourself as a traffic cop responsible for directing the traffic among the groups. If a technical stakeholder asks you a question about a decision the business makes, let the business answer if you don't know. You don't have to answer or even try to answer every question.

Also consider delegating responsibilities. If you're running the meeting, consider enlisting the help of another BA to take notes; facilitating the meeting is difficult enough without having to take notes on top of that. At the end of the meeting, the note-taker can turn over the meeting transcript to you so you can summarize the meeting minutes.

If you're using a conference call, consider having the note-taker logged into an instant messenger (IM). This way, if attendees on the conference bridge lose audio connection, they can notify you through IM.

When Paul managed a group of BAs, he'd work for his BAs in requirements workshops. The arrangement was that during the meetings, Paul would take notes in an outline, manage the IM traffic (and conversations), and handle the parking lot. The BA facilitating the session could assign Paul a task at any point during the meeting. After the meeting, Paul would turn over the outline to the BA, who would then have a good transcript of the meeting. This arrangement let the BA concentrate on facilitating instead of taking notes.

Wrapping things up by assigning action items

Before you leave the workshop, make sure you assign action items and agree to a time for their completion.

When assigning action items (tasks), follow this advice:

✔ **Ask the person to take the item.** Even though it's usually clear who needs to take which action item, asking is good etiquette. It also makes good business sense because people are more invested in tasks they agree to than in those foisted on them. Actually asking is one of the best ways to get stakeholder buy-in.

✔ **Agree to a deadline.** Instead of saying "You must complete that by Friday!", ask the person assigned the task when he can provide the answer. If his answer falls within your preferred time frame, great; you get what you need, and he feels like he's participated in setting the due date. If he states a date after your deadline, ask why. He may have a very valid reason, and you need to understand that your ideal deadline may not be reasonable. If he doesn't give a good reason, though, you need to explain why you need the information on a particular date. Sometimes further explanation is all that's necessary to get the stakeholder to agree to your deadline. If for whatever reason the date can't be met by the person, consider reassigning the task to another team member to keep the project moving forward.

After the meeting, distribute the meeting minutes to the meeting attendees (and anyone else who asks to be informed) so they can confirm the discussion and especially the key decisions affecting the direction of the project). Good practice is to distribute the meeting minutes within 48 hours of the requirements workshop.

Brainstorming

Brainstorming is a technique you can use to generate a large number of ideas in a short period of time. In brainstorming, you present a question, dilemma, issue, or whatever you're gathering info for and have participants voice their ideas without censure or modification. Brainstorming works by sparking new ideas as everyone hears everyone else's contributions. The result is synergy, and it's awesome.

When conducting a brainstorming session, make sure you and your participants follow these rules:

✔ **Let the ideas flow creatively and encourage the same from the session participants.** When looking at other people's responses, speak out what comes into your mind, no matter how crazy it may sound. If you hear or see something that reminds you of something else, it's your duty to share it! Your creative thought may spark someone else's creative thought.

✔ **Don't shut down any ideas.** No idea is a bad idea — not yet, at least. If you start saying, "We can't possibly implement that!", you run the risk of stunting the session. Participants may stop being so free with their ideas if they think they'll just get shot down. Yes, some of the ideas may be crossed off the list eventually, but they must be on the list to be crossed off.

A related concept is to praise ideas to encourage continued participation. Use it judiciously, though; praising may cause people to stop being creative and start trying to think of similar ideas to get the same praise.

✔ **Don't criticize or edit rules.** Just because someone decides mid-session that he doesn't like the rules doesn't mean he can change them or criticize them. This isn't a playground; you can't take your ball and go home.

✔ **Build on others' ideas and have participants do the same.** If nothing is sparking you, and you feel as though you're left behind, read through the list of brainstormed ideas again. If some people aren't participating, ask them questions like, "Jeff, what do you think about the situation?" The important thing is to bring stragglers into the discussion.

To help everyone feel comfortable with sharing ideas, start the session off with all participants writing their ideas down independently. Then open the session up by having them verbally share ideas. At the end, ask the participants to check their lists and see whether any additional items can be added.

Considering Focus Groups

If an elicitation technique was ever a top choice for the retail business domain, focus groups would likely be it. A retail operation's business structure is built on needing to solicit opinions from external customers, and focus groups do just that. *Focus groups* are sessions designed to elicit opinions on products from randomly selected individuals representing a particular demographic or viewpoint.

When creating a focus group, consider the following points:

✔ **Figure out the topic you want to cover.** Doing so helps you figure out who you want to pull into the focus group. For instance, if you're eliciting people's attitudes and opinions about diapers, you probably want to involve parents of young children (and specifically, the parents that change the diapers).

✔ **Consider holding the session off-site.** By scheduling the focus groups away from corporate headquarters, you accomplish two things:

• **Helping participants feel more at ease:** The idea of having the corporate big brother looking over their shoulders may make people feel inclined to sugar-coat their opinions or to hold back.

• **Maintaining the company's anonymity:** You may not want the people in the focus group to know whose product you're evaluating. This strategy helps keep a company's direction a secret. If people in the focus group are talking about the company's product, they could leak information about it that you don't want the general public to know.

✔ **Have an independent facilitator monitor.** These people are trained to be impartial and to drill into the information you need to get, so use them. If the facilitator isn't independent, he may goad or push the attendees into a direction that supports a company's hypothesis. If your facilitator is a BA assigned to Project X, and the members of the focus group are condemning the Project X application, the facilitator may feel inclined to start defending it.

✔ **Engage the members of the group.** Ask them for suggestions on what they think would be a great solution. Although you may not use exactly what they suggest, they may give you a solution or something that sparks a solution.

Doing Interface Analysis

If you think interface analysis is the act of analyzing the interfaces, you can go to the head of the class. But realize that you're dealing with more than just the user interfaces. An *interface* is a connection that your project (or application) has with a user, another computer system, or a piece of hardware.

You most often use this elicitation technique with software solutions because understanding the number of interfaces the project interacts with is critically important. With this knowledge, you can present your project estimate with facts rather than a guesstimate like "small," "medium," or "large." Using interface analysis, you have an artifact showing the number of interfaces.

When performing this technique, mine the documents (flip to the earlier section "Document Analysis" for the lowdown on document analysis) to look at the *impacts* (what other areas, applications, systems, people, hardware, and other projects it interacts with; if the interface is a connection between the solution for your project and something else, the impact is what needs to be done in order to interface properly with that the something else). For instance, look at Figure 7-1 to see how creating an application needs to find all the interfaces. In this figure, the stakeholders have identified three interfaces for a maps application: User Interface (the people who need to interact with the information and application), System Interfaces (the GPS satellites, which makes it possible to get position), and a Hardware Interface (which enables the user to charge the device).

Think about the interfaces Apple had to deal with for just one app in the iOS 6 upgrade. The maps application had to have a new user interface, a system interface with the mapping services, and a hardware interface to the new iPhone.

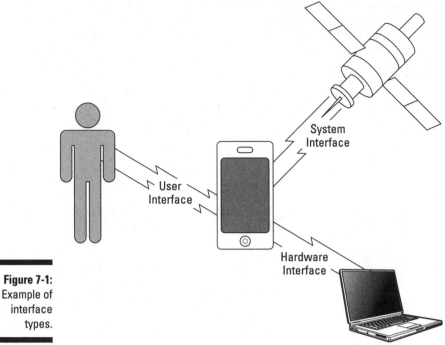

Figure 7-1:
Example of
interface
types.

Illustration by Wiley, Composition Services Graphics

As the BA, you need to think about these interfaces because even a seemingly small request from a stakeholder can turn into a much larger project. The more interfaces there are, the more people you have to work with to make sure the interface is working as needed.

Here are some questions to ask to find interfaces and help you determine the extent of the impact:

✔ Where does the information we need come from?

✔ Where is the information sent?

✔ How do we move the information from system to system (hardware interfaces)?

✔ Who uses the system? What kind of user? What kind of experience level?

Prototyping

In *prototyping,* you create a model of the proposed solution. In business analysis, a *prototype,* or *mockup,* generally means a representation of a computer screen and examples of how the user will interact with the application to accomplish a task to solve the business problem. The BA creates the prototype, usually with help from the technical team.

Prototyping is a great tool to communicate what a software solution will look like. You just need to make sure that the solution doesn't come before the underlying problem has been identified. Sometimes, a stakeholder draws a picture showing you what he thinks the solution should look like. That initiative isn't necessarily bad, but it puts the cart before the horse. In this situation, you still need to understand what the underlying problem is within the business domain.

Here are the reasons why prototyping is so great:

- ✔ **Prototypes give users something tangible to review.** People are visual. Many people are interested in seeing what something looks like, and the prototype fits this bill.

- ✔ **When done properly, prototypes can speed up the project lifecycle.** If a picture is worth a thousand words, prototypes save a lot of talking. In fact, in a commercial off-the-shelf (COTS) system, BAs often start with prototypes because the screen has already been designed. The changes to the screen and the configuration will be modified on the mockup.

Be careful about using prototypes too early in the project. Users may get caught up in the aesthetics of the screen and want you to make the fonts sans serif or something like that. Unless someone presents a valid reason for changing the aesthetics, remember the purpose of the prototype: You're only trying to understand how the solution should function. In addition, make sure everyone knows the prototype is just a picture. Some prototypes may look, and even feel, like a real system. People tend to think the system is already built and ready to be used, but it hasn't.

That said, sometimes aesthetic changes matter. Paul once created a dashboard for his manager that showed the health of the manager's projects with green, yellow, and red boxes. Unfortunately, the manager was colorblind, so the red and green boxes weren't useful. *That* is a valid reason to change colors!

You can work with three different types of prototypes, which we explain in the next sections.

Throwaway prototypes

You may be shocked that we'd suggest you throw away something you took a long time creating, but that's essentially what you do with *throwaway prototypes*. Throwaway prototypes are just pictures. You may draw them on a whiteboard or with an application like Microsoft Word or even on a napkin.

These may be kept as artifacts, but they are thrown away in the sense that they are not used to build the system directly. Sure, they're useful graphics, but that's the extent of it. The development team starts to build or update the application from scratch because the prototype can't be *leveraged* (it doesn't include code that developers can use when programming the solution).

Figure 7-2 shows an example of a throwaway prototype for a computer application. What's hard to notice is that it's just a drawing. Nothing more. That means the developers have to start coding from scratch.

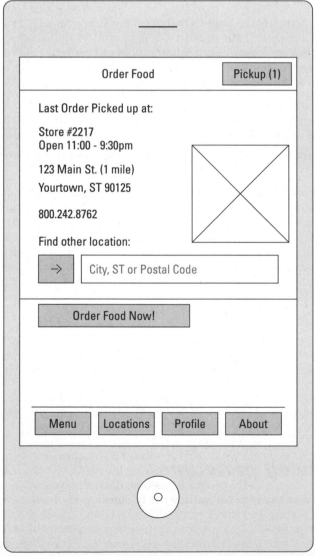

Figure 7-2:
A throw-
away
prototype.

Illustration by Wiley, Composition Services Graphics

Ricardo Nascimento
205, 5th Avenue SW - Suite 400
Calgary, Alberta T2P 2V7
Canada

Shipping Address/Adresse d'expédition:
Ricardo Nascimento
205, 5th Avenue SW - Suite 400
Calgary, Alberta T2P 2V7
Canada

SDcvtZRFfR

Invoice for/Bon de livraison pour

Your order of/Votre commande du:September 25, 2013   Invoice number/N° bon de livraison DcvtZRFfR October 7, 2013
Order ID/N° commande: 702-4988626-6398613

Quantity/Quantité	Item/Article	Description/Description	Our Price/Notre prix	Total/Total
1	Business Analysis For Dummies (** P-1-A181F576 **) 1118510585	Paperback	CDN$ 20.05	CDN$ 20.05

	Subtotal/Sous-total		CDN$ 20.05
	Shipping and Handling/Frais de port		CDN$ 0.00
	GST/HST/TPS/TVH		CDN$ 1.00
	PST/RST/QST/TVP/TVD/TVQ		CDN$ 0.00
	Order Total/Montant total		CDN$ 21.05
	Paid via/Payé par Visa		CDN$ 21.05
	Balance Due/Montant du		CDN$ 0.00

This shipment completes your order.

You can always check the status of your orders from the "Your Account" link on our home page.

Thanks for shopping at Amazon.ca, and please come again!
Cette livraison complète votre commande.

Vous pouvez à tout moment consulter l'état de votre commande grâce au lien "Votre compte" sur notre page d'accueil.

Merci de faire confiance à Amazon.ca Revenez nous voir!

Amazon.com.ca, Inc. 410 Terry Avenue North Seattle, WA 98109-5210
GST Registration Number/N° enregistrement TPS 85730 5932 RT0001 / QST Registration Number/
N° enregistrement TVQ 1201187015 TQ0001 / RST Registration Number/N° enregistrement
TVD 85730 5932 MT0001 / PST Registration Number/N° enregistrement TVP PST-1017-2103

0/DcvtZRFfR/-1 of 1-//UPS-VANBC/econ-ca/3820433/1011-18:00/1008-11:11

JM8

Page:1 of 1

When you make throwaway prototypes, follow the concept of "just enough." That is, spend only enough time on the prototype to get the project team to understand what needs to be done, and then move on. Time is tight, so you don't want to spend any longer than is necessary.

Evolutionary prototype

Evolutionary prototypes let the development team leverage the effort of the analysis; basically, what starts as a prototype turns into the actual solution. The advantage with this approach is that the expectations from the business are solid. They see the actual front end of the solution, and the developers make the necessary changes as the team works to clearly define the solution. Many times, the development team is involved in the creation of the front end and can guide the team on approaches.

Simulation prototype

Simulation prototypes are sort of like throwaway prototypes on steroids. Ultimately, the development team can't leverage these prototypes for code (although at the time of this writing, some simulation tools are allowing some code snippets to be exported like in an evolutionary prototype). The advantage with the simulation is it gives the business stakeholders something tangible to walk through. Users can interact with the solution and see how it works as they click and navigate through the proposed solution. There is discussion about simulation tools in Chapter 4.

Reverse Engineering

Reverse engineering refers to looking at the solution to figure out how it works. Basically, you work backward from the solution to understand the data, processes, and business rules. Reverse engineering is more common than you think. Have you ever looked into a Microsoft Excel formula to figure out where it's coming up with the calculation? Congratulations; you've reverse engineered!

Usually, reverse engineering is used to examine software or software components to figure out how they're processing business rules, where they're sourcing data, and how they make decisions. Basically, you want to understand how the software is supporting the business.

The use of this elicitation technique is increasing across the field because of all the *legacy systems* (old computer systems) sitting around. These systems need to be updated or replaced completely. Applications built on the mainframe 30 years ago were never expected to last as long as they have, and technology has progressed so far that these systems have to be reverse engineered so people can figure out how they work.

Here are some more-specific situations in which reverse engineering can be helpful:

- ✔ **When you're not sure what is happening within your code or need to understand how an old computer system calculates a certain field:** Business users may ask about how the system supports the business process, or what business rules are being enforced, which means you have to go in and figure it out.

- ✔ **When the software documentation is out of date:** In fact, you may not even have any documentation. Without up-to-date documentation on how the software works, you may have to go into a system and trace the code logic to find out why, say, the system performs a calculation a certain way.

- ✔ **When business users aren't aware of the business rules being enforced:** The business may have changed in the years since the rules were hard-coded into the application. You may have to walk business users through the system to find out what rules are being enforced and how they need to be changed.

- ✔ **When you're interfacing systems and need to know the correctness of data in each system:** This challenge is one you face when you create ongoing interfaces or one-time data migrations. For instance, in order to comply with e-mail regulations, you need to make sure opt-out preferences are always correct. If you do a migration, you need to go back and double-check that the old and new settings match.

Don't hesitate to ask for help with reverse engineering. If you don't understand where or how to look through software code, enlist a developer on the project team. He will have a good idea where to start looking for the rules, data, or enforced processes.

Choosing Competitive Analysis

Competitive analysis is a technique to examine your competitor's products and services and evaluate them against your products and services. The result is seeing how your offering stacks up against the competition.

The thought behind this technique is that external customers will not accept or adopt your product if it doesn't offer at least the minimum number of features and functions that your competitor's product offers. If a competitor's

Product B has features X, Y, and Z for $199, and you roll out a similar Product B that has only feature X but is the same price, how often do you think consumers will buy your product? Think about companies in the mobile phone industry. They're always looking to see what features and functions their competitors are offering so that they can offer more features or a better way to accomplish the same feature for a similar or lower price.

The BA performs the competitive analysis and then presents it to the project team, perhaps in a comparison table (our product versus their product) or a SWOT (strengths, weaknesses, opportunities, threats) analysis.

When performing competitive analysis, think through the following questions:

- ✔ **What features does our competitor have on a similar product?**

- ✔ **What are the most important features to customers, and how does our product stack up against the competition based on those features?** Hint: Use focus groups, which we discuss earlier in the chapter, to understand what the external consumer really cares about.

- ✔ **Can we exploit our competition's lack of features we already have or develop features neither of us has?**

- ✔ **How can we position our features/functions in a way that puts our product in a better light?**

When performing competitive analysis, make sure you aren't your own competitor. If you offer a lower-priced product that has almost the same functionality as one of your premium (higher-priced) products, you may be stripping away sales from the premium product, essentially competing against yourself.

Chapter 8

Uncovering and Analyzing Needs

· ·

In This Chapter

▶ Understanding the differences between company and stakeholder needs

▶ Finding the business problem and figuring out whether to solve it

▶ Innovating solutions that speak to the business's needs

· ·

*N*eeds are things that someone wants but doesn't have. At some point, a person with needs (or an organization with business needs) may decide that having a specific need unmet is unacceptable, and she'll look for a solution to fill it — which is where you come in. This chapter walks you through how to figure out what those real needs are (not what the stakeholders just tell you they are) so that you can be a solution-provider, defining the right solutions and making them valuable.

Investigating the Needs

Although business analysts (BAs) help provide valuable solutions, their key goal is actually to help stakeholders meet their business needs. Investigating the real need becomes a critical activity for ensuring good business analysis because the decision to meet these needs becomes the requirement (for a refresher on requirements, flip to Chapter 5).

The thing is, stakeholders often express their needs in the form of a solution, so you must put your best sleuthing skills to use. To start with, you want your stakeholder to explain what her problem is. The solution the stakeholder proposes ("You know, I really need X") may be a good solution, but it may not be the best solution. You may find she actually needs X to do Y to get Z. Perhaps the best solution doesn't give her X; instead, it skips Y and gets her to Z directly! That solution fills the real need more quickly and cheaply. X was just her means to an end; she really needed Z.

But not all needs can be filled by a solution directly; you may find that the best solution is a problem-resolving one rather than a need-providing one. If the stakeholder has to drive some or much of the effort herself (through skill or expertise, perhaps) to meet her need but is having trouble doing so — she really did need to do Y herself — then providing X is the best solution. It solves her problem in doing Y, which meets the need for Z.

Either way, you must figure out what's best for meeting the need most effectively by digging into those requests to unearth what's really motivating the stakeholder's search. She needs something for a reason; find out why! The following sections help you do just that.

Discovering a company's specific business needs

You must consider the needs of a company by interviewing company leaders. Just be sure that when looking to discover these *business needs,* your research is focused within the context of what the business is trying to achieve or do, not just on what the leaders are trying to do. If you let your team start working on solutions that meet stakeholder's needs without making sure you're serving an important business need, your project may not be the best investment. (You can read more about stakeholder needs in the later section "Searching out stakeholder needs.")

To find the business needs, ask questions! Start with the person at the company who requested that you embark on this project to find out why, what, and "what for" the requestor is asking in the first place; then let the research take you where it will. (In this case, *what for* means "to what end," not "why.") If stakeholders aren't clear, consider using the following to clarify:

- ✔ **Analyzing the mission:** Most companies have a mission, and a company's leaders have a vision and sense for what the company must do to achieve that mission, so start there. Ask around or perform some document analysis (see Chapter 7) to discover what the mission and vision are. Are they clearly articulated? Is the company going in the right direction — delivering on its mission, achieving impact, and adding value? As a result, is it realizing benefits? Is the company's performance at a level that suggests the future vision is in sight and likely to be accomplished? If the only answers you get to these questions are "no," "don't know," "not to the extent it could or should be," or even just "not yet, but getting there!", the company definitely has mission-related needs! *Tip:* A company's annual report, website, or internal strategy documents often have this info.

- ✔ **Scrutinizing the market:** Companies generally operate within or serve a particular market or set of markets; they focus on solving a specific set of problems or providing services to clients or customers, typically within a given domain. To gauge market-related problems, ask questions. What problems is the company solving? What clients or customers is it serving? What solutions (products or services) is it offering? Are those audiences excited about those solutions because they successfully solve their problems, or do they have a lukewarm response because the solutions only scratch the surface? What's the customer experience when dealing with the company? Are customers happy or frustrated? Are other competitors solving their problems better or less expensively?

Consider also that a company may be operating within or serving markets not in line with its mission. If so, find out why and determine whether it should continue doing so. Branching out, expanding, and pursuing new markets are totally acceptable, but is that outreach a discovery experiment, or does the company need to redefine its mission at some point to reflect new directions and strategies? If so, how does redefining it affect its organization, operations, or enterprise architecture? What else may need to change?

✔ **Looking toward the company's future:** In addition to maintaining its status quo, a company typically has targets to shoot for each year — annual goals and objectives set by executives who monitor the progress. That means that even if a company performs and progresses effectively and accomplishes its overall mission, it periodically gets new goals, objectives, and milestones to achieve for continued success. Those items are the next set of company needs you can look for. Ask these questions: What are the specific goals and objectives for the next year? How about the next 3 or 5 years? What are the critical milestones? What are the key performance indicators? Are they being met?

✔ **Identifying obstacles:** Like any entity trying to accomplish a set of goals, the company likely faces problems or challenges in achieving its goals. Stumbles, tripping points, and hurdles always pop up along the way. Consider what those challenges are. The company may be facing competitive or legislative concerns; it may have to confront regulatory inquiries, operational issues, or perhaps financial or cash-flow challenges. Legal guidelines, operating standards, a host of requirements, and terms may come down from external stakeholders, business partners, and suppliers. The company needs solutions to those problems and support for its efforts.

Each hurdle may translate to a need of some sort: a need to meet a requirement, a need to comply with a law or regulation, or a need to find opportunities and rise up to competitive challenges. Explore where the company struggles to accomplish its goals by using appropriate elicitation techniques, applying critical thinking, and asking good questions: What's stopping progress or operations? What requirements have others presented, and what's the company's position on each? (For details on elicitation techniques, check out Chapter 7.)

Breaking down obstacles

After you've pinpointed an obstacle, identify its characteristics to get the whole picture. Is the company compelled to meet certain requirements, or are they merely suggestions? What's the risk to the company of not complying versus changing processes or products so that it does? What exactly are the guidelines?

If stakeholders themselves are having a challenge, figure out what business-level goal, objective, or outcome they're working to support or achieve. Do the stakeholder challenges affect the business results? What do they or the business need in order to do better or differently? Continue your analysis by evaluating organizational support structures. Every company has organizational and operational groups that, together, do the work of the business. Each group has a role — whether formally defined or not — that is (or should be) aligned to the company's mission, vision, and corporate strategy. When analyzing the organization to identify business needs, you need to do three things: Identify how each group fits into the business as a whole; determine whether each group is performing its role effectively and efficiently; and diagnose whether, together, all groups are covering all the business's needs or whether they're suffering a gap in processes or outcome somewhere. Here are some questions to ask:

 ✔ Does the role that the group is playing and the work it's doing make sense for what it and the business are trying to achieve?

 ✔ Does the group align to the bigger picture or conflict with it? Is the group missing, adding, or duplicating anything important?

 ✔ Is the group collaborating and progressing work with other organizations efficiently? Is it passing any work to or getting work from other groups in a way that creates cost or inefficiencies?

Each individual group may work fine within itself, but if together the stakeholders aren't getting the job done in a way that's best for the business, they may have a problem. It may not be any one stakeholder's or group's individual problem, but in the larger context or bigger picture of how all those stakeholder pieces fit into the overall corporate puzzle, you may identify an undelivered outcome, missing process, or a broken service line.

Conversely, you may find a group responsible for something that the company doesn't need. Sometimes organizations or stakeholder groups evolve over time, but they keep doing tasks they've always done just because they're on autopilot or don't realize how new processes may help or hamper others. You may have a unique opportunity to look across groups end-to-end and see them in a more holistic, business delivery light than stakeholders would be able to see themselves. Defining an organizational structure or business architecture issue that needs to be addressed can be a valuable outcome for the business and is a real achievement for you as a business analyst.

Figuring out that something important is missing from (or unnecessarily added to) the business can be a tiny operational detail or a strategic organizational concern. Depending on the specifics, it may be a nonissue to fix, but it may require executive-level discussions on workforce staffing levels, group charters, or leadership roles — potentially a political hot potato. If what you find has senior-level impact, the way you share your findings may require some finesse. If you think you may have identified a sticky situation, seek some guidance from a mentor who can advise you on the appropriate communications approach and next steps. Do some stakeholder analysis (which we cover in Chapter 3) and keep your business-savvy wits about you.

Asking performance-related questions

If you've exhausted the mission-investigating questions in the preceding section and still aren't clear on what the company needs, begin by simply inquiring about its performance with questions such as the following:

- ✔ What areas of service or operation are currently monetized? What's the profit margin? Is it enough or too much? Has it changed?

- ✔ What's the revenue trend in each area? What does that trend indicate?

- ✔ What surprises the business leaders? (For example, are certain products not selling as leaders thought they would?)

- ✔ What did the company expect to perform differently, and what needs to change?

- ✔ Strategically, is the company serving the market or operating in the domain that it should be?

- ✔ Are customers or clients offering concerns or suggestions? If so, has the company done anything about them? Identify what happens if the business does or doesn't implement a specific suggestion or fix a certain problem. Would the business still achieve its desired outcome? What's the impact of a hit or a miss? How serious are the concerns raised to the business?

Searching out stakeholder needs

Each stakeholder — department, group, or leader — has a specific part to play that's in line with a company's corporate mission: Deliver effective operations, enable innovations and creative problem-solving, or provide valuable products and services. As the BA, you're charged with finding out how that's going for the stakeholders and whether their needs are being met so they can meet those of the company.

Subsequently, if stakeholders are having challenges playing their parts effectively, you're responsible for finding out specifically what they're trying to accomplish and what's preventing them from doing that effectively. You must know what their specific tactical or operational goals, problems, and needs are. These *stakeholder needs* come to light when you focus on what the stakeholders are trying to achieve operationally and what they can't easily or effectively achieve (and why). In the following sections, we help you uncover stakeholder needs and figure out how stakeholders interact with others.

Identifying what stakeholders need

The easiest and best place to start when discovering stakeholder needs is with their primary, bottom-line job(s). Find out what their objectives and responsibilities are — in other words, what do they need to do? Are they doing it? Is it going well? Are they achieving what they're expected to? If not, what's not going well? What are they having trouble with? Find out how they can tell whether they're meeting their goals. Do they measure something to find out for sure? Use the same approach to discover stakeholder needs as you do to discover business needs: Just ask the right questions. (The earlier section "Discovering a company's specific business needs" has details on the right questions for that topic.)

- ✔ What are the stakeholders' roles, goals, mission, and vision for the future?

- ✔ Are they on track? Do they have milestones or deadlines that they're trying to meet or beat? Are they following certain processes or procedures to get there?

- ✔ What tools or resources do they use, and what don't they have that would help them do their work better, more quickly, or more cheaply? Why don't they have those things? What have they found that's effective, and what issues or concerns are in their way?

- ✔ If they're using software solutions as part of their work, what are their *user goals* (the reasons they interact with the software)? Are their user goals being met? Does the software hinder them or help them?

Dig into stakeholders' day-to-day events; evaluate their typical processes, identify their end-products and outputs, and look at the inputs they get from others in the first place. See what's sufficient and streamlined, and question inconsistency and repetition.

Understanding how stakeholders work together

After you have stakeholders' specific work identified (refer to the preceding section), you also need to consider stakeholder *intersections* or *interfaces,* the points at which groups cross paths or individuals interact with other groups. Organizations sometimes share files or information and collaborate on processes to deliver products or results. These situations may be efficient, or different factors may create frustration. Here are some important questions to ask when exploring how groups cross paths:

✔ What requirements are others throwing at a given group, and how do those affect its ability to perform?

✔ What specific guidelines, regulations, or interfaces does it have to deal with, deliver, or meet? Is it integrated effectively for collaboration where it needs to be?

✔ What gaps does it have? Is it missing processes, people, or technology? What manual hoops does it have to jump through to get information passed back and forth?

✔ Has it noticed any inefficiencies it wants fixed? What does it need, or what could it be doing differently that would enable it to achieve its goals?

Uncovering the Root Cause

The genuine problem or opportunity that the business seeks to address is the *root cause* problem, and it's not always that easy to uncover. You typically have to ask a lot of questions to get down to that root cause because your stakeholders often report symptoms rather than the real cause. A BA's best question is "why?" "Why 'why'?" you ask. The question "why" has an incredible capability of getting someone to talk about and expand on her problems. It works like this: If a stakeholder suggests a solution or a symptom instead of telling you her real need, asking "why" gets her to identify the reason she's suggesting it. You get her rationale for the solution she's proposed, or at least a hint of another problem or issue in her way.

Don't ask just once. Ask stakeholders "Why?" a few times; you get all sorts of helpful details about their challenges. Push them to talk, and they'll explain how they're blocked in their ability to meet their needs. Ask a few more times, and they provide information about those blockers. Eventually — usually by the fifth time you've asked "why" — you get to the root cause of the problem. And that's the one that your solution has to be custom-designed for.

Getting stakeholders to go from what they want to what they need can be tricky. One way to handle the situation is to let them know you're happy to take care of their request, but you want to get it right for them: "Help me help you." Let them know that you need to understand the background and surrounding situation to give them the best solution. To help you, here are five really great questions you can ask that let you zero in on the precise need, problem, or opportunity:

✔ **What are you asking for?** What solution do stakeholders want? You can show your interest (and get more info) by asking them to elaborate a little. Have them describe in slightly more detail what solution or resolution they think they need. Get their solution vision; understand what they're thinking of or how they see it at the end.

✔ **Why are you asking?** Why do they need the solution they're asking for in the first place? What were they trying to do; what's broken, painful, or missing? Is something impacting their ability to do an important task?

✔ **Why now?** Have they been living with this issue for a while, or did it come up recently? What's the impact of the problem; what damage is it causing? If they've been dealing with the problem for a while, what finally pushed them over the edge to ask for a solution now; has the impact been increasing over time? Is there a reason they didn't ask earlier? These questions identify the *business driver* (the business reason why the organization approved this project) or the reason stakeholders have realized they must have a solution or pursue an opportunity: They can't live with the situation anymore and can't just ignore it. The driver is important to prioritization (if stakeholders make many requests) and to solution design.

✔ **What for, or to what end?** What will you use the solution for? If you had what you're asking for, what would the result look like? What outcome are you looking for? What's the purpose of the solution? Asking these kinds of questions helps identify solution options.

✔ **What will you do next?** Asking "what next" pushes the stakeholder to share her real goal or business need; it uncovers her *secondary* or *downstream desired outcomes* — the ultimate thing or success she's trying to achieve. This question helps clarify whether the solution she's asking for is a real need or just a stop-gap or work-around she's come up with.

These answers give you the information that allows you to identify not only the real problem but also the real needs and goals that drive them. Now you can evaluate the problem and then solve it appropriately.

Evaluating the Problem

You've figured out the business's and stakeholders' real needs, and you know what problems stand in the way of their achieving their goals or grabbing an opportunity. Now you're thinking, "Great, let's go solve for that!" Hit the brakes. Before you go solving for anything, ponder this question about the problem and the need: "So what?"

Just because people have problems or opportunity challenges doesn't mean that you have to go solving them — at least from a business analysis perspective. So what if they have a problem? How important is having someone (you or your organization) solve it? Are you or your team in the best position to solve it, or would someone else be a better solution provider in this particular case?

When you're answering these "so what" questions, value (for both the stakeholders and the business) is a critical consideration. In business, an unlimited supply of problems is always lurking, yet your ability to solve them is constrained by a limited supply of time and money. As a business analyst, you need to ensure that the work products and solutions your team creates deliver the highest possible value to the audience while also making the most of your business resources.

Problems that are annoying to deal with or easy to fix may look like really attractive problem-solving candidates, but before you decide that little problems or easy opportunities are low-hanging fruit or quick wins, realize that their corresponding solutions may or may not be so small. Fixing an issue doesn't mean you've delivered overall value back to the business. You and the team may just end up wasting valuable resources by directing efforts to inconsequential or less-critical problems. Not one moment of your business's time or any amount of money should be wasted on low-value opportunities, so don't choose the wrong problems to solve; consider your rationale carefully. The following sections show you how.

Choosing a good problem to solve

Given all those problems or opportunities, how do you evaluate and choose the right ones? How do stakeholders define a good problem to solve? What's a "good problem," exactly? A *good problem* is one with real, attractive value-potential in its solution. Characteristics or qualities that distinguish a good problem from the not-so-good are subjective, so people may not always agree on the value-potential when evaluating.

A good problem to solve in the business sense may be defined by the product management team as a problem "in our target market," or by the IT development team as one with "potential to use cool technology," or by an internal program or project management office (PMO) team as one that would "improve processes for the project teams." In other words, what a "good" problem is completely depends on which stakeholder you're talking to. You should facilitate discussions with the team and stakeholders to define your selection criteria for good if such information isn't yet agreed upon.

If you ask the problem-sufferer to decide whether solving a given problem has value potential, realize that she'll always say yes because she feels the pain of the problem more directly. You should consider stakeholder perspectives, but ultimately you have to decide whether something is a good problem to solve from the perspective of the business.

Truly, identifying and deciding on the good problems to solve (or opportunities to go after) completely depends on how the problems relate to the company's strategic priorities, business and stakeholder needs, and the cost/benefit to be realized in solving them — its impact and opportunity.

Figuring out whether the problem matters

You don't want to waste time putting a solution in place that doesn't solve the problem, but you definitely don't want to waste time solving a problem that doesn't matter!

Internally, ask whether it matters that the problem-sufferer has a problem. If it does matter, why does it matter? Evaluate the problem for strategic or operational interest so you can select problems that matter in a big way. From an internal perspective, consider where the problem is occurring:

✔ Is the problem occurring in a core business process? Is it a process executed frequently or one that occurs only once in a while?

✔ Does it affect the business's ability to make decisions, execute work, or deliver end-products as efficiently and effectively as possible? What's the length of the delay? What happens to work around the problem now?

✔ How many people are affected by the problem? One or many? What's the level of responsibility or position of those people?

If a problem creates an inconvenience but doesn't significantly impact the business in time or cost, then it may not matter much. If it's causing frustration-only pain, your stakeholder may admit that solving the problem isn't that big a deal for the business (even if it bothers her a lot), and you can probably determine that the problem isn't important on the large scale. However, if the frustration occurs in a process performed regularly in an operation core to the business, you should pay attention. Frustration that builds over time wears on employees. Depending on other job factors, the business may have a strategic interest in solving the problem because businesses want to retain employees.

From an external perspective, assess how the problem situation compares, contrasts, or aligns with the business by considering the following:

✔ **Is the problem occurring in a market the business cares about?** Even if it's someone else's problem, it may turn into the company's opportunity to grab by offering your solution.

✔ **Is it similar to other problems already being solved, or is it a completely new problem area?** If it's similar, maybe it isn't worth investing time and money in. If it's new, it may represent a new opportunity that warrants those resources.

✔ **Is the problem-sufferer in a similar or same audience category as others already being served, or is she in a different market or audience that interests the business?** If the category is similar, you may be able to address this need more easily. If it's different, the business has to decide whether it's interested in pursuing a new market or audience. Entering a new market or audience takes more time, effort, and money.

✔ **Would the (potential) solution strategically align with the company's current or future planned operations, organizations, or other product and service offerings?** If not, does changing or extending its business model to take advantage of the opportunity make sense? If it's strategically aligned, then the opportunity should get high consideration. If it's new, the business needs to decide whether it wants to change its model to take advantage.

Another way to look at it: Do the problem-sufferers know they have that particular need or problem? If they don't experience the point of annoyance — if they don't or won't decide a problem is bad enough or big enough to do something about it — they'll never look for a solution. Problems too small to block a need or even create a hurdle may not be serious enough to compel the sufferer to find a solution and may not be good problems to solve.

However, if the sufferer is aware of the issue but unaware that solutions may exist, you may still have a good problem to solve. You can help enlighten her by sending to her marketing material that educates her about the availability and capabilities of your solution. Without awareness, the potential customer may never understand or value your solution. If you can create demand from your marketing, the problem in question may be a good one to solve. But if the sufferers don't know your solution is out there and don't look for it, solving the problem may turn into a wholly wasted opportunity.

If the problem clearly matters, look insightfully at the problem-sufferer: Ask all the questions about getting to the root cause and identifying the real problem. Then consider potential impacts or costs resulting from her problem(s). By analyzing each problem and studying its components (a process we cover in the later section "Creating a Problem Statement"), you can assess the relative level of pain the problem-sufferers are experiencing. Depending on how big the problem is, you can identify the value in pursuing a solution.

Determining the impact of the problem

The impact to the business is a major concern of most business leaders; it's what they worry most about. Decision-makers hearing about problems want to know why they have a problem, what the real impact of the problem is, and what the choice on whether to address it is going to mean. If it's a painful problem that impacts the business and its bottom line, it probably indicates some opportunity or value to be found and may very well be a good problem to solve.

Evaluate the extent to which the problem impacts the business and understand the value that solving the problem may bring to the business. Appraise the depth and breadth of an internal problem's cost to the business and the commercial potential in solving an external problem by getting stakeholders to provide information about why a problem is a problem. This strategy gives you a good sense of the business and stakeholder needs the problem is preventing.

Good elicitation encourages stakeholders to share what they're trying to do but can't (at least not easily). Elicit the relative levels of pain they feel with their problem and identify the level of motivation they have for solving it. With that information also comes the underlying drive or pressure they feel for meeting the need(s) in the first place. What are they trying to achieve? Why? What is and isn't working? What do they need that they don't have?

When problems get in the way of your stakeholders or you yourself, you can quantify the pain and measure what's lost in leaving the problem unsolved by identifying what your stakeholders could have been doing if they weren't managing the problem. Ask what could've been achieved. Measure the cost of frustration; quantify the impact of not realizing important goals, missing objectives, or meeting needs. Did they lose time, experience inefficiency, or add extra people to get work done? Did they lose revenue, miss sales, or lower production volume?

Establishing the costs and benefits

Even if the problem is painful, you also have to consider what potential business risks and value potential lie in this problem or opportunity. In any decision-making situation, you have to consider two factors: costs and benefits.

By identifying pain, you've found the source of costs. Stakeholders were motivated to explain the experience of their situation; you can translate this information to cost. But you also need to identify benefits.

Using "so what" questions is a terrific technique for eliciting benefits information. Ask a stakeholder, "So what difference would having a solution make?" Her answer gives you a sense for the attraction or interest she feels for finding or pursuing a resolution. She may share specific ideas she's come up with for solving her problem. You can then follow up with the question "Is the difference important enough that you'd pay for a solution?" to identify the potential for the opportunity.

If the answer is no, she wouldn't pay, then the problem doesn't offer much opportunity. However, if her answer is yes, maybe she'd pay for a solution, then an opportunity may exist. In that case, your next step is to determine how big that opportunity is. Evaluate whether it's a solution worth pursuing by quantifying the opportunity with additional cost/benefit analysis (head to Chapter 5 for the lowdown on cost-benefit analysis). Consider both audiences:

✔ **The problem-sufferer (either internal or external stakeholder):** Estimate her cost of having the problem, the cost and benefit of purchasing or adopting a solution, and — most importantly — the price(s) she would or wouldn't be willing to pay for either low- or high-end solutions. That same consideration applies to both internal and external audiences: Would the department or organization be willing to pay or alter the way it works in order to change its situation? Would it allocate money from its budget to fix the issue or develop and sponsor a business case to do so?

✔ **The solution-provider:** Identify the investment required to generate a solution and drive the desired use and benefit after the solution is deployed, either internally or externally. Appraise the development and distribution costs for creating and supporting the solution; the number of expected users/buyers (anticipation of market or internal-audience size); and particularly the potential revenue, cost savings, profit, and return.

This analysis doesn't have to be detailed and researched. Depending on the audience and the amount of information available, creating a broad back-of-the-envelope, order-of-magnitude estimate may be perfectly acceptable. Just be sure to answer this question: Is it worth the investment of resources?

Consider all aspects of solution cost/benefit against each problem. Choose to solve problems worth solving because leaving them unsolved is costly. If you can deliver solutions that create beneficial value, seize the opportunity.

Creating the Problem Statement

After the business has decided a problem is worth pursuing, you should create a problem statement. A *problem statement* is the conglomeration of four key elements into one expression to convey the issue at hand:

✔ Root cause problem

✔ Impacted stakeholders/product users

✔ Impacts of the issues

✔ Effects a successful solution must include

The problem statement is a critical component of a project's statement of purpose or charter. (Read more about these documents in Chapter 10.) The reason to write a problem statement is so that all members on the project team are absolutely clear on what they're working on solving. If different team members understand the problem differently, you may end up having to address conflicts while creating and prioritizing requirements for the solution.

A problem statement generally follows the format of "The problem of W affects X, the impact of which is Y, so a successful solution would be to Z." Here's how to figure out how to put it all together:

- **"The problem of [statement of problem] . . .":** What's the goal or need of the audience; what's the root cause problem your target market is trying to solve? What do stakeholders struggle with; what concerns do they have? Which detailed or lower-level problems are buried under bigger problems? Are the important issues called out?

- **". . . affects [users and/or stakeholders] . . ."** Who specifically is impacted? This list isn't limited to just the problem-sufferer; it includes others also affected directly or indirectly.

- **". . . the impact of which is [statement of issues, costs, or other impacts]."** Lacking a solution (preferably yours), what are the impacts and outcomes suffered as a result of the business problem? (In other words, what's the business driver; why may the company be compelled to solve the problem?)

- **"A successful solution would be to [important benefits that would successfully solve the problem]."** What characteristics and qualities does an acceptable and/or compelling solution include? What would a (generic) solution do or have that addresses or resolves key issues and needs? A solution providing these benefits or capabilities would be just what the users need, with post-solution results or outcomes adding value.

A good example of a problem statement may be

> The problem of customers smoking in our rooms affects other customers, who don't appreciate the smoke and smell, and our housekeeping staff, who spend significantly more time cleaning smoking rooms versus nonsmoking ones, the impact of which is low customer satisfaction, reduced occupancy rates, and increased cleaning costs. A successful solution would be to eliminate smoking and smoking effects from our hotel rooms and readdress those impacts.

Focus on features or functions most valuable to the business strategy and to the customer. Articulate customer-focused problem statements, not business-focused problem statements. For example, the problem statement in the hotel-based example relates to the customers, not the hotel occupancy decline.

Creating the Solution Position Statement

A *solution* (or *product*) *position statement* is a description and positioning of a specific solution approach. It generally follows the format of "For the target audience of U who need V, the new product W is a solution that will do X. Unlike alternative Y, our solution does Z." As we note earlier in the chapter, an important element of a good solution is that it solves a real problem worth solving and ultimately provides value back to the audience using the solution. That task may sound simple, but it can be challenging. Therefore, use the problem statement (see the preceding section) and the solution position statement together to validate the value.

One reason to create a solution position statement is to explain the proposed solution to leaders; it makes a great elevator speech, with all the points summarized clearly and succinctly. But solution position statements also align all the project stakeholders toward the project goals and objectives. By clearly articulating what you're creating, what you ultimately intend to provide or sell, and to whom (as well as why they'd be compelled to use it), you can create incredible clarity around the team's objectives and delivery goals. This clarity appropriately drives requirements definition and prioritization.

The problem statement characterizes the issue and what the right solution must have to solve the problem, but after your team decides which way is best to solve the problem specifically, you must characterize your choice with a solution position statement. Describe what the specific solution is and explain why, given these custom features and design, it is in fact (once complete) the right solution to meet the need.

If you've never created a solution position statement, use the following framework:

- ✓ **"For [target audience] . . ."** State the target user, market, or customer by naming its role or characterizing its group.

- ✓ **" . . . who [statement of the need or opportunity] . . ."** Describe what the target is trying to achieve or do while it's having the problem. Rather than state the problem directly, state the need your target audience will have the opportunity to meet.

- ✓ **" . . . the [name of new product or business] is a [solution or business category] . . ."** Set the context for the solution by portraying the kind of product, solution, or new business venture (if pursuing large opportunities) it is. State the category the solution belongs to so the audience members understand its relevance and relationship to their needs.

- ✓ **" . . . that [statement of key benefit — the compelling reason to use the solution or do business with you]."** Highlight what the solution offers that will motivate or most interest the audience. This piece is the must-have outcome of value — the persuasive benefit. Provide the reason why this solution is the right solution by stating how the solution meets the need.

- ✓ **"Unlike [primary competitive alternative] . . ."** If the target didn't have your solution, what solution(s) may it look for or consider instead? State the current environment or competitor products to beat, or internally, the unacceptable situation (what the company has now) to fix.

- ✓ **" . . . our product [statement of primary differentiation]."** Distinguish and sell the solution. Besides the fact that it meets the most critical need, what other interesting or attractive features are included? List key marketing points or functionality that addresses the problem statement. Establish why stakeholders would want or need this function. What sets it apart? What are the key differentiators?

When developing solution position statements, speak to your market's need, not your business's need and then align the features and functions closely to that positioning. Don't add bells and whistles to a solution if they don't make sense for its purpose, or you'll waste time on things that don't add value.

For the hotel example in the preceding section, an effective solution position statement may be something like the following:

> For our visiting customers who don't appreciate secondhand smoke, hotel rooms that stink, or smoke-damaged linens and furniture, the no-smoking policy is a new policy for our hotel and guests that prohibits smoking in all our U.S. hotel rooms to address customer experience and our occupancy decline. Unlike our current policy, which allows smoking in some rooms, this solution will eliminate the impact of cigarette smoke in our rooms and on our customers, provide a cleaner environment for our guests and staff, and increase guest satisfaction with our hotel and customer service policies.

Notice how this solution statement concentrates on the benefits realized for the guests, not housekeeping. The solution statement for housekeeping would concentrate on the savings realized by spending less time cleaning the rooms in between guests.

Knowing When You Have the Right Solution

Solutions deliver or help stakeholders achieve outcomes. People don't create or use solutions just for fun; they do so because the solutions bring notable value. Commercial solutions find success when they provide so much value that people see it, appreciate it, and are willing to pay something for it. The following sections help you determine the value of solution options.

Validating the value of the solution

One way you, as a business analyst, can help the business hedge its bet that people will see and appreciate the value in the solution you're working on (prerequisites to the decision of whether they'd pay for it) is to validate the value of that solution. Figure 8-1 shows you a *solution option value validation model,* a graphical way to do just that.

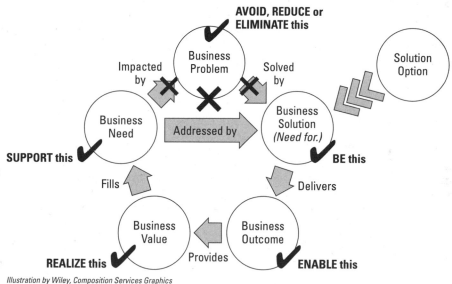

Figure 8-1: Solution option value validation model.

Illustration by Wiley, Composition Services Graphics

As you can see in Figure 8-1, a solution option must do all of the following to be successful:

- ✔ Support and address the business need, whether that's a user goal or an activity.
- ✔ Avoid, reduce, or eliminate the business problem and its impacts.
- ✔ Operate effectively and include expected or necessary capabilities.
- ✔ Deliver results during use that enable achievement of the business outcome.
- ✔ Provide additional value beyond the business outcome so that the audience appreciates that the option is a successful solution that fills the need.

All five requirements must be met for solution success. As long as the option you decide to put in place as the solution does those things, it will be a successful business solution.

Taking your audience into consideration

If you have more than one potential option for solving the problem, selecting one requires evaluating and comparing one's potential against the others'. Just how successful one solution is depends on how satisfied the business and other audiences are with the value they decide that option has. Your audience probably wants to understand that value before they want your solution.

Just as when you're evaluating the level of pain in a problem (as we discuss in the earlier section "Evaluating the Problem"), the evaluation of a solution's value can be subjective. For instance, some people may find value in cutting-edge innovations and novelty items because they get pleasure from having something new and cool or in doing things they haven't thought of before. But overall, value is realized when your solution provides your audience with outcomes or benefits that are better, faster, and cheaper than what they have (or don't have) now.

Thus, the audience for your solution — whether buying, adopting, or sponsoring and funding — wants to know, "Why should I consider this solution? What's the value to me?" (This solution requirement is otherwise known as *WIIFM:* "What's in it for me?") Before selecting one particular approach to solve the problem, be sure you know what your audience members value:

- ✔ **Does the solution option need to just solve their problem or to go above and beyond?** What's their vision for the solution in terms of form, function, and permanence? For instance, if they need a boat to cross a lake, which are they thinking of: raft, kayak, canoe, rowboat, motorboat, speedboat, yacht, or cruise ship? A raft can do the bare-bones job of getting them from A to B, but the other options do so with more bells and whistles. Identify, create, and innovate key functions and features for a useful, desirable solution.

- ✔ **What do they really need (versus want)?** Maybe they want a speedboat, but a rowboat would still meet the need to get across the water. (Chapter 5 has details on distinguishing needs from wants.) What are the critical outcomes that the solution must deliver, according to your audience? Identify what the users would do with the solution that would make it helpful and valuable toward solving their problems or meeting their goals. Then, how perfect does it need to be right now for the audience? If more than one group benefits, who has the most influence over use or revenue? What does that group need most?

✔ **Which option is the best solution option for multiple audiences?** This answer depends on what's best for the business, for the users, and for any other beneficiaries, given all the issues and tradeoffs. For example, given all the options and constraints at the lake, maybe the motorboat is best because it's least expensive of the faster options, bringing value to the boater because she doesn't have to row and value to the buyer with its lower cost profile.

Setting Your Solution Up For Success: Getting Clear Objectives

"If you don't know where you are going, then you probably won't end up there."

—Forrest Gump

All your work defining and framing the right solution has probably created expectations around what it is and what it will most likely look like. You've clarified and articulated the problem; you've identified different solution options; you've figured out some key features (or criteria) necessary for the solution to be valuable and right; and you've positioned them accordingly with a powerful solution position statement. (For tips on any of these steps, refer to the preceding sections.) This solution is going to be just what the audience needs, and you expect the audience is going to love it. You're on the path to success.

But to what extent will your expectation be the reality? How will you measure success? The expectations your stakeholders have going in — whether your team has set and provided them upfront or stakeholders have developed expectations independently — are the success criteria for your solution. Those criteria are how your solution will be measured, evaluated, and judged. The following sections help you clarify what objectives the solution must meet.

Objectives are quantitative or measurable indicators that reflect the outcome and value desired from achieving a goal. All objectives together define the measurements of success. They describe what's expected, the specific level of expectation (how much), and by when the achievement is expected.

Eliciting and articulating clear objectives

Your solution must hit the stakeholders' success criteria, which means you need to know what those criteria are and aim your solution at them. That is, "begin with the end in mind," as Stephen Covey said. Goals and objectives need to be clearly stated so that everyone knows what the targets are and can work together effectively to achieve success.

When a project is initiated or a problem needs solving, the sponsors or stakeholders very often have goals and objectives in mind. To uncover these pre-existing objectives, ask the appropriate parties directly:

- What's your vision of success?

- If this project is successful, what will happen and by when?

- If the solution is successful, what will be different? What will be gained or realized and by when?

- What are you trying to achieve with the solution and by when?

- What do you expect to be able to do with the solution?

- What do you expect to see from or when looking at the solution?

- What do you expect to get or have after deploying the solution?

Use the elicitation skills and techniques in Chapters 6 and 7 to draw out their expectations and objectives.

Sometimes, however, stakeholders may need to react to something instead of creating objectives from nothing — they'll know what they want when they see it. If that's the case, you can help stakeholders identify their objectives visually by defining them yourself first. To identify appropriate solution objectives, you can start by extracting objectives from the following goals by using the provided sample questions:

- **The business has its needs met and is successful in achieving its objectives while using the solution defined.** This business analysis goal will be met if you define an effective problem statement.

  - How many users must be served, and which needs must be met? By when?

  - What impacts need to be eliminated and to what degree? What outcomes or objectives must be achieved? By when?

  - What capabilities must be in place when the solution is complete, and by when?

- **The solution you create actually works.** This business analysis goal will be met if you define an effective solution position statement and double-check it with the solution option value validation model in Figure 8-1 earlier in the chapter.

- What does it mean to you if the solution is working? What does "working" look like?

- How rapidly does the solution operate, or how quickly do you expect to achieve your outcome? How usable or user-friendly is the solution?

- What's your expectation of value? What will come of the solution, or what will you get from the solution after using it?

As we note in the earlier section "Knowing When You Have the Right Solution," a solution option must meet all the requirements in Figure 8-1. Explore each of those requirements, working with stakeholders to quantify exactly what, how, and when specific results are to be achieved.

✓ **The solution team actually builds and delivers the right thing in the first place.** You'll be on the path to meet this BA goal after you articulate clear solution objectives!

- When do you need the solution completed? At what point are you expecting a draft or pilot solution versus a final permanent solution?

- What level of quality do you expect? How good or perfect does it need to be by a certain time?

Assess and interpret what you come to know from your analysis. After you have a draft, sit down with stakeholders to review for validation. From the collective set of BA goals and all the different business, stakeholder, and solution requirements collected to date, deriving solution objectives in case stakeholders have trouble articulating them should be pretty easy.

Getting clear with SMART objectives

One of the most frustrating things that can happen between two parties is that they think they've reached understanding and agreement when they really haven't. In those cases, both parties may walk away from the initial conversation thinking they're talking about the same thing but later realize they were talking about two distinctly different points or different levels of acceptability or achievement within the same points.

The way to eliminate that issue is to be SMART about quantifying the objectives and then articulating them clearly and validating with stakeholders. SMART is an acronym that stands for "specific, measurable, attainable, relevant, and time-bound":

✓ **Specific:** The objective is clear and unambiguous and explains to the (future) project team exactly what's expected.

✓ **Measurable:** The objective gives concrete measurements to assess your progress against the objective and determine whether you've met it.

✔ **Attainable:** The objective can be reached. It must be realistic; otherwise you're setting yourself up to fail. *Note:* Sometimes "agreed-upon" is also suggested as the *A* here; if stakeholders don't agree on an objective, it's not necessarily a good one.

✔ **Relevant:** The objective has to matter to the organization. *Note:* If the *A* changes to "agreed-upon," the *R* typically switches to "realistic."

✔ **Time-bound:** The objective provides a time frame of expected achievement. This criterion often affects your solution option design choices or decisions. An objective to identify 150 new customer leads within three months may require a whole different solution than the objective to identify those leads over the course of 2 years.

For more examples of SMART objective criteria, take a look at Chapter 9.

The value in defining SMART objectives is that the team members understand clearly what they and the solution will be measured against, providing a basis and justification for making specific choices and decisions. Without the SMART objective, each member of the team may have her own perspective on levels of acceptability, which can cause conflict and frustration. If you set an objective only to "raise scores," then an increase of 1 percent would be technically acceptable. But if the sponsor feels that anything below a 10 percent increase isn't really an increase, you have a mismatch. SMART objectives ensure everyone knows exactly what's expected; they set the expectations of stakeholders so those people know precisely what the solution will and won't do for them and are clear on how performance — and success! — will be measured.

Some examples of SMART objectives for a hotel looking to address smoking problems include the following:

✔ Reduce customer complaints related to smoking policy by 90 percent within 1 month of policy rollout.

✔ Increase occupancy for the last 6 months of the year to prior year occupancy rates.

✔ Reduce housekeeping costs by 15 percent for the last 6 months of the year.

Part III
Selling the Plan and Keeping It on Track

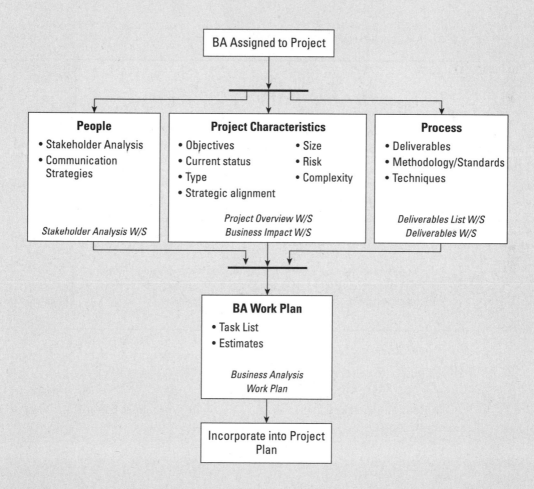

BA Assigned to Project

People
- Stakeholder Analysis
- Communication Strategies

Stakeholder Analysis W/S

Project Characteristics
- Objectives
- Current status
- Type
- Strategic alignment
- Size
- Risk
- Complexity

Project Overview W/S
Business Impact W/S

Process
- Deliverables
- Methodology/Standards
- Techniques

Deliverables List W/S
Deliverables W/S

BA Work Plan
- Task List
- Estimates

Business Analysis Work Plan

Incorporate into Project Plan

Find out how to maximize the business analyst–project manager relationship at www. dummies.com/extras/businessanalysis.

In this part . . .

✔ Understand what a business case is, why you want to use one, and how to create a compelling case that gains stakeholder buy-in.

✔ Explore what scope is and why creating and sticking to the scope is so important to your project.

✔ Recognize scope creep (what happens when scope changes) and learn how to properly manage expectations during the change.

✔ Understand the importance of business analysis planning. Plan for your projects by focusing on the people, project characteristics, and project processes in your organization.

Chapter 9

Making the (Business) Case

In This Chapter

▶ Knowing why you need to make a business case in the first place

▶ Including all the right elements in your business case

▶ Understanding and writing effectively for your audience

▶ Choosing the right presentation

A business case is a compelling argument you give in order to get approval to embark on your suggested course of action for addressing the business need. So what's included in a business case? Is it a document? A presentation? Who's it for? When do you develop a business case, and what level of detail should you provide to support your opinion or case? This chapter answers these questions and more and provides a rationale for how a business case can also be used effectively as an analysis technique.

Before You Dive In: Breaking Down Business Case Basics

A business case outlines an opportunity and a recommendation to invest resources to take advantage of it. Think of the business case as your marketing or sales brochure for your idea. It may be your one shot to get approval for a project that may have a significant strategic, structural, or political corporate impact. A compelling case requires enough facts about the recommendation to make it credible and the correct positioning for the audience or reader to buy into it. The following sections show you the pros of creating a business case (consider it our business case for business cases) and help you nail down your audience and business case structure.

A business case can take various forms, including a formal or informal document, a presentation, or a walk-through of a simulation. We cover presentation considerations in the later section "Presenting the Business Case."

Looking at the benefits of writing a business case

The primary purpose of a business case is to sell a viable solution for a clearly defined business problem or new product to the company that's hired you. It's part of enterprise analysis (more about that in Chapter 2) at the point when you identify the problem or finalize the solution and request funding for it.

Not all companies require you to develop a business case, although most organizations do if you request funding above a certain amount. Even if a business case isn't mandatory, you may still find value in writing one for these reasons:

- **To provide insight into the viability of your solution or idea:** At a minimum, writing the executive summary and mission statement (we talk about those elements in the later section "Defining and Presenting the Opportunity") can give you incredible insight into the viability of a solution or idea you're considering. Creating these items also helps you organize and collect your thoughts and validate what may just be a gut feeling that this solution is correct. Writing the business case out also provides a foundation for further analysis and solution development.

- **To support a feasibility study:** A *feasibility study* is an analysis effort to determine whether the opportunity can be reasonably achieved. Presenting a strong business case can garner you support for conducting this study.

- **To prioritize projects:** Sometimes you need to conduct one or more projects to achieve the final solution, and the business case helps you prioritize them. For these types of complex projects-within-projects, the business case can explain for project team members the overriding strategic goal and mission of the project so that the subprojects have a context. Having this type of documentation is extremely valuable even if it isn't required for project approval.

Even if a business case is approved, it may be cancelled or changed after further analysis is conducted, so you may need to develop a follow-up business case. Some business cases are actually written to just to get approval to research and analyze an idea further.

Playing to the crowd: Knowing your audience

The most important question you must answer before creating your business case is "Who am I trying to convince?" The audience for the case drives all aspects of it, whether that audience is one, some, or all of your stakeholders. (For a complete understanding of performing stakeholder analysis so you know who you're writing for, see Chapter 11.) Here are the primary considerations you should keep in mind about audience members when writing a business case:

- **Knowledge level about the opportunity:** If members are familiar with the issue and context, you don't have to go into great detail in your case. If they have no education, background, or framework for the subject, though, you need to provide significantly more details in the business case. Specifically, you need to find a way to compare the subject to something the audience can relate to. Say you're trying to make a case to a company regarding launching a new accounting software program for individuals (versus the staff or company as a whole). If the audience doesn't know anything about launching programs on the individual level, you can compare this process to something members already know, such as when they went from only developing programs for large companies to developing them for small companies as well. Reminding them that they've changed markets before in a similar way can help them be open to learning about the new market.

- **Decision-making authority:** Know whether the first reader is the final decision-maker or whether the case needs multiple levels of approval or a committee's approval. Your understanding of all the stakeholders participating in the approval process is critical in making it relevant for each of them. You may need to provide information that is relevant to some stakeholders and not others.

 If you're making one presentation to individuals with different information needs, you should focus on meeting the needs of the ultimate decision-maker. If your case will go through multiple reviews and approvals, tailor the case's executive summary for each individual.

- **Passion for the product or problem:** Knowing your audience's level of passion for the case is critical. If you know audience members are passionate about the contents of the case, don't spend much time trying to get them excited; they're already there. For example, consider the famous scene in *Jerry Maguire* where Jerry comes over to his girlfriend's house, says hello, and then goes into a lengthy apology speech about how horrible he's been. Finally, he's silent and she just says, "You had me at hello." The point is, sometimes less is more.

If the audience perceives your case as just one more project to review and sign off on, then you've got an uphill battle. Add information to your case that gets audience members excited. Find something to relate the project to that they have passion about. Give them a reason to care — a reason to say yes.

✔ **Desire for details:** Some people are *i*-dotters and *t*-crossers; they closely read everything they're given. Perhaps they're risk-averse and scared to make decisions without knowing every minute detail. (Or maybe they're just thorough.) Others prefer to skim through written messages or skip everything but the pictures. Knowing which category your audience members fall into is vital so that you can provide the right level of detail for your audience. If you've written cases for your audience before, then you may have a good sense of the level of detail each person needs. If you haven't, though, ask around. You can most likely find other people in the organization who've presented to your audience. Find those people and get guidance on how to proceed.

You must write your business case while keeping all audiences in mind by including points that address all audience members' needs. Achieving this goal may mean you have to have two different summaries, depending on the audience reading the business case. Consider how brilliantly written the best animated movies are. If you've ever watched one with a child, you know that you laugh at totally different times than the child does; that's because the movie includes inferences and even animation features to endear different audiences. When your business case audience is made up of disparate groups, you have to walk the same line.

Following basic business case structure

Regardless of audience, most business cases include the following three categories of information:

✔ **Defining and presenting the opportunity:** Here's where you clearly make your case with a persuasive outline of the recommendation, a statement of key points, and the bottom line conclusion. Present the opportunity at the highest level of definition and positioning.

✔ **Justifying the recommendation:** Provide the top-level evidence that assures the audience that your recommendation is the right course of action. Give an overview of your evaluation criteria and the results that support your conclusion. Most notably, compare and contrast the options considered and clearly position the recommendation as the winner — the most compelling course of action.

  ✔ **Supporting the documentation:** The supporting documentation allows your detail-appreciating audience members to see the evidence with their own eyes and confirm the validity of your analysis, assumptions, and conclusions. Support and prove the key points of your argument by providing the details for review, including the analysis, description, and factual results for every option analyzed while deriving the conclusion.

Each category features sections that provide increasing levels of supporting details, as you can see in Figure 9-1. We describe those categories in detail in the upcoming sections.

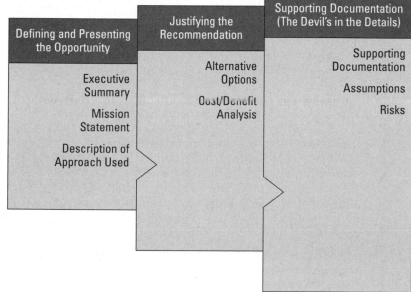

Figure 9-1: Be sure to include the three main information categories in your business case.

Defining and Presenting the Opportunity	Justifying the Recommendation	Supporting Documentation (The Devil's in the Details)
Executive Summary	Alternative Options	Supporting Documentation
Mission Statement	Cost/Benefit Analysis	Assumptions
Description of Approach Used		Risks

Illustration by Wiley, Composition Services Graphics

Defining and Presenting the Opportunity

The top level of the business case is the definition and presentation of the opportunity. The goal of this category is to capture the interest of the audience and gain its immediate support. Although you want all categories to accomplish this task in a way, piquing interest is really the only goal of this section; if you don't capture audience members' interest at this point, they won't proceed through the case. That's why positioning the opportunity in the best way possible, based on the audience you seek approval from, is critical. Your positioning should indicate that you're passionate about the opportunity and believe in its viability.

This category of the business case includes the executive summary, the mission statement, and the description of the approach used, which we cover in the following sections.

Executive summary

The *executive summary* is the cover page or opening scene to your story — your *hello*. It's the first thing that's read, so it's the most critical section of the business case for most audiences. Therefore, it must be concise. Keep it to one page; any longer, and chances are you have too much information. The objective for this section is just for the reader to be interested enough to keep an open mind and continue reviewing the rest of the document.

We say "most audiences" because some readers are purely financially driven. They tend to skip the front-end sales pitch and flip to the cost/benefit analysis first. (Read more about that piece in the appropriately named "Cost/benefit analysis" section later in the chapter.)

Your executive summary should include the following parts:

- **The current situation and opportunity:** Describe what is going on in the business or in the marketplace that necessitates action. For new opportunities or products, discuss why the time for this new product to be developed is now. Give a very high-level (big-picture) description of the opportunity — your two-to-three-sentence *elevator pitch* (a synopsis short enough to be delivered during an elevator ride) that sums up the opportunity.

  For example, yearly training for remote employees may be the opportunity for which you're providing a business case. Your elevator pitch may be, "Some of our employees don't have the knowledge or skills to perform their jobs, and we must find a solution or we'll be forced to hire new staff that are already trained. The time delays and mistakes are costing us significant delays in product rollouts that we can't afford to continue. However, due to the employees' dispersed location, bringing them to a central location for group training is difficult."

- **Business drivers behind the recommendation:** *Business drivers* are the primary business reasons that you're presenting the recommendation; they explain how the business will be impacted if they're approved. For example, if the business wants to provide training to a particular group because the lack of training is causing a business problem, the business driver would be the impact to the business of the group's mistakes or ineffectiveness.

If you have positive financial statistics, include the ones that support your case most effectively in this area. We recommend not including all cost/benefit details or all statistics (such as return on investment) in the executive summary unless your organization's template requires it; only include those stats that directly relate to the business success in this section.

- ✔ **Recommendation description:** The *recommendation* is the solution you're proposing to take advantage of the opportunity. Describe it at a very high level in this section — in just enough detail for the audience to be able to articulate it to someone else. For example, if the opportunity is to provide at least one training class per year for all individuals, including those who can't travel or who are remotely located, two potential recommendations to meet this goal may be a live virtual training class and an interactive self-paced training module.

The executive summary isn't the area to describe the exact classes being held, the technology to deliver the virtual classes, or the classes' development. You include those details in the identification and prioritization of alternative solutions and the supporting materials sections of the business case, which we address later in the chapter.

If you feel your case is extremely compelling and you think your audience members will be so moved by the executive summary alone that they may sign off on the case right then and there, you should add a page for signature approvals to it. You can present this package as a cover letter to the entire business case.

Mission statement

The *mission statement* is the combination of the goal and objectives of the opportunity. The *goal* is the business driver stated in the executive summary. The *objectives* are quantitative or measurable indicators that indicate whether the opportunity has achieved its goal or the problem has been solved.

Setting SMART objectives

When writing objectives, you must make sure they're SMART. No, we're not shouting at you; *SMART* is an acronym. Although you won't find a 100 percent standard definition for the letters, we use the commonly accepted *specific, measureable, attainable, relevant,* and *time-bound:*

- ✔ **Specific:** The goal must be clear and unambiguous. Explain to the project team exactly what is expected: "Identify new customer leads for product X." In this case, you know exactly what type of customer leads you need to get.

✔ **Measurable:** The goal's threshold for success must be something you can concretely measure: "Identify 150 new customer leads" tells you precisely how many customer leads you have to generate (versus a more general goal like "Identify more customer leads"). The reason you create a measurement is to assess your progress to the goal and to know when you meet it.

✔ **Attainable:** You want to make sure the goal you set can be reached — that it's realistic. For example, if you sell F-22 Raptor fighter jets, identifying 150 new customer leads may not be attainable (the market isn't large enough), so you'd want to bring that number down.

✔ **Relevant:** The objective needs to be relevant to the organization and matter to the organization. An objective to "Make buttermilk pancakes for the entire staff" may be attainable and specific (it did specify *buttermilk* pancakes, after all), but is it really relevant to the organization's mission or strategy? No. A better example may be "Identify 25 new leads per month."

✔ **Time-bound:** This part of the objective tells you when you need to measure to see how well you achieved (or — gasp — not achieved) your specific goal: "Identify 150 new customer leads within the next two quarters." As an organization, you know when this objective needs to be in place and when you need to measure whether you achieved it. Additionally, you can measure at stages along the way, such as by 6 months after project implementation.

For example, if a business driver states the goal as "the organization wants to offer training to business analysts (BAs) who work remotely and can't travel," some corresponding SMART objectives may be

✔ Training courses on project scoping are offered to all remote workers by the end of the first quarter.

✔ Eighty percent of the BAs complete at least one training course by the end of the third quarter this year.

✔ No travel costs will be incurred this year for any training courses attended/completed by remote workers.

Using key performance indicators

Another approach to defining the mission statement is through the use of *key performance indicators,* or KPIs. KPIs are also objectives, but they relate to the ultimate desired outcome for the business versus the desired outcome for the project. The KPIs are those measurements that most effectively predict success. They include those performance measures that are key to identifying that a solution is (or isn't) performing.

In the training example, the objectives are about delivering training for BAs without travel, but if your desired outcome is to improve your scope process for projects, then your KPIs would be different from the objectives listed earlier.

For example, KPIs to improve your scope process may be the following:

- Students must achieve a 95 percent or higher score on the course exam.
- Business problem statements will be accurately described in every scope document.
- Ninety eight percent of all external agents will be identified at the time of the original scope.

The mission statement and the corresponding measurements depend on the opportunity for which the business case is being written and the audience that will be reviewing it for sign-off.

Description of the approach used

If the audience members aren't convinced to approve the project after reading the executive summary or mission statement, they may simply want to know all the information before signing off. However, they may have other concerns — perhaps they're not comfortable with the information that was summarized, or they don't know or trust you as the writer because they don't know you. The *description of the approach used* section is really about credibility for the development of the case. It's an opportunity to reinforce why the audience should rely on the information contained within the case.

You achieve this goal by describing the following:

- The individuals who provided background for the opportunity and business drivers
- The steps taken to validate the business driver
- The experts or external vendors researched to provide solution options
- Where data was compiled from to support the cost/benefit analysis
- The level of analysis effort and significant activities performed to recommend the solution

 To combat the problem of unfamiliarity with the writer, try to relate this case to a previous successful case that you were involved with and that the audience is familiar with. Attach yourself to success to enhance your reputation with the audience.

Justifying the Recommendation

Justifying the recommendation is about describing the recommended solution and comparing it to the alternative solutions considered. Also included in this part of the business case is the cost/benefit analysis for the final recommendation. The following sections break down the components of this piece of the business case.

This part is important to include even if you think the audience will be compelled to approve based solely on the executive summary. Most projects have delays between the time they're proposed and the time they actually begin, and this information provides detailed supporting documentation for the project team and committee later. You can also use it as a starting point or as supporting documentation for the business analysis effort for the project(s) resulting from approval.

Identifying and prioritizing alternative solutions

You should highlight and compare each option that you've considered to the others so the reader is aware that you've vetted alternatives. For most options, the comparisons are financial in nature, but they can also include time to market, strategic alignment, feasibility rankings, brand image, company politics or culture, technology response time, customer satisfaction, or any other metric that's critical to achieving success. You should compare how well each option supports the KPIs or other objectives outlined in the mission statement (refer to the earlier section "Mission statement" for details on these topics). Table 9-1 shows some appropriate comparisons for the KPIs outlined in the business driver example in "Defining and Presenting the Opportunity" section earlier in the chapter.

Rarely does a problem or opportunity have only one solution; one option for comparison should always be to do nothing.

Table 9-1	Sample KPI Comparison		
Solution Options Considered	*% of Students Expected to Achieve 95%+ Test Score*	*% of Students Expected to Write Excellent Problem Statement*	*% of External Agents Identified at Time of Original Scope*
Virtual live training	99%	90%	85%

Solution Options Considered	% of Students Expected to Achieve 95%+ Test Score	% of Students Expected to Write Excellent Problem Statement	% of External Agents Identified at Time of Original Scope
Self-paced online learning	85%	80%	65%
Students read various white papers and reference materials	70%	60%	50%
Provide no training	50%	40%	40%

You should also show a financial comparison for the information in Table 9-1 (you can see financial comparisons in Table 9-2). At some point, the cost to achieve the goals stated may outweigh the cost of doing nothing or providing a less-than-optimal solution. To compare the financial implications in that example, you have to know how an analyst's lack of proper skills and training in scope impacts the business on average.

For example, falling short in the KPI related to identifying external agents can ultimately cost the company more than offering the training would. By missing a stakeholder group, the untrained BA puts the solution at risk of not meeting the needs of that stakeholder group; that situation will require reworking, causing the project to incur additional costs. When you rule out the "provide no training" options, the financial cost of training is obviously less of a consideration than selecting the most effective means of transferring knowledge.

Table 9-2 shows a financial comparison of the options in Table 9-1. Assume that the company has 100 BAs that require training, and each works on approximately five projects per year.

Table 9-2	Sample Financial Comparison		
Solutions Considered	Cost for One Class for All Students	Benefit Expected	Net Cost/Benefit Estimated for Year 1
Virtual live training	$100,000	$425,000	$325,000
Self-paced online learning	$50,000	$325,000	$275,000
Students read various white papers and reference materials	$10,000	$250,000	$240,000
Provide no training	$0	–$500,000	–$500,000

Including a cost/benefit analysis

Cost/benefit analysis is an estimation and evaluation of net benefits associated with alternatives for achieving defined goals and is the primary method used to justify expenditures. It's also a critical piece of the business case.

You may or may not need to include a detailed cost/benefit analysis for each alternative in the business case. Some opportunities may warrant having just the final recommendation fully documented in this section. The audience and the opportunity drive the level and complexity of the details required.

A good rule of thumb is that, if the recommendation is obvious to and will mostly be accepted easily by all individuals responsible for approval, you can simply include the details for only the final recommendation. However, if two or more options are viable solutions, providing more detail in this section gives the audience members the additional information they require to make an informed decision.

If the opportunity is technically or otherwise outside the expertise of readers, though, you should include more details to allow them to become comfortable with your recommendation. Companies are looking for a positive return on their investment in a project, and most organizations have minimal financial measurements for the opportunity to achieve before it can be considered cost justified. Therefore, the additional details can help companies predict financial impact even when the recommendation — "software should be easy to use," for example — isn't easily measurable.

Where most analysts stumble in writing a business case is in knowing how much analysis is enough but not too much. (You don't have to fully analyze each recommended option to the point of absolute certainty.) A business case is a vehicle to gain approval to move forward, which means more analysis occurs after approval but before the project is actually developed or software is purchased. Committing the resources to fully analyze a solution before approval doesn't make sense. However, not doing enough analysis can result in approval for significantly less funding than is ultimately necessary. Through experience, you'll become better at aligning the appropriate analysis effort and the amount of the funding request with the final estimates for the actual results.

Understanding financial terminology and metrics

Here are a few of the terms and financial metrics you should be familiar with as you develop a business case:

- ✔ **Tangible/intangible:** You can quantify *tangible* costs and benefits in financial terms, market share, employee satisfaction measures, or by any measurable scale. *Intangible* costs and benefits must be documented subjectively. Examples of tangible and intangible costs and benefits include the following:

- **Tangible costs:** Labor and material costs, overhead, and decreased quality and production

- **Intangible costs:** Customer, employee, or vendor dissatisfaction and loss of potential customers

- **Tangible benefits:** Increased revenue or income, increased production or quality, and reduced cost

- **Intangible benefits:** Goodwill and customer, employee, or vendor satisfaction

✔ **Goodwill:** An accounting term describing an intangible benefit received by an organization when its customers and investors have a positive feeling or impression of it. Although goodwill isn't included in the net cost/benefit calculation, you should include it in the description as supporting text to justify or support why an alternative wasn't selected. You may also refer to it in the risk section.

✔ **Sunk costs:** An accounting phrase describing expenditures that are in the past and shouldn't have any bearing on future decisions. An opportunity may be a continuation of another project, but any sunk costs associated with the prior project shouldn't be included in the calculation for the current business case.

✔ **Cash flow:** The availability of assets at any given time in an organization. The cost of developing a project and the resulting ongoing or operating cost should be offset by the positive revenue or cost savings over time. The cash flow analysis shows the initial cash required to develop and implement and the expected returns over time.

✔ **Payback period:** The length of time required to recover the cost of making the change or developing a new product. Most organizations have a minimum requirement for a project to be paid back in order to be approved based on the amount funded.

✔ **Return on investment (ROI):** A financial performance measure used to evaluate the efficiency of a number of different investments. ROI is calculated by dividing the profit or savings of an investment by the cost of the investment over time.

Estimating techniques

If multiple alternatives are being considered, each alternative must be analyzed and documented using the same approach. This step is extremely important for options where a financial comparison is being shown.

Determining the costs and benefits means estimating two main categories — one-time cost of change and net impact to ongoing operations — as you can see in Figure 9-2. The source of cost that is usually most obvious is the one-time cost of change. The less-obvious (but equally important) cost is the difference between the cost of the current business process and the cost of the recommendation after it's in place at some future time: the *net impact to ongoing operations*. These two categories make up the overall cost/benefit of the proposal, which may reflect a positive or negative cost/savings after calculated.

Figure 9-2: Components of business case cost estimates.

Illustration by Wiley, Composition Services Graphics

The current process is considered your *AS-IS* process, and the future recommendation is your *TO-BE* scenario. For a brand new initiative, you have only a *to-be* cost or savings. These costs are composed of the ongoing or operating costs of the new recommendation plus the costs to get it built, implemented, and working in place. Figure 9-3 shows the flow for comparing the AS-IS and TO-BE.

Quantifying ongoing/operating costs and benefits

Initiatives can impact people, processes, or systems and should be analyzed individually to ensure that all aspects have been included. After you've identified and quantified all costs and benefits for each impact group, the total of these items makes up your current and future ongoing/operating costs/benefit cost or savings. The difference between these items is your cost justification or comparison for each option.

Process-related impacts

Review your processes to identify the elements that may change because they're directly impacted by the problem or solution. New processes may be identified, or some existing processes may be eliminated. In Figure 9-4, you can see an example of a change in a process from current state to future state; the third tier expands, and the fourth tier is eliminated.

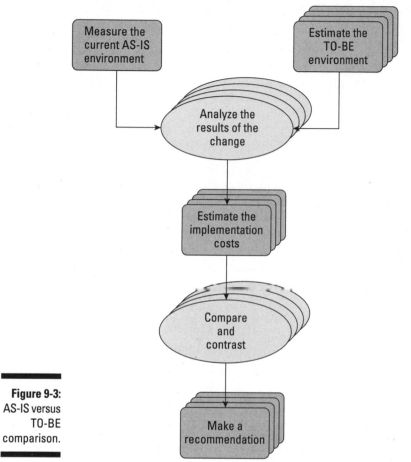

Figure 9-3:
AS-IS versus
TO-BE
comparison.

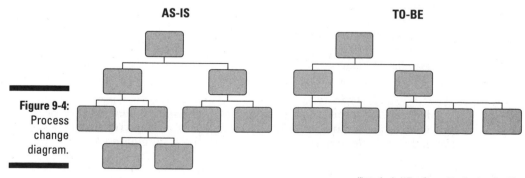

Figure 9-4:
Process
change
diagram.

Identify outcomes and critical workflows needed for the change, if possible. As much as you can at this stage, determine the specific workflows and activity steps that may be impacted; doing so helps substantially in quantifying the cost/benefits.

If you can identify the actual costs/benefits of the current AS-IS process and the estimated costs/benefits of the TO-BE process, you and your audience can evaluate the recommendation objectively. Changes to processes may include savings in efficiencies or effectiveness, savings due to activities being eliminated, or costs for new activities. The actual costs or savings realized depend on the option being evaluated.

For example, say that an opportunity is proposed to change the production and distribution of student class certificates so that the students receive an electronic certificate rather than a printed one. The ongoing cost differences between these alternatives include those listed in Table 9-3.

Table 9-3   Cost Difference of Moving to Electronic Certificates

	AS-IS	TO-BE	Difference
Time to print certificates for each class	2 hours	0 hours	2 hours
Salary of personnel to produce certificates	$15/hour	$15/hour	$0
Subtotal of salary cost	$30	$0	$30
Cost of materials and shipping	$50	$0	$50
Net (cost)/benefit of automating certificates	($80)	$0	$80

For this scenario, you need to find out the potential customer satisfaction of students receiving a printed color certificate versus an electronic one. If they're unhappy with the electronic certificate but won't take any action, the financial impact is zero. However, if they avoid future classes or tell others to because of this change, you have to include the estimated negative impact in the analysis.

People-related impacts

The business objectives of an initiative may impact the people in the organization or target market. To identify people-related impacts, consider the following:

✔ **Who or how many are impacted:** Look at the problem or opportunity as well as the solution to identify the people who are impacted.

✔ **What the transition from the AS-IS to the TO-BE means for them:** Identify whether the impacted individuals will have to learn new processes or skills to perform the new process and whether they'll remain employed or be transferred to a different business area.

After you identify the change impacts to people, you can quantify the related tangible and intangible costs and benefits, which may include all costs associated with labor, such as salary, benefits, and management support costs. Only consider the ongoing or operational costs of the change as related to people at this point. We discuss the initial cost to implement the solution in the upcoming section "Quantifying implementation costs."

System-related impacts

You may find in the business case stage of a project that a specific technology hypothesis is in place for the solution. Considerations when analyzing impacts to the target system(s) include

✔ System user/production

✔ Outsourced contracts

✔ Operational support

✔ Hardware

✔ Software

✔ Licenses

✔ Maintenance fees

✔ Network cost

The cost to develop the new system or changes are included in the one-time implementation costs and aren't part of the ongoing/operational costs.

Quantifying implementation costs

Implementation costs are one-time costs associated with a brand new initiative or a change to an existing one. These costs include — on a broad level — the cost of developing or producing the opportunity as well as the transition costs to move from the AS-IS to the TO-BE.

Just as you identify the process, people, and systems for the ongoing/operational costs, you can use these categories when analyzing the implementation costs:

✔ **Process change costs** may require organizational readiness assessments or a change management plan, and that adds cost and time. We discuss these types of transition requirements in detail in Chapter 15.

✔ **People-related implementation costs** include costs of managing the change and training (such as communication programs) and human resource activities to relocate, hire, or terminate personnel.

✔ **System-related implementation costs** include the development or enhancement to the technology and any simulation, prototypes, or pilots required during development.

The implementation costs of switching from printed class certificates to electronic certificates include the following at a minimum:

✔ Analysis time to design the certificates

✔ Development cost

✔ Testing costs

Assuming these costs total $15,000 and the cost savings per class is $80, the change will have a payback after 188 classes. The automated certificate should be maintenance free for at least 2 years, with minimal changes required to the format expected every third year at a cost of $500 per change. The organization holds approximately 200 classes per year; Table 9-4 shows the cost/benefit recommendation at a high level for the next 6 years:

Table 9-4   Implementation Costs of Making Certificates Electronic

	Year 1	Year 2	Year 3	Year 4	Year 5	Year 6
Implementation costs	$15,000					
Maintenance costs			$500			$500
Ongoing (costs)/benefit	$16,000	$16,000	$16,000	$16,000	$16,000	$16,000
Net realized	$1,000	$16,000	$15,500	$16,000	$16,000	$15,500

The Devil Is in the Details: Providing Supporting Materials

The details section of a business case provides all the supporting documentation and diagrams for the recommendation. You usually include only the details of the recommendation, but you may want to add details of some alternatives if they were close in comparison or the audience may be interested in seeing them. The following sections explain the types of details in this part of the business case.

Addressing supporting documentation

The amount of detail that you include in a business case is primarily driven by the audience of the business case. If the business case serves as a repository for the details of the opportunity, then you want to include all supporting documents regardless of whether the reviewing audience will utilize them.

The types of supporting materials include the following:

- ✔ **Problem statement:** The executive summary and mission statement discuss the problem, but they may not include all components of a fully defined problem statement. The *problem statement* is a structured way to represent the problem or issue causing the organization "pain." Here's a quick review of the statement's basic structure (for details on creating a problem statement, flip to Chapter 8):

    The problem of [*description of the problem*] affects [*name(s) of the stakeholders affected by the problem*], the impact of which [*description of the impact of the problem*]. A successful solution would be [*list of key benefits of a successful solution*].

    Putting these components together in a properly defined problem statement for the electronic training classes example would look like this:

    The problem of having employees in remote locations affects the remote students who cannot attend the in-person training classes, the impact of which is missed requirements in their analysis and a delay in product rollouts. A successful solution would be to provide training that doesn't require travel to improve requirements analysis, thereby reducing errors and increasing product rollout.

- ✔ **Solution position statement:** The *solution position statement* represents the expected results if the solution is developed and implemented. It focuses on the business impact. Again, you can find detailed information about building a solution statement, but the general structure is this:

    For [*name of the target customer*] who [*statement of the need or opportunity*], the (or a) [*solution or product name*] that [*statement of the key benefit or the compelling reason to do business with*]. Unlike [*primary alternative or current situation*], this solution [*statement of primary differentiation*].

    Using this structure to create a solution position statement for the electronic training classes example, you get something like this:

    For students working in remote locations who need training and can't travel, a virtual training program will provide the knowledge necessary to improve their requirements gathering efforts that will result in fewer missed requirements and faster product rollout. Unlike self-paced online training, which has limited opportunities for practice, the virtual training has a faster ramp-up time to begin realizing the value.

- ✔ **Background or evidence of need:** These items are the details behind how the opportunity originated and may include summaries of discussions and meetings related to the opportunity and impacts to the business.

- ✔ **Approach or plan to implement:** If an implementation plan is required and has been developed at the time of the business case, include it in this section even if it's only a high-level outline at this point.

- ✔ **Any other relevant data:** Depending on the opportunity, an internal and/or external communication plan or a change management plan may be necessary. Also, if you consulted an expert who provided supporting documentation, this part is the perfect place to include a copy of his report.

Noting your assumptions

Whenever you're developing estimates for the cost/benefit analysis, you make assumptions. Some estimates are based more on factual data than others, but almost every item in a cost/benefit analysis is an assumption that should be visible in the details.

Give the reader all the assumptions used in the estimates. For example, if you're assuming that an existing process takes 5 hours to complete, and the new process will take 1 hour to complete, you should document in this section how you determined that assumption. Did you have a similar improved process that readers can refer to, or did you guess using some other reference point?

Here are some examples of assumptions:

- ✔ Cost of labor won't change during the duration of the project.
- ✔ Resources will be available for the duration of the project.
- ✔ The skills required are available in the marketplace at the cost estimated.
- ✔ The software vendor will respond to problem calls within 4 hours.
- ✔ The software vendor won't sell the software rights to another vendor for at least 2 years.
- ✔ Laws won't change the way the business operates.
- ✔ The technology to be used will continue to be available and supported by its manufacturer.

> ✔ Demand for the organization's product will continue as forecasted.
>
> ✔ Competition won't install a similar automated system.

Documenting risk

Just like assumptions, any estimate for costs/benefit analysis should include details about any risks. Which risks to document depends on their likelihood and the potential impact the occurrence of such risks would have on the business case. The intent is to provide guidance for the reader to make the most well-informed decision possible based on all information available at the time of writing.

Some assumptions are actually risks, whether they do or don't occur. For example, an assumption listed in the preceding section is that laws won't change the way the business operates. If an opportunity is related to the implementation of tax changes for the next fiscal year, the laws may change such that the system would need to be updated again. In this example, the risk would be "If the laws do change, the potential financial impact realized is $15,000."

You have to do an estimate for a given point in time based on what information is available at that time. However, you should make the readers aware of all potential implications that may impact their decision.

Never leave out known risks that may have a significant impact just to win approval. Although doing so may achieve the immediate goal for the opportunity, it may put the business in serious jeopardy and will surely destroy your credibility.

Presenting the Business Case

The visual image of the business case sets the tone with the audience. What do you want it to say? Will you present the business case in a leather-bound book or a white binder with a typed cover page and colored standard tabs? Do you have a full-scale prototype or hand drawings of your idea to present with your case?

Some organizations have standards for important review documents, business cases, and templates that you must adhere to for internal use. If your company doesn't have such standards, the project's audience, size, priority, visibility, and strategic importance should guide your presentation decisions.

If you're presenting a small case to just your manager, perhaps a single-page executive summary and a sketch to support your idea is perfectly sufficient. If your audience is a team of department leaders, though, presenting color Microsoft PowerPoint slides outlining the executive summary and justification sections (and handing out hard copies for discussion purposes) may be more appropriate. You can provide the details for individual review in a three-ring binder, with tabs for each option. Leather-bound books may be reserved for *C-level* cases presented to chief executives, their teams, and boards of directors.

Chapter 10

Creating and Maintaining Scope

*J*ust as each project has analysis and design phases, it also has a scoping phase. *Scope* is all about understanding what is and isn't relevant to your project. It's about working with your stakeholders to set clear limits and project boundaries and making sure you all remain on the same page about them.

A properly set and enforced scope is a key part of a successful project. Scoping the boundaries of a project, as well as all the elements you should address and analyze given any constraints, puts you in a better position to estimate the time and other resources the project will take. After all, you only have so many resources (time, funds, and people) with which to achieve the project's goals.

Although scoping can be a challenging skill to master, you probably already set scope in other areas in your life without even thinking about it! For example, if you're buying a house, you may set the boundaries for the location ("no house outside a 10-mile radius from work") or have a certain price range in mind. Setting those boundaries keeps your house hunt focused on options that meet your goals.

Ideally, you work jointly with the project manager (PM) on the project scope. The PM is usually responsible for the work breakdown structure (WBS), the budget, the schedule, the human resources, the project risks, and the milestones. On the other hand, you as the business analyst (BA) take care of designing, compiling, and enforcing the data flow diagram, the use case diagram, the stakeholder analysis, the business risks, and the high-level business processes. In this chapter, we give you the lowdown on determining, documenting, and debating changes to your scope.

Making Sure You're Scoping the Right Solution

On the most simplistic level, organizations undertake projects to either solve a problem or achieve a growth objective. One of your jobs as the BA is to help the organization understand the real problem or real opportunity it's facing, which is actually the beginning of scoping a project.

Figuring out the real issue isn't always as easy as it may seem. Stakeholders are smart. As they come across problems, they often devise their own solutions to them. In many cases, their solution fixes the problem even though it's no more than a temporary bandage. We call this kind of fix a *work-around*; it's a solution, although not the most ideal one. Work-arounds affect scope because they don't always address the real problem; if the real problem or solution isn't correctly identified, you can't correctly set scope. So you have to dig a little to get beyond any work-arounds in order to set the scope for implementing a true solution.

To get beneath the surface of a work-around, start by asking the stakeholder "why" questions: "Why did you start using this work-around?" "Why does this fix work for you?" The more you ask "why," the more you understand the real problem the stakeholder faces. You can also walk your stakeholders through the creation of a scope diagram that sets the boundaries for their projects (we cover scope diagrams later in this chapter). For even more strategies for discovering the real issue, turn to Chapter 8.

Paul was once on assignment helping out delivery drivers in the business domain of a package delivery company. When one of the managers found out about Paul's IT background, he asked whether Paul could make a change to a report so he could sort it in a different way. The manager needed to more quickly compare the drivers' assistants' availability (which was on a printed report) against a list of drivers (which was on a computer screen). However, by asking "why" questions, Paul discovered that the real problem wasn't the sorting of the printed report; it was the scheduling action. So instead of fixing the printed report (which would have been a work-around), Paul determined that the solution to address the real problem was an interface between the two systems that could match the assistants' and drivers' schedules. Figuring out the real issue first allowed Paul to set the proper scope.

Recognizing Relevant Stakeholders

You must work with your stakeholders to create the appropriate scope. The more people you bring into your scoping sessions, the better. Involving all the people or representatives that are affected allows for a greater perspective on the project; you get different opinions from different people during the scoping process. In addition, everyone understands and has input on the project boundaries (the scope) and is therefore in agreement moving forward.

A scope is like a contract on a house. All the aspects of the house purchase are outlined, and the expectations are set going in. The buyers and/or sellers can change the contract to affect the price or timeline, but both parties have to agree to any modifications. It's very similar in project scope. Expanding the project scope may affect the budget, timeline, and/or the specific requirements, so all parties need to sign off on changes.

Uncovering stakeholders by asking project-specific questions

Suppose your manager comes to you and says a stakeholder initiated a request to have the company logo printed on the invoice. Pretty simple, right? But this situation presents a lot of concerns you as a BA should have and express. Which invoices would the logo appear on — online? E-mail? Printed? What size is the logo? Is it registered or trademarked? Do different customers receive different logos from different company divisions? Who (or what department) owns the invoice printing process today? And you haven't even started to address getting permission from the legal department. The answers to these questions help you determine which stakeholders need to be involved. Here's a sample list for the logo project:

✔ The legal department because the logo contains the ® mark, which comes with a set of restrictions and has to be approved

✔ The company's different divisions because they use different logos; certain customers purchase products from only one division

✔ The billing department for invoices and manufacturing for products because these departments own the printing process

By knowing all the stakeholders, you can then form the basis of what you are (and aren't) going to study.

Your various stakeholders will probably identify more parties, systems, and hardware than will actually be in the project scope when the project gets underway. That's fine. You end up adding those extras to the "out of scope" section we detail later in the chapter. Stakeholders must be clear and in agreement on any item's placement, regardless of whether you identify the item as within scope or out of scope.

Discovering key stakeholders in different parts of the organization

Many organizations are arranged around functional-based or organizational-based segments (sometimes known as *silos* or *stovepipes*). People tend to think of these segments as vertical slices of the company, but many processes or projects go across those silos. For example, look at how a customer's order goes through multiple silos in Figure 10-1.

Figure 10-1:
A customer order going across multiple organizational silos.

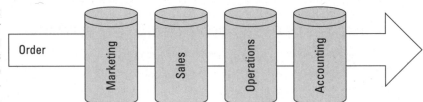

Illustration by Wiley, Composition Services Graphics

The problem with this arrangement is that a project that one silo undertakes may make another silo's process less efficient. When scoping, you have to consider all the parties you need to include and how changes may impact everyone.

The easiest way to make sure all stakeholders are on the same page is to bring in everyone that is or may be impacted by your project. If you're trying to improve the customer order process in Figure 10-1, you bring in stakeholders from the marketing, sales, operations, and accounting departments. By having all these parties in the room, you make sure they all have a say in ways to make the process more efficient.

Some techniques you can use to identify who you need to have in the room are stakeholder analysis, brainstorming, swimlane process diagrams, data flow diagrams, and interface analysis. We explain these techniques in Chapters 7 and 13.

Ensuring That the Scope Aligns with Key Business Drivers

As we discuss in Chapter 9, *business drivers* are entities that have a major impact on the performance of a specific business, and identifying them is critical to scoping your project properly. Business drivers

✔ Reflect the performance and progress of your business

✔ Are measurable

✔ Can be compared to a standard, such as a budget, last year's figures, or an industry average

✔ Can be acted upon

You need to make sure that your scope and the identified problem/opportunity align with the business drivers. You don't want to end up with a project with requirements that don't support (or worse, that conflict with) the drivers. Doing so can lead to cost overruns and scope creep in the best case and complete project failure in the worst case. (We discuss scope creep later in the chapter.) For example, if your business driver is to increase customer satisfaction, you probably won't add requirements for changing the way employees report their expense accounts.

Business drivers vary among organizations. To understand what drives your specific project and organization, ask questions such as the following:

✔ What organizational units will be involved with the project? What systems and departments are going to interface with the project?

✔ Which individuals within those organizational units am I going to work with? What is their stake in the project? How am I best going to work with them?

✔ How do the various organizational units work with each other?

✔ How are the subject matter experts (SMEs) going to interact with the project team? How are they going to interact with the technical team?

✔ How are the technical systems developed within the organization? What are the methodologies used?

✔ What deliverables and what level of detail does the implementation team expect from the business analysts?

This stage is where you ask perhaps the most important question in the project: "Why is this project being done?" Knowing the answer helps you establish the context surrounding the project and helps you understand why the organization is undertaking this project.

The information you get from these answers can help you organize the drivers to understand them further. Business drivers normally fall into one of eight categories:

✔ **Revenue:** Companies often undertake a project in order to increase revenue. If the company you're working with is publicly owned, chances are that increasing shareholder value is a big business driver.

Not all organizations are driven by revenue. Nonprofit organizations may have other primary business drivers; for example, a nonprofit hospital's primary business driver may be customer service or compliance.

✔ **Cost:** Another reason organizations undertake projects is to decrease the cost of doing business. For instance, say a database marketing company mails out thousands of catalogs multiple times each year. If it can target the folks most likely to respond to its offerings and/or switch to a more cost-effective delivery method (such as e-mailing an electronic catalog), it may save money on catalog sales. When focusing on the cost business driver, remember to include stakeholders that may have insight about or be impacted by this decision, such as the customer service department. Ultimately, the business driver of cost may override customer service, but that department should still be included.

✔ **Customer service:** Organizations often look to increase customer service and provide better service than their competition. Customer service is one of the biggest drivers for one of the premier outdoor gear and apparel retailers, REI, and it shows in the company's return policy: Return anything at any time if you aren't 100 percent satisfied.

✔ **Compliance:** Sometimes your own organization doesn't initiate the project; instead, a governmental organization or a regulatory body dictates what you must do. Sometimes companies have to change some form of the organization or enterprise in order to be compliant with new mandates.

Sometimes, from the business side, being noncompliant is more cost-effective than spending the money to be compliant. For instance, suppose a company faces a $5 million project to be compliant with a governmental regulation. But if the company gets caught being noncompliant, the fine is only $50,000. From a return on investment (ROI) perspective, the company is still better off getting caught 99 times than paying the cost to implement the compliancy! However, the company's image may suffer if it's found willfully negligent, so the cost to implement may be necessary from a publicity standpoint. Oh, the decisions business analysts deal with!

✔ **Brand:** Another business driver may be maintaining brand standards. Companies that have a well-respected brand may want to enhance or not damage that image, so they may decide to undertake a project even though it costs them money.

✔ **Time to market:** Organizations generally want to get their products to market faster than their competitors because doing so can mean name recognition. For instance, people often use brand names like Xerox and iPod even if the photocopying and MP3 devices they're using aren't actually those brands. When you're the first one in the marketplace, you establish the criteria for the rest to follow.

Not all companies prioritize this business driver. Some organizations wait until the first product is already out before they leap into the market with a similar product. They want to see what works and what doesn't and then develop their product accordingly. (Note, however, this strategy may backfire if the first-to-market product is accepted with great fanfare.)

✔ **Agility:** Some organizations realize that the strongest companies aren't necessarily the ones that survive; the most agile ones are. Companies that are able to adapt to changing conditions and markets are the ones that continue to do business year after year after year.

Consider how automobile companies are changing with the rising cost of oil. They're looking at alternative fuels to power vehicles because the market is changing; more and more buyers have a greener outlook on automobile power and don't want to burn gasoline. The more quickly the companies can change and give their customers what they want, the more likely they are to be in the marketplace for years to come.

✔ **Fulfillment time:** *Fulfillment time* is the elapsed time between the order being taken and delivery of the order. Look at what Apple's iTunes did for the music industry: It changed the expectation of when customers could get their music. Now customers expect to be able to purchase and download items instantly instead of waiting to go buy them at the mall.

✔ **Market reach:** Many of the projects undertaken by business analysts in the late 1990s and early 2000s were *global* projects that rolled existing legacy applications out globally. This trend occurred because organizations recognized the need to extend their reaches to new consumer markets. As they did so, they also faced new challenges of rising costs. So eventually, after they had the global reach, many of those companies started selling similar products in multiple markets. Take, for instance, Ford's decision to sell the 2012 Focus model both domestically and internationally instead of making different models for different markets. Doing so helped Ford be more competitive and reduce costs.

Identifying Interfaces That Are Part of the Project

When you're scoping, you want to be able to find all the interfaces that are part of the project. You need to consider three types of interfaces: user, system, and hardware. The following sections give you the details.

Look to the data flow diagram and use case diagram to find interfaces. In a data flow diagram, the curved data flow lines from external agents are your interfaces; people are user interfaces, systems and external organizations are system interfaces, and pieces and hardware are (you guessed it) hardware interfaces. In a use case diagram, any association line from an actor that crosses the automation boundary into a use case is an interface. You can read more about both types of diagrams in Chapter 13.

User interfaces

The *user interfaces* are how the user interacts with the solution; they often take the form of mockups (see Chapter 13). Although many interfaces are technological in nature, non-computer items such as a steering wheel and an accelerator pedal are also user interfaces (for a driver to interface with an automobile).

Your user interfaces come from external people who need to interact with your solution. When you create a user interface, you have to think about the system user because the success of the interface is determined by how well it works for the person (or people) using it. Ask the following questions about your users:

- Who are the people we are interfacing with?
- What is their education level?
- What experience do they have with the solution?
- Are we dealing with different levels of people (for instance, regular customers, preferred customers, elite customers)?
- Do any of these individuals have disabilities? (508 compliance would be critical.)

Knowing the answers to these questions (and this list is just a start) helps you determine the level of effort you need to put into the project to create these interfaces.

System interfaces

The *system interfaces* are the interfaces your project has with other computer systems from either external organizations or other departments within your organization. To identify system interfaces, listen for terms like "batch interface" or "real-time interface" when eliciting information from your stakeholders. Doing so will uncover external agents that are systems and require a system interface.

Here are some questions to ask to find system interfaces:

- What systems are we interfacing or communicating with?
- Where are we getting our data?
- Who are we sending information to?

After you know the system interfaces, you still need to understand the data passing through the interface. Although you don't have to comprehend it to the level of the data types and lengths, you need to get an idea of how long completing analysis of each interface takes.

Hardware interfaces

Hardware interfaces are the interfaces that go from your project to a piece of hardware somewhere — say, a printer or a television (yes, television). To identify hardware interfaces, listen for the mention of technological devices (either on the sending or receiving end) during your elicitation sessions and make sure they're reflected in your diagrams. Your project may end up outputting information to the printer or mobile device, and you have to be aware of that. It's an interface, too.

Some questions to ask to find hardware interfaces include the following:

- When we capture data, where does it go?
- How will we display that information? Who needs to see it?
- Where will the information in our application come from?

Defining Scope with a Data Flow Diagram

Sometimes, trying to explain what's within scope by using just words becomes very difficult. That's where a *scope diagram* (version of the data flow diagram in Chapter 13) can be helpful. Instead of just taking notes, you can actually structure your findings graphically in a scope diagram to help you make sense of everything. The scope diagram has three parts:

- The rectangular boxes represent *external agents* (sometimes called *actors*). These agents are the people or the systems with which your project (what you're analyzing) will interact. They're external to your project, so you don't study their internal processes. The only thing you can do is change the interface with the external agent.

- The curved lines are the data flows into and out of your area of study that connect to the external agents. They show information (or data) going into and out of your project and represent interfaces.

- The circle in the middle is your area of study — your scope. You work on all the requirements inside the circle to be able to process information and send and receive it to your external agents.

In business analysis lingo, a scope diagram is sometimes called a Context Level Data Flow Diagram.

The diagram in Figure 10-2 shows the area of study ("Reserve Hotel Room"), the people or departments you interface with ("Reservation Systems," "Guest," and so on), and the interfaces themselves ("Name, Dates of Stay," "Availability, Price, Confirmation," and so on). The beauty of this data flow diagram is that, when in place, it becomes an artifact you can share with stakeholders and project managers. When those people ask about new requirements, you have a scope you can return to in order to verify whether their requests fit within the boundaries of the original project or constitute a new request.

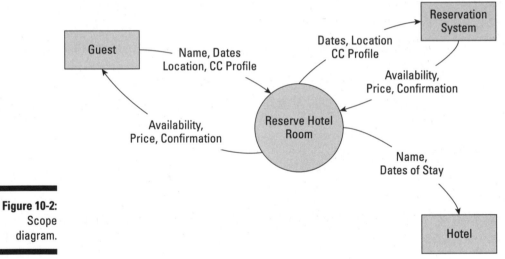

Figure 10-2:
Scope
diagram.

Illustration by Wiley, Composition Services Graphics

The diagram looks pretty simple, and you may be tempted to just jump right in and start drawing circles and lines. But those circles and lines represent aspects of your project, so be careful what you draw; it's going to sign you up for what you work on! Here's an easy five-step process to create a scope diagram (we cover each step in detail in following sections):

1. **Identify parties and systems that will be impacted by the project.**

2. **Identify information (data) flows among the parties or systems.**

3. **Gain consensus on the scope for the project.**

4. **Give the project a descriptive name.**

5. **Finalize the scope diagram.**

Identifying parties and systems that will be impacted by the project

In this step, you want to list all the people, systems, and other external entities (such as external companies or regulatory agencies) that your project impacts. Based on the project statement of purpose (see the later section "Stating the purpose of the project"), come up with a list of these entities. These parties become your external agents.

Perform this activity with your project team. Having multiple people in the room helps bring in additional viewpoints that you may not have thought of on your own.

Consider the invoice logo example we introduce in section "Uncovering stakeholders by asking project-specific questions" earlier in the chapter. You bring in the project team and identify all the parties or systems. Write these groups down in rectangles on the shared workspace (whiteboard, flip chart, sticky notes on the wall, or whatever)

Remember, you're simply identifying parties or systems that may be impacted by the project. You haven't fully defined the scope yet. As you work through the scoping process, some of these agents may fall off. The important thing is that you capture your team's thoughts about what impacts may happen with this project.

Identifying information (data) flows among the parties or systems

Next, you want to understand what information or data passes among these external agents. At this stage, you only want to understand the data at a high level. These data flows aren't the detailed data elements but rather the big-picture representations of what passes among the different external agents. As you identify them, add curved lines to your diagram, like in Figure 10-3.

For instance, the billing process accesses the invoice template from accounting prior to creating the customer invoice and sources charges from sales.

Continue identifying all the data flows until you've completed the diagram. At this point, you have only rectangles and flow lines.

At this stage, you may find that some external agents don't belong or don't connect with any data flow lines to any other external agents. That's fine. These stragglers are good candidates for specifically listing as "out of scope." Customer Service is one of those external agents we can identify up front as being out of scope.

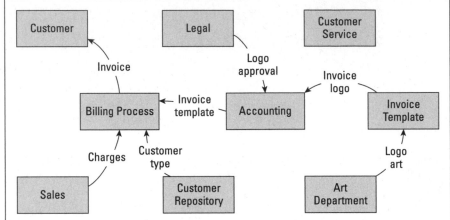

Illustration by Wiley, Composition Services Graphics

Figure 10-3:
Identification
of data
flows
among
external
agents.

Gaining consensus on the scope for the project

Now you can have the discussion as to what will be studied to create a solution. You have a diagram with rectangles and curved lines, but still no indication of what is in scope (though you may have identified a few out-of-scope items). When you agree as a project team on what the scope is, you circle the rectangles you're going to study as part of your solution as shown in Figure 10-4.

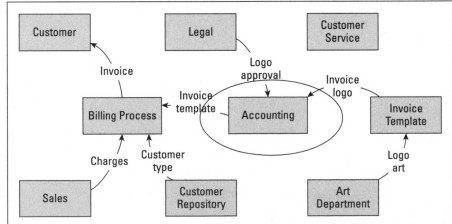

Figure 10-4:
Gaining
consensus
on scope.

Illustration by Wiley, Composition Services Graphics

At this stage, you can see that the only impacted party is the accounting department, so it becomes the group you analyze to determine a solution to the problem area. The circle now tells you a couple of additional items about the scope:

✔ Any of the external agents who don't share a data flow directly crossing the scope circle are out of scope for the project efforts. In Figure 10-4, this category includes the customer and the sales, customer repository, and art departments. You can officially list them as out of scope for this project.

Any time you take something out of a project, list it as out of scope to avoid any confusion about its status later in the project.

✔ The diagram shows you interfaces. Any data flow lines the circle crosses become user, system, or hardware interfaces. (Head to the earlier section "Identifying Interfaces That Are Part of the Project" for info on these types of interfaces.) You may have to create these interfaces or modify existing ones.

All your requirements for changes or creation of new processes exist inside the circle. The external agents connected to the project scope interact with your project, but you have no control over them. For instance, in Figure 10-4, legal is an external agent. Although it may be internal to your organization, it's external to your project. You aren't going to study the processes to determine how the ® mark gets approved for your logo.

Giving the project a descriptive name

Making sure your project's name is descriptive ensures that everyone understands what this project is undertaking. Consider the difference between Project Print Logo and Project Xf89K6-5. You can understand what the project is doing just by reading the name rather than a nondescript number.

In some organizations' cultures, though, numeric names are just as descriptive as words. In one organization Paul worked for, the culture dictated using terms such as Project 1024 or Project 1132. People in that organization understood which project numbers related to which corporate initiatives. If that is indeed your organization's culture, go with it.

Finalizing the scope diagram

For better clarity and readability by stakeholders, many business analysts list the high-level processes that will most likely be studied as part of your scope.

You may study the software, hardware, manual or automated processes, and possibly the creation of new processes. For example, on the print logo project, some of the high-level processes may be "approve logo," "determine customer type," and "charge customer."

In this stage, you formally remove the items that aren't in scope and document them as such. In addition, any flow lines connected from one external agent to another external agent outside the project circle are documented as out of scope for the project because your project has no control over communication between those external agents.

Using Project Initiation Documentation to Clarify Scope

Documentation created at the beginning (or *initiation*) of a project is called *project initiation documentation* — some organizations call this a *project charter* — and it helps clarify what the project is all about. This documentation contains seven sections: project statement of purpose, project approach or methodology, project objectives, problems and opportunities, risks, project assumptions and constraints, and high-level processes. (We give details on these parts in the following sections.) With each section, collaborating on the initiation documentation as a project team is helpful; the more time you spend refining this documentation, the more accurate your project scope and estimates will be.

Stating the purpose of the project

The *project statement of purpose* explains why the organization is undertaking this project. This section of the documentation is the only one that should be written by the project *sponsor* (the one going for the project funding) rather than the project team. The project sponsor is very clear on the purpose of the project and understands why it's being undertaken. (Theoretically, at least. If the sponsor has a hard time explaining the purpose, that may be an indication that you're going to face a rough project.)

Remember the following points about the statement of purpose:

✔ **It can be a text description anywhere from a paragraph to a couple of pages long.** The size depends on the complexity of the project and the organization's standards. Some organizations have templates for a more structured description outlining required and optional information.

✔ **It must be formally written so that everyone on the project team understands the project the same way.**

✔ **It describes what is to be accomplished, not how.** At this point in the project, you simply need to understand what the problem or opportunity is, not how to solve it. Keeping the project team members aware of these terms helps guide them in their thinking.

✔ **It contains three deliverables:**

- The current environment

- The problem or opportunity the organization faces

- The approach that will be used to address the problem or opportunity

If the project sponsor hasn't written the statement of purpose or is having a hard time explaining herself clearly, you can help by rewriting the statement to communicate why the project is being undertaken. Just make sure that if you're involved in the writing, the project sponsor signs off and takes accountability for the project!

Describing the project approach or methodology

This section of the project initiation contains a brief description of the approach the project team uses to complete the project. The BA helps with this documentation to get the project team to an understanding of how the organization is going to approach undertaking the project. Generally, the approach contains four main areas:

✔ **The name of the methodology to be followed:** This designation can be anything from an industry standard (such as Six Sigma or Lean) to a custom in-house methodology.

✔ **The tasks the project team will perform:** This part describes the activities the project team will undertake as part of the work it delivers on this project. It briefly outlines the major work areas the team will perform. Examples include a feasibility study, gap analysis study, and business process mapping exercise.

✔ **The tools to be used by the project team:** Even if you're using Microsoft Word as a documentation tool, you should record that here to set expectations on what people will receive when this project is complete. We discuss more tools and techniques in Chapter 13.

✔ **Other related documents:** You may reference documents and project artifacts in the project approach that you don't actually write. These extras may be project plans, schedules, or budgets, for example.

Listing project objectives

The *objectives* are the business's reasons for initiating the project. When you write objectives, you want to be SMART about it. (*SMART* is an acronym for *specific, measureable, attainable, relevant,* and *time-bound*. For more on these SMART characteristics, flip to Chapter 8.) As the BA, you write your project's objectives, so you need to see how well they align to these criteria as you go.

Be careful to not go too deeply into requirements when identifying your objectives. Although there's no hard-and-fast rule, your objectives are generally longer-term goals. Requirements are the expectations applied against the problem or opportunity.

Articulating problems and opportunities

A technique some BAs use to help clarify scope is to gather the project team together and have them articulate the problems and opportunities the business area faces so that the BA has a better understanding of these issues.

As a BA, you normally document problems and opportunities in a table like Table 10-1. Keep in mind that not all problems translate into an opportunity, and not all opportunities stem from problems (as you see in the third row of the table).

Table 10-1	**Problems and Opportunities**	
ID	*Problem*	*Opportunity*
1	Users frequently misspell words when creating text messages.	Create a solution to recognize the word and automatically correct it for them.
2	Users are using more data on their unlimited data plans than our infrastructure can handle.	Switch them over to a shared data plan.
3		Introduce pay-by-phone options for retailers rather than credit cards.

Outlining risks

Understanding and analyzing the risks of a project is an important part of identifying and documenting the project scope. Risks can be project-related and/or business-related:

✔ **Project risks:** *Project risks* are potential problems that may impede the completion of a project. They include situations like losing a key person prior to the completion of the project or having a team inexperienced with a *commercial off-the-shelf* tool (or *COTS* tool, a pre-packaged, one-size-fits-all solution that may or may not have the ability for customization). Project risks are managed by the project manager.

✔ **Business risks:** *Business risks* are risks that may impact the mission of the business area. Examples include having the release of the product go so well that the company can't keep up with orders. You as the BA manage the business risks.

Identifying possible risks and response plans ahead of time puts you in a better position to react to a changing project. If the project falls behind schedule, you can swiftly focus your time more effectively on the areas that are the neediest because you'll have already anticipated them instead of being caught by surprise. In addition, you should already know which pieces of the project can be postponed without business failure. In the following sections, we show you how to categorize risk responses and factors and list them in a handy table.

Risk responses

Knowing what the risks are is one thing; knowing what to do about them is another. When identifying risks, identify a response as well so you know how you're going to act if and when a risk actually happens or so you can put controls and checks in place to prevent a risk from occurring in the first place. According to the Project Management Institute's *A Guide to the Project Management Book Of Knowledge,* 5th Edition (PMBOK 5), you can respond to a risk in four ways:

✔ **Avoid:** In this response, you change the project to eliminate the threat. For example, say that you want to put in a new software solution that allows customers to purchase products online, but this is being developed in a software program that the development team is unfamiliar with. To avoid that risk, the team can either change the software and develop within the expertise of the staff or utilize developers that are experienced with the desired software.

✔ **Transfer:** Shift the risk to another party. Perhaps you transfer the risk of creating the online purchasing system to a consulting company. The consultants are contractually bound to create the system, not you. They accept the risk.

✔ **Mitigate:** Reduce the probability or impact of the risk. You don't have experience in coding web pages, so you send your development team to an intensive two-week training in website coding.

✔ **Accept:** Choose to accept the risk and develop a contingency plan. You put the online purchasing program in place, and your contingency plan is to drive customer traffic by using social media to promote the new site.

By thinking ahead, you're prepared with a clearly thought out response plan so you can react with level heads instead of responding to the risk in the heat of the moment and making an uninformed (and possibly emotional) decision.

Risk factors

The last items you want to document surrounding a risk are the *risk factors*. They include the risk's *probability* (likelihood) and *impact* (effect on the project).

As the BA, you bring the project team together and, through conversation and educated guessing, get members to agree on the likelihood that the risk will happen as well as the impact to the project or organization if it does.

Putting all the risk information together

After you've spent the time documenting the project and business risks, what value do they have? Well, with the probability and impacts documented, you can prioritize the risks and concentrate on those you feel will be most likely/have the highest impact. Consider the risks shown in Table 10-2. You have a list of the risks for the project, as well as how you plan to respond to them if they happen.

Table 10-2		Risks and Responses			
ID	Risk	Response Type	Response	Probability	Impact
1	Key developer leaves before the project is complete.	Mitigate	Pair up developers and cross-train.	Medium	High
2	Unfamiliarity with the new application may delay project dates.	Transfer	Hire consulting company to implement software.	High	High

Specifying project assumptions and constraints

An *assumption* is a premise that you believe is true at the beginning of the project and will remain true throughout the life of the project. An example may be, "We assume the technical personnel will be able to integrate the new tool into our legacy systems." Assumptions are an important concept because they become the truths under which the project operates.

When you're eliciting and people laugh or roll their eyes at someone's assumption, that's a signal that they don't believe that assumption to be true. When that happens, classify the assumption as a risk instead.

A *constraint* is a restriction or limitation on the proposed solution. For instance, when creating the project scope, a large constraint on a project may be the organization's requirement that you use a COTS tool. Another constraint may be a due date — the project must be completed by the end of the second quarter of next year.

Documenting high-level processes

High-level processes give the project team a good idea of the complexity and size of the processes under study. They also become the starting point for your process decomposition diagram (discussed in depth in Chapter 13).

When documenting the high-level processes, you want to use a verb and a noun (a *noun phrase*) such as "submit lead" or "inquire shipping status."

When naming your processes, take time to think about what the process actually accomplishes. Use a strong verb like "record," "submit," "update," or "remove." Stay away from words like "manage" and "move" because they're vague. And whatever you do, don't use the word "process" to name a process!

Identifying who's responsible for each deliverable

To keep track of who's responsible for each deliverable outlined in the project initiation document, use a chart like the one shown in Table 10-3. (This chart can also serve as a summary of who does what in the scoping activities.) Identify the participants along the top row and the deliverables in the left-most column. Then note the degree of responsibility for each person:

✓ **Responsible (R):** Those who have to do the work in the task.

✓ **Accountable (A):** The person who ultimately has to answer for the task getting completed; only one person can be accountable for each task.

✓ **Consulted (C):** Those whose opinions and information you seek.

✓ **Informed (I):** Those who are kept informed on the project.

Table 10-3	Project Initiation Documentation RACI Chart				
	Project Sponsor	*Project Manager*	*Business Analyst*	*SME*	*Project Team*
Statement of purpose	RA	C	C	I	I
Project approach or methodology	I	RA	R	I	C
Project objectives	C	RA	R	C	C
Problems and opportunities	C	RA	R	C	I
Risks	C	RA	R	C	C
Assumptions and constraints	C	RA	R	C	C
High-level processes	C	C	RA	C	I
Items not in scope	C	R	RA	C	C

Indicating What Isn't Covered: Items Not in Scope

Although the idea that anything not listed in scope is out of scope may seem obvious, some items you want to specifically document in the project initiation documents as being out of scope. These items tend to be ones that people may think are in scope but actually aren't. If you don't document their out-of-scope status upfront, you may waste valuable resources exploring problems and solutions that aren't within the boundaries of the project.

Consider the case of the project team making changes to its website as part of a 12-month project. During scoping, both the customers and the customer service department were identified as external agents for the project. However, communications between the customers and customer service happened by phone and therefore weren't going to be handled by the website. Although this communication was recognized as being beyond the control of the website project, it was never actually documented as out of scope. Eight months into the project, a business stakeholder suggested bringing live chat functionality into the project so customer service could handle customer inquiries by using the website. Because nothing indicated that this functionality was out of scope, the project underwent multiple unnecessary meetings and impact analysis to determine whether it could be brought into scope.

Getting Agreement on the Scope

Getting clear agreement on the scope is very important because you're dealing with so many different stakeholders with so many different opinions. When you get agreement, it results in the scope being

- ✔ **Manageable:** You can achieve what you want to achieve within the given time frame.

- ✔ **Focused:** The project team can focus its efforts on the analysis and deliver the best solution instead of being spread too thin and creating less-effective and irrelevant solutions.

- ✔ **Well understood:** Knowing in detail what the stakeholders are trying to accomplish and spending time to understand the problems and the business domain go a long way to ensure you fix the right problem.

- ✔ **Set up to produce a good ROI for the company:** ROI has different meanings in different organizations. In a for-profit enterprise, it's usually associated with dollars and profitability. For a nonprofit organization, ROI may be something more like "If I work on this initiative for 6 months, we will be able to help 5 percent more people per year."

Failing to take the time to make sure everyone understands and concurs with what you as a team have set as the scope may spell disaster for the project. To get agreement from all the stakeholders, be sure to do the following:

- ✔ Have a formal review of the scope.

- ✔ Discuss and make any necessary changes.

- ✔ Obtain sign-off of final document from the project sponsor.

Avoiding Scope Creep

Scope creep is what happens when your project experiences changes and increases beyond its original mission. Your job is to make sure your team stays on track by referring to all your documentation anytime a question about scope comes up. You don't necessarily have to say "no" to every request for a change; you just have to put each request up against your original documents to see whether it's a fit. If a stakeholder requests a new requirement (say, to add a frequent-stay program to the original scope of the hotel reservation project in Figure 10-2 earlier in the chapter), you'd refer to your documentation in order to determine whether that's something you originally signed up to work on. You can say "yes" to out-of-scope requests; just understand what happens when you do so by comparing each request to your documents.

When evaluating change requests, consider the *project management triple constraint:* scope (what work you can do), time (the amount of time you have to complete the work), and resources (the people and money you have to complete the work you signed up for). When a proposed change affects any one of those items, it impacts one or both of the other two.

The following sections show you how to figure out whether a change request will cause scope creep and lead you through creating a process for administering change requests.

Spotting scope creep

To identify scope creep, follow these steps:

1. **Examine the agreed-upon scope diagram for the project you're working on.**

2. **Determine whether the request is within the area of study (the circle) or fits within the data flows and existing external agents.**

   If so, it's not scope creep; it's an additional requirement you need to account for. If it doesn't fit, it's scope creep.

3. **Perform a rough estimate of the impact to the scope, time, and resources.**

   For instance, adding new requirements may do any of the following:

   • Necessitate additional time and/or resources (whether that's financial or people resources).

   • Remove existing items from the scope and replace with the new items.

4. **Request that the stakeholder complete an official change control document (see the following section) detailing the change and the reason for the request.**

5. **Estimate the change and report back to the stakeholder and the project team the change in the project scope, time, and resources necessary for the change.**

   The project manager decides whether to accept the change into scope.

You want to perform a rough estimate at this stage or at least advise the stakeholder of the consequences of adding new items to scope. You don't want to spend a lot of time determining exact figures because every estimation task takes you away from your primary purpose — analysis!

Formulating a change control process

Change control is a process by which the project scope is changed. As with any project, you need to establish a formal change control process. Although some stakeholders may dread filling out change control forms because they think the forms are a waste of time, you need the forms so you can understand the rationale behind the change. Change request forms create official artifacts for the request. Plus, when stakeholders have to fill out documentation every time they want to request a scope change, they're less likely to continually submit ridiculous requests they don't feel are necessary for the business.

The more stakeholders request and ask for change estimates, the more time the project team spends estimating changes rather than performing the analysis work for the project. Although you want to establish a good working relationship with stakeholders, you have to balance your estimates and helping on new stuff with the original requests and project scope.

Any official change request should contain the following items at a minimum. The first four fields are filled out by the requester; the last two are for the project team's use:

- **Requester name and contact info:** The requester is the stakeholder who is making the request. Contact information lets you contact the person regarding the status of the change and links the change with the stakeholder who will end up testing it during user acceptance testing.

- **Request date:** Listing the date the request was submitted is important for understanding impacts. If the request comes in one week before a 12-month project is to be rolled out, instituting the change may be virtually impossible. If the same request is submitted one week into the same project, the change may be much easier to make. The submission date may also align with other work packages (when solutions are being created), lessening the impact.

- **Change description:** Of course, you need the stakeholder to describe the change she wants to make. Make sure the project team understands what is meant by the change. If not, members will need to make assumptions when they estimate the change to the project. These assumptions could be wrong and have negative impacts for the entire project. Go back to the stakeholder for clarification.

- **Reason for the request:** This field explains why the stakeholder feels this change is necessary. The project team compares its estimates against this area to determine whether the change will have a good return on investment.

- **Estimated impact to the project:** The project team determines the impact to the project by increasing the amount of time, adding additional costs to the project, and/or removing existing items from scope to fit in this item. *Remember:* Any change in time should come with a change in implementation date.

- **Assumptions:** As part of the estimate, the project team completes a list of assumptions it made when estimating the change to the project. Any acceptance of the change request must take the assumptions into account.

You may also want to track other items as part of the change control process:

- Time completing the change request took

- Change request number (for traceability and identification)

- Resources required

- Who was responsible for creating the change request impact estimate

- Date the change request was approved or denied

- Sign-off from the project manager, project sponsor, and person submitting the change request.

Chapter 11

Creating Your Work Plan

You may think the mandate "make a work plan" is part of the project manager's (PM's) role because the PM is responsible for the overall plan of the entire project. But as the one involved with business analysis on the project (whom we refer to as the business analyst [BA]), you're responsible not only for making sure that your activities — eliciting, analyzing, and communicating the requirements — are strategic and fit together in a detailed plan of their own but also for working with the PM to ensure that your efforts fit it into the overall project plan.

Planning, like other business analysis tasks, is a team event. You shouldn't sit in a room alone, think through all the factors that go into your plan, and then emerge with a finished work plan that you hand over to the team. You need to collaborate with many stakeholders throughout the project, involving them in your planning and getting their buy-in.

In this chapter, we explain how to create a work plan — including outlining the key components of every plan — and look at project-specific characteristics, people, and processes.

Hashing Out Work Plan Basics

Like snowflakes, no two projects are exactly the same, even though they may look alike at first glance. Whether projects are large or small, complex or simple, going through the planning process with every project is critical.

How long will it take?

Creating a work plan is the only reliable way to determine a good time estimate for a project. Early in his career, Kupe would start sweating when someone asked, "How long will the analysis effort take?" because his answer was always a complete guess. On one project, he suggested 4 weeks. The PM said, "We don't have that long, so how about 2 weeks?" Without any backup (a work plan), Kupe had to agree. He worked many hours of overtime and did a lot of scrambling to meet the deadline. He got smart on the next project, saying it would take him 8 weeks when he really needed 4; predictably, the PM reduced the timeline to 4 weeks, so Kupe ended up right where he wanted to be. He felt pretty proud of himself that he had gotten one over on the PM. Eventually, though, the PM caught on to him and started slicing even more time away from the project. This psychological game may be fun, but it's not the way to conduct business. You have to come to the table with an intelligent plan to show why you need the time you're proposing, and then you can negotiate based on factors of time and resources.

Having a well-thought-out and well-backed-up approach for how to attack the project, what techniques you plan on using, and how much time you estimate those techniques will require gives you a solid, realistic negotiation tool and eventual map to success.

Without a work plan, any estimate that you give in terms of cost, time, or resources is just guesswork. With proper planning, your estimates are based on hard facts and data, making them not only more accurate but also effective as a negotiating tool. If you are asked to reduce the estimated project time, you can have a conversation with the team to ask for additional resources that help reduce the time to completion or to determine which of the outlined tasks you can cut to reduce the overall analysis effort.

Considering the key components of a business analysis work plan

Dwight Eisenhower once said, "In preparing for battle, I have always found that plans are useless, but planning is indispensable." Of course, business analysis isn't quite the same as war (usually), but the main idea of this quotation still applies: Going through the process of planning is a critical task; actually documenting a plan is less critical (although in some cases it may be required). Whether you write out a plan or not, the important thing is to thoroughly think through every component of the work plan. Here, very briefly, is a rundown of the vital work plan components:

✔ **A stakeholder communication plan:** Your *stakeholder communication plan* indicates how you're going to elicit and communicate requirements with all stakeholder groups. We discuss how to make and use this plan later in the later section "Taking It to the People: The Stakeholder Communication Plan."

✔ **A list of deliverables to be produced:** Your list of *deliverables* includes documents, services, and products you (and possibly other team members) must produce in order to effectively analyze and communicate the requirements of the project. We discuss considerations for determining your deliverables throughout this chapter.

✔ **A detailed list of tasks:** These are the tasks you need to perform to elicit, analyze, and communicate the requirements. Get as detailed as you need to with this list in order to estimate your time accurately to your stakeholders and managers. We discuss how to create this list later in this chapter in "Compiling Your Work Plan."

Sometimes estimating is helpful: Break down the tasks you need to accomplish and sum up the total. For example, if completing a use case takes you 8 hours (Chapter 13) and you have to create 10 use cases, you could estimate your work at 80 hours.

✔ **An estimate of time and cost:** All together, the stakeholder communication plan and lists of deliverables and tasks help you determine the time and cost estimates for you and your stakeholders. We explain how to compile these estimates in "Compiling Your Work Plan" later in this chapter.

Planning is unique to each individual. Everyone has different strengths and weaknesses and different knowledge and experiences. Something that may take experienced BAs 4 hours may take novice BAs 8 hours. The person doing the work needs to be the one giving the time estimate whenever possible.

Using a framework to create your plan

Starting a plan from scratch is pretty difficult, especially if you're just starting out in the business yourself. Even those who have been at this business awhile can easily overlook something if they aren't careful. The Business Analysis Planning Framework, shown in Figure 11-1, is a guide we've designed for BAs to use when they need help building an intelligent business analysis plan. It aids you in thinking through all the considerations and variables for each project regardless of when you join the project team. Think of the framework as a checklist to make sure you have everything you need.

We've broken up the work plan into three areas — people, project characteristics, and process — represented by the three boxes in the middle of the figure and each outlining the variables you need to consider for that specific area within your project:

✔ The *people* represent all the individuals or groups that are involved in the project that you need to interact with.

✔ The *project characteristics* include specific attributes of your project, like the project scope, budget, constraints, and key milestones.

✔ The *process* includes things, such as the *project methodology* (a model for how you complete the project) and deliverables, being used for the project.

Together, all three areas help you determine what tasks and deliverables you need to complete for the specific project and how long they'll take you.

You may be asking, "Do I have to think of all this stuff for every project, even though many projects are the same?" The answer is yes. Although many projects look and feel similar, never lose sight of the fact that each project is different (remember those snowflakes).

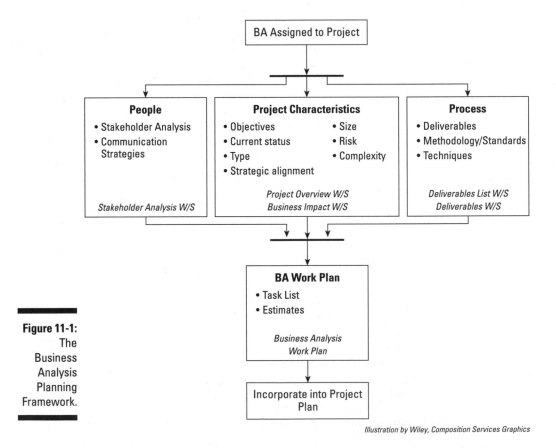

Figure 11-1:
The
Business
Analysis
Planning
Framework.

Illustration by Wiley, Composition Services Graphics

This framework is meant to be fluid and flexible, allowing information to flow as it will. Although the flow of the framework appears to have linear qualities, you don't necessarily gather data in a set chronological way; rather, you may get some information that leads you to jot down some tasks to start, and then you may add to that list later after you've talked with someone else.

Perusing the Project Characteristics

The project characteristics are attributes that impact the tasks to be performed, the deliverables to be created, and the way you develop your plan. In the following sections, we go over key characteristics you need to consider for each project. We also offer tips on areas that BAs often miss during planning.

Identifying project type

The type of project impacts the categories of requirements you elicit, analyze, and communicate (more on requirement categories in Chapter 12). To find out more about the different project types and how they impact requirement categories and the work plan in general, read on.

The BA profession has an ongoing joke about people asking for "typical" things. The answer is always "It depends" because no one-size-fits-all list actually exists. In the following sections, we offer examples of the kinds of tasks each type of project needs, but really, the task list you come up with is always unique to your project and based not only on the type of project but also on all the other variables. Bottom line: As a BA, you need to know all the tools available to you; think through all the variables related to the people, project characteristics, and the process; and then determine what tasks you need to complete.

Software enhancement or maintenance projects

In software development, *software maintenance* refers to modifying software products after delivery in order to correct faults, improve performance or other attributes, or to adapt the product to a modified environment. These projects are about more than just fixing bugs, though. With these projects, you can implement new features or make performance improvements to keep software up-to-date in a changing, competitive environment. In other words, a software maintenance project can involve any changes (reactive or proactive) to existing software or systems.

Here are some examples of enhancement and maintenance projects:

- ✔ Adding a new feature or function to an existing system
- ✔ Implementing a business policy change
- ✔ Correcting a problem with the current system or improving the performance of operational software
- ✔ Porting (moving software components) operational software to a different hardware platform

Maintenance or enhancement projects vary in size and complexity, which means your work plan does, too. Planning for commonalities across the board with these types of projects is significantly challenging because so many variables are at play, but here are a few tips to keep in mind when outlining your work plan and time estimates:

- ✔ **What to focus on:** Spend time focusing on eliciting, analyzing, and communicating functional and nonfunctional requirements more than any other requirements. (For information on the difference between functional and nonfunctional requirements, head to Chapter 12.)
- ✔ **How to deal with fast-path or emergency requests:** These requests can waylay a project very easily if you're not careful. To keep your project on track and on time, consider creating the documentation after implementation to save time upfront.
- ✔ **How to deal with other important requests:** Perform a cost/benefit evaluation to determine whether the request is viable. If it's not, you can cut the request from your plan (Chapter 9).
- ✔ **How to do analysis of multiple requests for a single release/iteration:** For these projects, you have only one chance to get it right. Perform code-level analysis and build in checkpoints to reduce the risk of redundancy, conflict between requests, and the introduction of errors into production. A *checkpoint* is a time in the project when you review deliverables to make sure they're aligned with the original project objectives and scope. A review of the functional requirements document prior to building the solution is a great example of a checkpoint.

COTS projects

People buy commercial off-the-shelf (COTS) software to save development time and cost. A company can implement a COTS package as-is, customize the package (change the code or add-ons to the existing functions), or configure it (change settings within the tool but not the tool's internal code) upon installation.

The ideal scenario when working on a COTS project is one in which you can elicit and analyze business requirements from the stakeholders before selecting a package. In reality, however, some companies purchase software packages and then ask your team to implement the software after the fact.

For COTS projects, your primary focus is on business requirements — including the business processes and data requirements. You should do less work on functional and nonfunctional requirements unless you're customizing the system.

If you take on a COTS project, the tasks you need to build into your work plan after you've determined the business need are typically as follows:

✔ **Performing a gap analysis on the existing functionality for the business process to be changed:** By performing a *gap analysis* (which examines the difference between the current state of affairs and the desired future state) of the goals, the data requirements, the process mapping between the current process and the process associated with the COTS product, and usability, you can help determine whether a COTS product can be implemented as-is or needs customizations. This process is the *as is* or *how* analysis. (We cover analysis types in Chapter 5.)

Regardless of the size of the COTS product (how many people are using the system and how many features are incorporated in the system), make sure your work plan gives you enough time to determine the need and impact of customizations or operational process changes. If customizations are necessary, they can get expensive and cause upgrades to be lengthy.

✔ **Confirming the recommended solution and determining whether customization is necessary:** This is the *to be* or *how* analysis.

Outsourced or offshore development projects

Today's projects usually include team members in multiple locations and often involve outsourcing. These projects have a higher difficulty and risk of failure because of potentially conflicting culture and communication norms (not to mention the logistical matter of managing varying time zones). Stakeholders in different locations can negatively impact the momentum and the team's ability to all have a clear understanding of the goals and direction of the project. Often, formal planning is necessary to successfully ensure that everyone is clear on how the analysis effort will be conducted. In general, you work with the business directly to understand its needs rather than with development team members in another country.

For these types of projects, plan more time for meetings based on the physical location(s) of all stakeholders.

When dealing with outsourced or offshore development projects, include these kinds of tasks in your work plan:

✔ Conduct a feasibility study to give the team members a sense of what they can accomplish.

✔ Define key objectives and measurements for success so members can point back to them during the project to ensure they're on track.

✔ Gain agreement (including a formal review process) for the deliverables.

✔ Create a project glossary for all appropriate terms and definitions.

✔ Document and discuss all assumptions, risks, and constraints.

✔ Define clear acceptance criteria for requirements.

✔ Plan activities for team-building communication with the external team.

Additionally, you and your team should look at ways of supplementing your communication efforts by using collaboration tools such as those found in Chapter 4.

Keep in mind that the decision to outsource or use offshore development is often made outside your project's scope and your control. In this situation, your team needs to clearly prioritize the requirements and take an approach to incrementally work on one function or feature at a time. Because many off-shore development teams are in different time zones from the users and the rest of the team, working on a small subset of features at a time is more manageable than trying to complete the requirements for all features. Working in small chunks makes it more manageable for the team.

Data warehouse projects

A *data warehouse* is a solution that brings together information from diverse sources and puts it in a format that stakeholders can easily access when making complex business decisions. A data warehouse supports a company's tactical and strategic goals.

Data warehouses are useful for trend analysis, forecasting, competitive analysis, and targeted market research. Data is often summarized by specific subject area, function, department, geographic region, time period, or all of these.

Most data warehouse projects fall into the "large project" category (see the later section "Tackling large projects") and result in a substantial project planning effort for you as the BA. These projects often have a company-wide focus — not a department-specific one — which means users throughout the company use them in one way or another. The business priority for the project depends on what critical decisions need to be made to address a business threat or opportunity.

Include these types of tasks in your data warehouse project work plan:

✔ Identifying what information the data warehouse must contain, identifying who should have access to it, and making sure users have the right level of access. (*Note:* The structure of the data warehouse and the amount of data to be manipulated and stored can impact what kind of reporting is available.)

✔ Identifying and prioritizing subject areas to be implemented.

✔ Managing the scope of each subject area iteration or release.

✔ Validating the data accuracy and consistency during the extract/transform/load (ETL) process.

✔ Defining the correct level of data summarization.

✔ Establishing a data refresh schedule that's consistent with business needs, timing, and cycles.

✔ Researching and reviewing available COTS business intelligence tools used for complex reporting.

✔ Planning for a user-friendly, powerful desktop query tool for users to access data without IT assistance.

✔ Planning for the user training and support needed to learn how to use tools and access data.

✔ Ensuring thorough testing is done prior to user acceptance testing (UAT), which we discuss in Chapter 14.

Process improvement projects

Companies find competitive advantages by looking closely at their business processes and determining whether they need to make changes to improve their business operations. Depending on the changes to be made, those changes may occur in small segments over a long period of time (*evolutionary changes*) or may be made at one time (*revolutionary changes*). As a BA, your evaluation of the business process may result in a recommendation for software changes, procedural changes, organizational changes, or personnel changes.

The tasks you perform when completing a process improvement project include analyzing the current process, capturing metrics as a baseline, identifying the problems, and identifying solutions that fix those problems to achieve better performance.

Reengineering — another approach to changing a business process — happens when you start from scratch to ask what the organization needs in order to succeed instead of fixing something that already exists. You ignore current roles, *silos* (departments in organizations that are compartmentalized and don't talk to one another), and outdated business rules, and challenge assumptions to create enterprise-wide changes. Reengineering implies that you're innovating dramatically to design new, streamlined processes.

Tasks related to process reengineering projects include the following:

✔ Performing root cause analysis (see Chapter 8) to find out the real problem that exists within the business

✔ Brainstorming (turn to Chapter 7) with the project team alternative approaches to address the problem area

✔ Choosing the best approach that solves the business problem

Infrastructure projects

Infrastructure projects are internal technical upgrades that impact systems, hardware, platforms, or tools in order to improve the technology that supports the business and the information technology (IT) efforts. Typically, these projects are called *IT projects* because they're driven and sponsored by IT departments.

Tasks to include on your work plan include the following:

✔ Assessing how software interface changes (even small ones) may impact usability

✔ Assessing how the project may impact user productivity and whether training may be required

✔ Determining whether any change to a work process needs to be made based on the project

With infrastructure projects, the changes often affect stakeholders, external customers, or suppliers. Business analysts are involved to manage requirements and expectations of these changes among all project stakeholders. Here are some things to keep in mind:

✔ BAs sometimes underestimate or miscommunicate business impact, technical risks, and priorities, so be careful. In particular, don't forget about implementation considerations and transition requirements (user training, timing, and support). They're really important!

Although infrastructure projects aren't intended to change user functionality, user productivity often decreases during the learning curve as users get used to the new elements — something for you to definitely include in your work plan.

✔ Because these projects are technology improvements, they may often be delayed to make room for more business-critical efforts, assuming their delay doesn't significantly impact the business.

✔ These projects may be initiated because vendor support is no longer available.

Web development projects

In today's environment, many users expect feature-rich websites and applications accessible from anywhere with any web browser. They also expect functions to be delivered in short time frames. Think about the applications you use today, like online banking, social media, shopping websites . . . the list goes on.

Web development projects are customer-facing web applications that are targeted at consumers (for example, a customer order website) and are available inside or outside the organization. As such, they require some special considerations in your work plan.

When planning for this type of project, make sure to prioritize the features and functions. Doing so allows the team to work on and implement the highest value features first. Using an *agile* approach (building a highly skilled, tightly knit, self-managed, and collocated team that stays with the project from beginning to end and delivers software quickly) works well for these types of projects. (For details on the agile approach, refer to the later section "Agile development methodologies.")

Key stakeholders involved in these projects include usability experts, marketing product owners, and a customer representative or surrogate representative, such as marketing or business analyst (that's you!).

The following are some tasks to include on a web development work plan:

✔ Eliciting usability and security requirements (see Chapters 6 and 7 for the details on eliciting requirements)

✔ Use cases, user stories, wireframes, prototypes, and simulations (see Chapter 13 for the how-to on these techniques)

✔ Testing activities like UAT

Project size

Project size is a big factor in determining what tasks you undertake and how long you take to complete them. Factors to consider are the number of features you need to deliver, the number of people you'll interact with, and the number of people that will use the solution. Eliciting requirements from 1 stakeholder is less time-consuming eliciting than from 50. The following sections tell you what you need to know about the impact of project size on your work plan.

Handling small projects

These typically are much smaller in scope and may even be considered maintenance projects, or *tickets* (enhancement requests entered into a tracking system). Typically, they have a minimal amount of risk and exhibit the following characteristics:

✔ They require small amounts of effort, low cost, and touch only one or two systems. This limited reach makes the scope small.

✔ They involve a minimal number of people — sometimes just a developer and the BA — and don't have many interfaces with other systems.

✔ They're generally maintenance projects, designed to enhance an existing system, rather than implementations of new systems to support a business process.

When you plan for a small project, you don't need to produce the same number of deliverables (or level of effort) as you do for a large project, but that doesn't mean you don't have to make sure you're addressing the right business problem with your plan. Small projects can be motivating because you can see results in a fairly short time, but you can't skip critical steps in the planning process.

When planning for small projects, consider these aspects:

- ✔ **You may participate in both formal and informal processes, communication, and deliverables.** Some really small projects are often discussed in a hallway or drawn out on someone's whiteboard.

- ✔ **Even (or perhaps, especially) on a small project, you still need to understand the scope.** Without an understanding of the boundaries of the project, you can get distracted, off track, and lost in various streams of the work effort quickly.

    Defining scope is the most critical step, even for simple requests. If you don't understand the scope, you may opt for what appears to be an easy and obvious solution, rather than the *right* solution. For complete details on how to set and manage scope, refer to Chapter 10.

- ✔ **You must establish a clear purpose and objective.** Doing so ensure that you're spending the organization's (probably very limited) resources in the right place.

Tackling large projects

Large projects are sometimes referred to as *monster* projects. They typically have high business risk because more is at stake. If the projects fail, the business can lose a significant amount of money and/or lose out on an opportunity. Large projects exhibit the following characteristics:

- ✔ They require large amounts of effort, have a high cost and large scope, and last a long time.

- ✔ They involve lots of people.

- ✔ They can contain features with many dependencies — that is, one feature may be linked to others, meaning a change to it results in a change in many.

- ✔ They're mission-critical.

- ✔ They're complex.

Planning for monster projects is usually formal and may involve significant resources. New development efforts also have a high technical risk because the enabling technology may be unfamiliar to the business and internal IT resources or have complex system interfaces. These development efforts need the following from you:

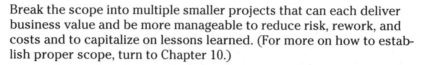

- Formality in process, communication, and deliverables

- Full discussion of the project with stakeholders, regardless of type

- Adequate time to formally plan the project with the project manager, an established methodology to guide planning tasks and deliverables, and collaboration with a lead IT/developer in the planning of the effort

- A clear purpose and objectives to define the scope and clear communication of scope boundaries to all stakeholders

Break the scope into multiple smaller projects that can each deliver business value and be more manageable to reduce risk, rework, and costs and to capitalize on lessons learned. (For more on how to establish proper scope, turn to Chapter 10.)

- A *feasibility study* (a study undertaken to uncover the strengths and weaknesses of the project, the environmental opportunities and threats the project poses, the resources required to create the project, and the project's success criteria) and prototype

- Thorough investigation of the business problem or opportunity and completion of all requirements categories (business, functional, transition, and so on)

- Thorough stakeholder analysis and communication plans

Other things

No matter what plan or methodology you find yourself working within, you still need to consider other aspects surrounding the effort. These are highlighted in the following list:

- **Business risks:** One common risk is time to market because it can impact the projects you work on. To address this type of risk, make sure you understand the priority among all the features that are requested within the project so that you can elicit, analyze, and communicate the high priority items first.

Work with the business stakeholder and development team to determine priority. Elicit features as *must-haves* and *nice-to-haves.* For example, the business may view having a log-in screen for an application as a nice-to-have, but the development team may require it as part of company policy, putting it in the must-have category.

- **Interfaces:** Does a technical solution not interface with another application? Make sure you know how many interfaces can be impacted; this knowledge drives the number of stakeholder groups, which can impact time and cost of the project.

- **Project complexity:** As the BA on the project, do you understand the business enough to ask the right questions? Do you need some expertise to help or time to get up to speed? To understand complexity, perform document analysis (Chapter 7) and look through the project scope documentation (Chapter 10). Doing so helps you develop questions for the business area. You can also conduct a web search to get an idea of business challenges and gather more information about the business domain.

✓ **Clear understanding of problem/opportunity:** If you don't fully understand the business problem or opportunity, you may need to take some time to get clarity so you can accurately understand the scope of the project. Ask the business directly what problem it's trying to solve or what opportunity it's trying to take advantage of. You can also try observing the business in action (more on the observation elicitation technique in Chapter 7). Doing so gives you a good idea of problems inherent in the process.

Taking It to the People: The Stakeholder Communication Plan

Projects are all about people; you work on projects for, with, and because of them. The people side is the biggest variable — and for us, it's the most exciting part of planning (even though it's far from being the easiest). Understanding the people you work with takes an ongoing commitment.

Because the people are the key to the project, communication is the key to the people — so much so that business analysis features a special plan-within-the-plan called a *stakeholder communication plan*. Creating this plan involves three key steps: Identify the people, get to know them, and get them involved.

Identifying the people

The PM may have already taken care of this step by the time you get onto a project, but if not, identifying stakeholders (one who has a "stake" in the project because he or she will impact or be impacted by it) is your responsibility. (You can read more about stakeholders and their stakes in the project in Chapter 3.) Here's a sample list:

✓ SMEs

✓ Management approvers/reviewers

✓ Executive sponsor

✓ Quality assurance (QA) team

> ✔ UAT participants
>
> ✔ Development team
>
> ✔ Architects

Tools to help you capture all the right people include the information data flow diagram and the context level diagram (refer to Chapter 10). These diagrams identify areas/departments that produce the data or are impacted by it. With that info, you can derive a variety of stakeholders that, without such a diagram, you may have unintentionally overlooked.

Projects involving multiple stakeholder viewpoints require an increase in management efforts by all parties, especially you, which means you have to be adept at balancing different perspectives. When viewpoints are in conflict, the ultimate decision-maker is the executive sponsor.

Getting to know the stakeholders

People want to work with those they know and share similarities with. Communication is easier (and problem-solving is just faster) when individuals have good relationships. You can better manage tasks when you're familiar with the team members' strengths. Therefore, a key way you can foster success is to get to know the stakeholders beyond just knowing their titles and roles in the organization.

Build relationships with your project team and business stakeholders before you get assigned to a project to help ensure project success. Go to lunch, grab a coffee, or chat in the hall with your teammates and other stakeholders. Do what you can to get to know the ones you work with before they're your stakeholders or project partners.

Objective characteristics

Here are some objective characteristics about your stakeholders that you want to know. These are characteristics you should keep track of for both current and future projects:

> ✔ **Physical location:** Any time zone differences affect meeting schedules, and location differences affect face-to-face meeting availability.
>
> ✔ **Availability for project work:** Remember that the project may be *your* first priority, but your stakeholders may have other projects higher on their lists. If a stakeholder is only available for the project a few hours a week, the project schedule must reflect this limitation.
>
> ✔ **Subject matter expertise:** A stakeholder's level of expertise helps determine how much of his time is needed for elicitation, reviewing, and approving requirements. This information also helps you formulate questions.

✔ **The technical team's experience with you:** If a developer or other team member has never worked with you and is unfamiliar with how you approach the analysis effort, plan to spend time explaining detailed needs in walk-throughs.

✔ **Experience on previous projects:** If the stakeholders have had good experience working on previous projects, they'll be very helpful. If they've had bad experiences or no experience, however, they may need more time to learn the process.

✔ **Preferred level of formality/mode of communication:** Is this stakeholder someone who likes casual communications/notes or very formal, documented work products? Does he prefer talking on the phone, using instant messaging, or having face-to-face conversations?

✔ **Decision-making authority:** Know who has authority to make decisions for this project. If key decisions aren't being made, make sure you raise that issue to the people who can make the call to keep the project moving forward.

Everyone's heard the golden rule: Treat others as you'd like others to treat you. For BAs, the *platinum rule* applies: Treat others as they'd like to be treated. As BAs, you need to adjust to your stakeholders' preferred mode of communication. For example, Kupe was working with a client right around the time he discovered text messaging (and his addiction to it). He texted the client about the project repeatedly throughout the week. Finally, she called him and said, "Kupe, stop texting me!" She didn't have a text plan, and he was costing her money! He made a huge assumption: that texting was a fine method of communication and that she liked it because he liked it. He should have confirmed whether she liked that form of communication before he started using it.

Subjective characteristics

You also want to be aware of some subjective characteristics. These are areas you want to know about but may not openly share:

✔ **Value to the organization:** If this stakeholder is the main (or part of the main) talent or revenue generator of the organization, he may get more respect than other employees. Think of those people in your organization who always get their way. Is it because they scream louder, have better political connections, or are they people who bring revenue into the business and therefore have greater needs based on that ability?

✔ **Culture/language:** Understanding the native language and culture of each stakeholder helps you improve communications. Learn local customs whenever possible, and be careful not to offend stakeholders in various cultures. Making connections on a cultural and personal level helps the whole process go more smoothly, so build time in for really getting to understand a stakeholder's customs.

✔ **Relationship to other stakeholders:** If negative issues exist between stakeholders, plan more time for building consensus.

✔ **Emotional commitment to the project:** If the stakeholder isn't excited about a change, plan more time for requirements elicitation and organization change management.

✔ **Technical team skill level:** If a developer on the team doesn't have much knowledge in the solution technology, plan for more detailed functional requirements.

✔ **Ability/speed of decision making:** Know your audience. Is this stakeholder comfortable making decisions quickly, or does he take more time and thought to come to a conclusion? In either case, make sure you take this characteristic into account. Give someone who needs time to come to a conclusion info ahead of time. For someone who likes to get information at the last possible moment, don't frustrate him by giving him information too early.

Getting stakeholders involved

Your plan isn't just about you; it exists to enable others to provide requirements and do their jobs effectively. Impact your stakeholders early and often so they turn around and impact your plan positively. Make sure your plan includes the steps and produces the information they need to make decisions and do their jobs effectively. Here are some considerations:

✔ **Make sure you set expectations of how much time you need from them during the project.** If you plan nothing else, plan that piece out — it's the most important.

✔ **Throughout the project, make sure everyone is aware of your status and their role in the analysis effort.** The PM may handle this task, but if he doesn't, you need to make sure you do. By reiterating this information, you don't end up at a critical milestone with an unfinished task because everyone *thought* it was someone else's responsibility.

✔ **Know how best to elicit requirements from each stakeholder.** Work with your stakeholders to verify that the techniques you plan on using are best for them, and keep checking in during the project to validate that you're using the best techniques for them. (For a rundown of elicitation techniques, go to Chapter 7.)

Down Argentine Way

Awhile back, Kupe made several trips to Argentina. On the first day of his first trip, the people were very nice but weren't really giving him the true story about what was going on. He tried to elicit the real problems and issues from them, but to no avail; he seemed to get only canned answers. He knew he had to connect better with team members or he wouldn't be successful. Then he noticed that everyone in the office kissed each other on the cheek as the group left for the day. "Brilliant," he thought; he knew how to become part of the group. Despite the fact that he's mostly a hug and handshake kind of guy (with kissing left for close family), he was determined to be one of the team. So the next morning, he saw a group of people, mustered up the courage, and went in for the kiss. He was sure everyone noticed how nervous he was, but it was like flipping a switch. At that moment, they realized he was a good guy and treated him like he was one of them. The rest of his trip went very well, and he made some great connections in Argentina. Because he was able to embrace their culture and customs, they embraced him — literally!

Putting together the stakeholder communication plan

When you've identified your stakeholders, know how to work with them best, and have determined how to get them involved, you can develop your stakeholder communication plan (shown in Figure 11-2), which includes these categories.

- ✔ **Stakeholder name/group and role:** These help you understand the role of the person and the number of people they represent. Additionally, based on the role they play, they may have specific responsibilities.

- ✔ **Location/time zone:** Knowing where stakeholders are located and their time zone helps you plan elicitation activities such as meetings and conference calls.

- ✔ **Issues/concerns/expectation and time/resource constraints:** Not all resources are 100 percent allocated to work on the project like you are. Additionally, some of them may have internal biases or hidden agendas that you have to plan for.

- ✔ **Requirements needed:** These are the expectations this stakeholder or group has of your project; it is what they expect to receive.

- ✔ **Communication/elicitation approaches:** This is your plan for how you will approach elicitation with this stakeholder.

As Figure 11-2 shows, the stakeholder communication plan puts all the important characteristics of each stakeholder or stakeholder group in one easy-to-access location. Recording details about your stakeholders and how they like to communicate is an important piece in figuring out how much time you should spend on which methods.

Stakeholder name/group and role	Location/time zone	Issues/concerns/ expectation and time/resource constraints	Requirements needed	Communication/ elicitation approaches
Ron White Project Sponsor	New York Headquarters office (EST/EDT)	Ron comes from ABC and may be biased toward his existing CRM package.	Clear objectives, budget, authorization/ assignment of resources	Interview with project manager
Julie Smith VP of Sales	New York Hqtrs	Julie comes from DEF and may be biased toward her existing CRM package.	Sales needs from CRM (data, processes, entry of opportunities and leads, reporting)	Interviews
500 Sales reps – one sales rep from each regional office will be assigned to the project	Located around the world. Regional offices in NY, Hong Kong, Sydney, and Paris	Usability, accessibility DEF's package currently offers mobile access but ABC's does not.	Day to day workflow, data needs.	Requirements workshop with the four regional representatives. Questionnaires, survey of entire sales force. Will need a training plan for those converting to new system.

Figure 11-2: A sample stakeholder communication plan.

Illustration by Wiley, Composition Services Graphics

The Process: Figuring Out How Things Are Done

When we say *process,* we are referring to the project processes that are in place at the company where you're working that you can use as a guide. For example, your company may provide defined templates and types of deliverables that you can use on the project. If so, you need to find out what your company's project methodology and standard deliverables are.

In this section, we discuss in detail four different methodologies: waterfall, agile, spiral/RUP, and RAD/evolving prototype. As the BA, you must figure out what needs to be addressed when planning under these project processes. Having familiarity with them helps you adjust and understand why certain deliverables are required; it also ensures that you plan the time to perform them.

Most companies use some form of these methodologies, often taking the best of each and sometimes coming up with a combined version that best meets the culture of an organization while focusing on business value. As the BA, your best bet is to have a number of available methodologies available and ready to use. Because every project is different, one methodology doesn't meet the needs of every project.

Asking the following questions can help you understand more about how you should execute the project with certain accepted processes, techniques, and document templates for deliverables. All this information goes into your work plan:

✔ What methodology will be used for this project?

✔ Are the stakeholders familiar with the planned methodology?

✔ Are the project roles and responsibilities clear?

✔ Is the process tailored appropriately for this project?

✔ What deliverables are required?

Waterfall

In the *waterfall approach*, the team completes each phase before moving on to the next. Table 11-1 lays out the different phases of the project. Note that each phase involves several tasks and roles and results in at least one deliverable.

Table 11-1	Phases of a Waterfall Project		
Phase	*Roles Involved*	*Tasks*	*Deliverables*
Planning	Project sponsor; BA; SME	Initiate project; define project scope; estimate costs, time schedules, and resource requirements	Project statement of purpose; project objectives; project scope document; funding approval
Analysis	SME; BA; data administrator; facilitator	Elicit detailed business requirements; bring multiple organization units to consensus	Detailed business requirements document

Phase	Roles Involved	Tasks	Deliverables
Design	BA; database designer; system designer	Lay out user interface; design database; design programs and interfaces	Screen layouts; report layouts; database definition; program specifications
Construction	Software developer	Write programs; unit test programs; create database	Completed programs; databases
Testing	QA tester; BA; SME	Test integration, system, and user acceptance	Fully tested software
Implementation	Software developer; trainer	Install software; set up parameters; train users	Production application
Maintenance	SME; BA; software developer	Perform impact analysis; design system modifications; make and install changes	System modifications and enhancements

The benefits of this approach are that it's a well-documented, structured, proven approach that focuses on eliciting business requirements before designing a solution. The limitations are that you have to complete each phase before starting the next phase, which makes it difficult to go back when problems arise. Plus, requirements tend to be documented in a long, textual format that often leaves the requirements open to different interpretations.

If you use textual requirements, plan on adding time for more-formal reviews so you can ensure everyone has the same understanding of a requirement. Consider supporting text with diagrams to enhance requirements understanding.

Agile development methodologies

As we note earlier in the chapter, the emphasis in an agile project is on building a tightly knit, highly skilled, *collocated* (in the same place and working side-by-side), and self-managed team that follows the project through from start to finish and delivers software quickly. Typically, the only formal project deliverables are the actual working software and the required system documentation that's completed at the end of the project.

The benefits an agile approach brings to your work plan include the following:

- ✓ Rapid feedback from users that increases the usability and quality of the application
- ✓ Early discovery of design defects
- ✓ The ability to easily roll out functionality in incremental stages
- ✓ The ability of future deliverable phases to capitalize on lessons learned in earlier phases (called *iterations*)
- ✓ A more motivated and more productive team because of face-to face collocation
- ✓ Knowledge-sharing for the duration of the project
- ✓ Adaptive analysis (techniques are employed as needed)

The following limitations can impact your work plan:

- ✓ Difficulty in coordinating large projects
- ✓ Slower buy-in for major project process change than often expected
- ✓ A tendency to not adequately document what's necessary after completion
- ✓ Difficulty in predicting exactly what features are possible within a fixed time or dollar budget

Agile development is *iterative* (that is, a repeating process), tightly *time-boxed* (has a fixed time for development), and geared for *dynamic requirements* (those that adapt and change) and frequent — usually daily — measurements. For more details on this methodology, check out *Agile Project Management For Dummies* by Mark C. Layton (Wiley).

Spiral model/Rational Unified Process (RUP)

The *spiral approach* requires the project team to perform risk analysis (see Chapter 9 for the step-by-step) before each iteration and to work on the portion of the system that has the highest risk. It also involves implementing portions of the system as they're completed. Benefits include the following:

- ✓ It's a risk-driven approach, addressing the highest risk areas first.
- ✓ It tries to eliminate errors in early phases.
- ✓ It provides one model for software development and maintenance.

✔ It works well for complex, dynamic, innovative projects.

✔ Reevaluation after each phase allows changes in user perspectives and technical architecture (the hardware and software pieces arranged so as to support the objective).

Of course, the spiral method has its limitations:

✔ It lacks explicit process guidance in determining objectives, constraints, and alternatives.

✔ It provides more flexibility than is convenient for many applications.

✔ It requires risk assessment expertise. Assessing and resolving project risks isn't an easy task. Significant experience in software projects is necessary for success.

✔ Rational unified process (RUP), an adaptable process framework, is not a single concrete "one size fits all" process, but rather needs to be tailored to a company's needs.

RAD/prototyping

Rapid application development (RAD) and *prototyping* are approaches that were developed to speed up the time needed to develop an application. RAD involves a short analysis or requirements elicitation phase (refer to Chapter 6). The team then starts the user interface design by developing a prototype very early in the project as a method of validating user requirements. A *prototype,* such as a mockup of a screen layout or a storyboard showing a series of screens, is a graphical representation of how a user interfaces with an automated system. Typically, prototypes are created for online screen interactions. For details on creating prototypes, head to Chapter 7.

Benefits of these approaches are that they give the end-users of the system an idea of how it may look and help the BA and SME clarify their mutual understanding of the recommendation. The drawbacks: Mockups presented too early in the project can cause SMEs to get distracted by the aesthetics of a screen and to forget to focus on core business requirements. And if a prototype is presented electronically, SMEs may get the impression that the solution is already built.

Compiling Your Work Plan

As you gather all the information about the people, project characteristics, and process, your plan takes shape. It determines how you go on to elicit, analyze, and communicate requirements, as well as what working products and deliverables you develop. By the time you're creating your work plan, you've determined the tasks to complete your deliverables, including estimates of your time and your stakeholders' time. All this information goes into your work plan.

Here are steps to take to compile your plan:

1. **Create the task list.**

   You can organize the task list by techniques, deliverables, stakeholder groups, or time sequence based on how you compiled tasks as you thought through the people, project characteristics, and process.

   Figure 11-3 shows an example of a set of tasks based on the use case technique (a technique we discuss in Chapter 12).

Figure 11-3:
Listing
your tasks
helps you
accurately
estimate
time in your
work plan.

Develop questions for business SME's in each department.
Scheduled a working elicitation session to identify use cases.
Conduct session.
Compile notes and create draft use case diagram.
Present draft for review.
Revise as requested.
Resolve use case conflicts.
Finalize use case diagram.

Illustration by Wiley, Composition Services Graphics

2. **Estimate analysis time.**

   After you have a complete task list, assign time to each task. Ask your project manager whether you should estimate *work time* (the actual amount of time required to do the task) or *lapse time* (the duration of the task). For instance, having a stakeholder physically sign off on a document takes only about 5 seconds; that's the work time. However, getting that stakeholder to actually complete those 5 seconds of work may take 2 weeks; that's the lapse time. Estimate realistically and conservatively; many people underestimate time required to complete tasks.

   If you have trouble putting a number next to a task, try breaking the task down into subtasks and estimating them. When tasks are specific, time estimates are more likely to be accurate.

Figure 11-4 shows an example of how to record time estimates for eliciting and communicating a use case accurately. Remember, your plan is a negotiation tool — that is, your time estimates are at the heart of your negotiations — so be accurate!

Tasks	Estimate
Develop questions for business SME's in each department.	2.0 hours
Schedule a working elicitation session to identify use cases.	0.5 hours
Conduct session.	1.5 hours
Compile notes and create draft use case diagram.	1.5 hours
Present draft for review.	1.0 hour
Revise as requested.	0.5 hour
Resolve use case conflicts.	2.0 hours
Finalize use case diagram.	1.0 hour
	10.0 hours = 1.5 days

Figure 11-4. Recording time estimates.

Illustration by Wiley, Composition Services Graphics

The larger the project and longer the time frame, the more difficult estimating is because there are a lot more moving parts. This fact is one of the reasons that iterative approaches have become more popular. They let you plan in smaller chunks, which means fewer moving parts. To use the iterative approach, you first estimate the current iteration. Perform the iteration and track actual time used, and then estimate the next iteration based on lessons learned from the first one.

3. **Lay the plan out.**

   You can build the business analysis work plan after you've completed the task list and listed a time estimate. You now have to lay out the tasks in order and understand the dependency each task may have on others — in other words, what tasks have to wait on others to be completed and what tasks can be done concurrently. Then you can include an overall time estimate for the whole project.

4. **Communicate your plan.**

   Get buy-in from your team, the business stakeholders, and your manager. Upon approval, your work plan needs to be incorporated into the overall project plan.

You can set your plan on a firm foundation by doing a couple of things:

✔ **Develop a good working relationship with your PM:** Know your own strengths and weaknesses, and then, before the project begins, get to know the PM. Also take time to discuss the characteristics of the project (objectives and stakeholders) to make sure you both have the same understanding. Also talk about the approach (waterfall, agile, and so on) to be used (read about these approaches earlier in the chapter) and discuss how you're going to elicit, analyze, and communicate requirements. Finally, have a chat about how the two of you can best work together.

✔ **Plan for contingencies:** As you discover new information about the people, project characteristics, and process, those changes impact your plan. So that these changes don't derail your project, preface all your plans with "This is the information I know now" and tell your team right away when you have to make any changes. Also develop a response for the high-impact, high-likelihood scenarios that may arise.

Part IV
Achieving Goals with Business Analysis

Doing the Right Thing for the Business

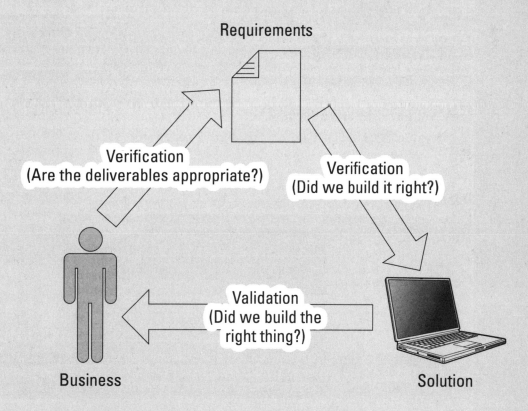

Requirements

Verification
(Are the deliverables appropriate?)

Verification
(Did we build it right?)

Validation
(Did we build the
right thing?)

Business

Solution

In this part . . .

✔ Examine the different categories your requirements fall into: business and stakeholder requirements, solution requirements, transition requirements, and technical requirements.

✔ Analyze and communicate the requirements for your project and ensure their traceability.

✔ Get to know various analysis diagrams and documents so you know which techniques are right for each situation you encounter.

✔ Understand the difference between verifying a solution (whether you built the system correctly) and validating it (whether you built the correct system). Discover how to complete the verification and validation processes and how to conduct a requirements review.

✔ Use transition requirements to devise a rollout plan for your solution and effectively implement it.

Chapter 12

Defining Solutions, Part 1: Taking a Closer Look at Your Requirements

● ●

In This Chapter

▶ Knowing how the requirements types vary and who uses the different types of requirements

▶ Understanding how different audiences have different needs for your requirements

▶ Tracing requirements and being versatile in your approach

● ●

So you've elicited your requirements — now you're ready to put into action the analysis part of your job description. In this chapter, we detail how to analyze and document the requirements you've found. Why would you want to analyze the requirements in the first place? When you look at the requirements strategically with your stakeholders, you ensure that you've communicated effectively with each other during the elicitation phase and that you write requirements that are clear, accurate, and thorough. Analyzing your requirements is like doing a little self-audit and housecleaning before moving on to actually designing and implementing a solution.

Business analysts (BAs) operate within two worlds: the business world and the technical world. As a BA, you use your knowledge of both to discuss problems, requirements, and solutions intelligently. Often your role is that of an intermediary, a translator, and a liaison among the different stakeholders and the worlds in which they reside. This reality becomes especially apparent when you need to actually categorize and craft the requirements.

A requirement is basically a condition or capability the business needs in order to solve a problem or achieve an objective. The documented requirement explains what the problem or opportunity is.

Categorizing Your Requirements

Requirements have attributes that make up and define the requirement. These attributes ensure that your stakeholders get what they need from the requirements. Not every stakeholder needs to know all the various attributes, however. Categorizing requirements lets you help stakeholders access just the information they need from all the information that surrounds a requirement.

Consider how you search for recipes: You may look for all dishes that include chicken, all dishes that can be grilled, or recipes that received ratings of four starts or better. In each selection, you could find grilled chicken (the requirement), but you found it in different ways. Your recipes are like requirements.

By categorizing the requirements, you're able to communicate the different levels of requirements to the appropriate audience. Business people can understand the requirements at their level, technical people at their own level, and so on. If you're a business person, you can choose to look only at the business requirements. If you're an approver, you can choose to look only at requirements that are ready for approval. Additionally, you can show progression of how a particular requirement at the business level is being solved through the functional requirements with traceability.

Getting the process started

Although categorizing becomes intuitive after a while, it may seem confusing at first. After all, the stakeholders just keep talking and talking, and you may have a hard time making sense of it. Here's a process to get you started:

1. **Capture the requirements.**

   This idea may seem simple, but the first step is to elicit the requirements from the stakeholder (flip to Chapters 6 and 7 for the lowdown on eliciting).

2. **Look for operative words.**

   Review your elicitation notes and look for key words that define the stakeholder's statement. If a stakeholder mentions technology or a technical constraint, for example, you know it's not a business requirement. Here are things to look for as you categorize:

   • **Business and stakeholder requirements:** Look for words and phrases that describe the *what*, such as "we need a way to" and "we need to be able to." These requirements don't mention technology or a solution, so you know they're describing what needs to happen. You may find yourself extracting these from the functional requirements by asking "Why?" frequently.

- **Solution requirements (functional and nonfunctional):** These requirements have solution-oriented language, such as "the system will." These requests often contain a solution component.

- **Technical requirements:** You hear technical language and jargon inside these requirements. For instance, "alphanumeric indicator" and "customer prospect table" are jargon-y terms that can tip you off to a technical requirement. Look for solutions of how the system is built.

- **Transition requirements:** Because these requirements focus on the tasks needed to go from the current state to the future state, look for temporary requirements, such as "Migrate the data from the old system to the new."

Note: You can get the basics on each type of requirement in Chapter 5.

3. **Clarify with the stakeholder.**

   Go back and have the stakeholder confirm her understanding of what you noted. This validation can prevent defects or misunderstanding later.

4. **Put the round peg into the round hole.**

   Document the requirements appropriately, putting the requirement into the correct category. You can read about documentation in the later section "Documenting Your Requirements."

If you still have problems determining which category is the correct one, try the tactics we outline in the next section.

Choosing the right category

Often, the challenging part for new BAs is correctly identifying which category any particular requirement falls into. If you get tripped up as you sort through your requirements, think of them as building on each other to help you figure out where they go in the order.

Consider the process you use when you purchase a car. You first need to understand the mission of the vehicle. Are you looking to cart around your kids' soccer team, or do you need an inexpensive commuter car? These needs are your business requirements. Next, you look for a solution by examining the different vehicle options, choosing which ones have the features, color, and style (functional requirements) and performance (nonfunctional requirements) you need. Finally, the manufacturer delivers a car with an independent suspension rocker arm wishbone suspension riding on P205/R16 Z4 tires (technical requirement).

Another way to help yourself categorize requirements is to figure out who reviews and ultimately uses the contents of which category. Table 12-1 is an example of a handy reference chart that outlines best practice standards, although the categorization can vary slightly from project to project.

Table 12-1:	Categorizing Requirements by Who Does What	
Requirement Type	**Elicited and Documented By**	**Reviewed and Used By**
Business and stake-holder requirements	BAs	Subject matter experts (SMEs), technical team, and testing team
Solution (functional and nonfunctional) requirements	BAs and/or technical team	SMEs, technical team, testing team, and BAs if not involved in the creation
Transition requirements	BAs and/or technical team	SMEs, technical team, testing team, and BAs if not involved in the creation
Technical requirements	Technical team	BAs, developers, testing team

Documenting Your Requirements

When you document your requirements, you're really just capturing the information and then presenting it for validation, sign-off, review, and so on. Although it can be a physical, formal document (like one you'd produce in MS Word or another word processing program), it can also take other forms. In essence, it's just a recording of what you captured in your elicitation sessions.

When documenting requirements, think of who you're talking to and what level of technical knowledge they understand. This understanding helps you craft the communication so it's on a specific audience's level. Use business language for business folk and technical language for technical folk.

Documentation doesn't necessarily mean you have to produce something text-based. Although your documentation certainly can be a written report, requirements can also be drawings, such as a workflow diagram.

Agile teams

Here's a note for *agile teams* (teams within the project team that deliver working solutions through iterative creation and development in a rapid time frame): The requirements may be hard to categorize when everyone works with everyone and the team members don't use the titles listed in Table 12-1 (as some agile teams do not); nevertheless, agile teams still need to understand the nature of the problem the business is trying to solve instead of just creating and implementing a solution. Understanding the problem is especially important because agile teams do things a lot faster. If the team doesn't "step back" and figure out the real problem, it could do the business a disservice. For more on agile teams, refer to Chapter 11.

The following sections help you understand the different requirement categories and what you should think about when documenting them. Head to Chapter 5 to understand the different types of requirements.

Documenting business and stakeholder requirements

When you write business and stakeholder requirements, you want to capture the problem or opportunity and explain what has to be done (rather than how you're going to solve the problem or take advantage of the opportunity).

As the person performing the business analysis, you're generally the main person capturing the business requirements because you have a unique ability to drill into the real problem or opportunity rather than just gather a solution request (which is why your process is called "elicitation" and not "gathering"). Stakeholders are also involved because they're the people from whom you elicit.

Business requirements exist at many points in the project, but you create them primarily at the beginning. In documenting the business requirements, include the following information:

- **Project initiation:** This category includes the statement of purpose, objectives, and risks of the project. It should capture what the purpose is, what the objectives are (what would make this project a success?), and what the risks are.

- **Information needs:** You can also call this information the *data*. It's the description of the information the business area needs in order to accomplish its business. So long as you stick to what the business is, you're still eliciting business requirements.

✔ **Business processes/activities:** These processes are the workflows the business performs to get its work done.

✔ **Business rules:** These rules are the constraints or conditions that govern how the business makes its decisions. They're the operating principles of the business.

Documenting solution requirements, both functional and nonfunctional

The solution requirements category is where the solution's design lives, which means the technical team can help write some of the functional and nonfunctional requirements. After all, these people are an integral part in the creation of the eventual solution, so having them on the project as early as possible is always good. For example, if your solution involves a computer application and you're designing user interfaces, bring your technical people into the functional requirements discussions. This strategy works on two levels: One, the tech people can help write the requirements in the proper language, and two, they can provide input on whether your prototypes and screen mockups are feasible, which gains their buy-in. Bonus!

Functional requirements

As we note earlier in the chapter, functional requirements answer the "how" questions, such as "How are we going to change the process? To answer these kinds of questions, your functional requirements should include the following info:

✔ **Design area scope:** The scope of what will be included in the design. Solution design may take on both non-automated solutions (like adding more people to the business area or redesigning the manual process) or automated solutions (creating a mobile app to allow people to order takeout food from a restaurant, for example). One technique you can use to create the design area scope is a use case diagram, covered in Chapter 13.

The design area scope may differ from the project scope because not all aspects of the project scope are completed at the same time. The solution may be split into different phases, each with its own design scope.

✔ **System functionality:** How the user interacts with the software. Think about the actions you perform and the reactions (or responses) the system provides back to you — this is the expected system functionality. You often document these items with use cases and user interface (UI) specification documents (which we cover in Chapter 13).

✔ **Data definitions:** What the business data looks like, such as allowable values, default values, and field lengths. For example, you may define that a customer's shipping state defaults to using the state code on their billing address, such that allowable values are AL, AZ, AK, and so on.

✔ **User classes:** The groups of people who will be using the new application software or process (internally or externally). Some examples include customers, prospects, guests, employees, senior management, line people, and call center representatives.

✔ **User interfaces:** Description of screen layouts, report layouts, and procedures. Remember to follow up any pictures with explanations of how the screen operates. For instance, Figure 12-1 is an example of a user interface prototype of a flight reservation system. When describing this interface prototype, you'd explain that the "Find Flights" button remains inactive until the users choose an origin, destination, and departure and return dates. This sequence is the behavior surrounding the screen.

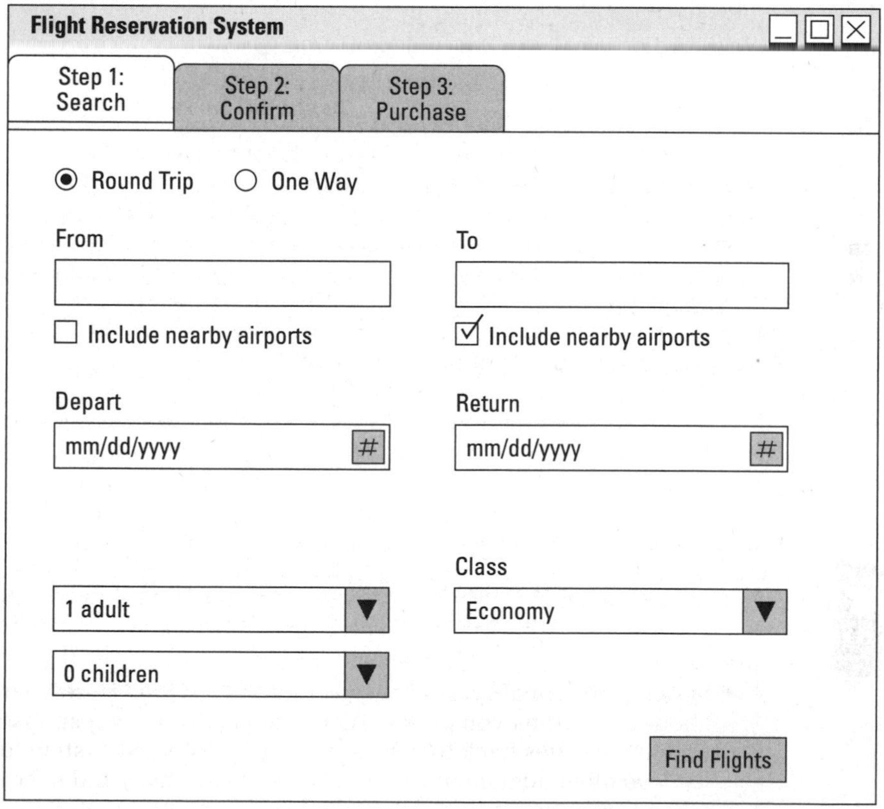

Figure 12-1: Prototype of a web page user interface.

Flight Reservation System

| Step 1: Search | Step 2: Confirm | Step 3: Purchase |

◉ Round Trip   ○ One Way

From

To

☐ Include nearby airports   ☑ Include nearby airports

Depart   Return
mm/dd/yyyy [#]   mm/dd/yyyy [#]

                                   Class
1 adult ▼   Economy ▼

0 children ▼

                                              Find Flights

Illustration by Wiley, Composition Graphics Services

When documenting functional requirements, keep the following in mind:

✓ **Document how you want the functionality to work rather than what specific tool you plan to use.** For example, making sure the flight reservation system in Figure 12-1 displays only return dates that occur after the departure date is a description of functionality; the fact that you'll use, say, a Java calendar code applet to calculate Today +1 is a description of a tool for execution.

✓ **Stick to the interactions between the computer system and the external agent (the user).**

✓ **Address the look and feel (the observable behaviors) instead of focusing on code design and implementation.**

You have to tread a fine line when you're documenting functional requirements. The language has to be nontechnical enough to communicate to the business SMEs so that they understand how the solution is going to operate. However, it still has to be detailed enough so the technical team knows how to create the solution, including all the exceptions/alternate ways to create the solution.

Documenting nonfunctional requirements

Nonfunctional requirements are just as important as the functional requirements when it comes to defining the look and feel of the solution. Nonfunctional requirements are a challenge because different people interpret them differently from organization to organization (or even from department to department in the same organization). "The computer system should be easy to use" may not mean the same thing to everyone. You need to understand a lot about the people using the solution and make sure your nonfunctionals document its performance.

You create the nonfunctional requirements based on your elicitations from the users, who they are, and what their expectations of the system performance are.

Make sure you elicit the nonfunctionals while you're eliciting the functional requirements. A lot of BAs gloss over the nonfunctionals and instead concentrate on the functional requirements. But the nonfunctionals are important because they support the functional requirements, telling you how well something must be done. Eliciting both requirement types at the same time ensures that user requests and requirements are technologically feasible.

When you create nonfunctional requirements, you need to think about things like the following:

✔ **Performance:** How well does the system perform? To understand the performance requirements, ask stakeholders questions such as "What are the number of concurrent users?", "What are the system or query response times?", and "What is the system's capacity in terms of memory, disk space, and data volumes?"

Remember to speak in the language your audience understands. Don't expect a response if you ask your business stakeholders how many hard disk partitions they need in their solution!

✔ **Security:** Who has access to the system, and how much access do they have? To understand the security requirements, ask questions such as "Which users are authorized to perform which functions?", "What is the privacy of the information being captured and stored?", and "What features need to be in place to log user access and authenticate users?"

A useful technique for communicating security access within your solution (the first item in the preceding list of questions) is to create a *security matrix*. This matrix shows your stakeholders which users can access which processes (sometimes called *use cases*) within the system. For example, a security matrix for an order system may look like the one shown in Figure 12-2.

✔ **Reliability:** *Reliability* is how the system operates based on the expectation of the end-user. Think about buying a car. You probably *purchase* a car because of the *functionality* (0–60 mph in 8 seconds, A/C, satellite radio, and so on), but you probably think about going to shop for that new car because of the *reliability* of the car (yours keeps breaking down, it's costing hundreds each month to maintain it, and so on). Similarly, you want to make sure you find out how consistently the business wants the solution to perform and what maintenance and support you need to make sure it stays that way.

Actor	Add item to shopping cart	Modify shopping cart	Update shipping status of shopping cart item	Update shipping preferences	Cancel order
Customer	Yes	Yes		Yes	Yes
Customer Service Rep	Yes	Yes	Yes	Yes	Yes
Order fulfilment			Yes	Yes	
Fraud Department				Yes	

Figure 12-2: A security matrix order system.

Illustration by Wiley, Composition Graphics Services

To elicit the reliability requirements, ask questions such as "When is the system expected to be available?", "What downtime does the system have for the administrators to perform maintenance, and when is the best time to schedule downtime?", and "What notification do the users need when the system is going down for maintenance? How much advance notice should they receive?"

✔ **Compatibility:** *Compatibility* refers to the extent to which the solution plays nice with other applications. To elicit compatibility nonfunctional requirements, ask questions such as "What common standards, common technology, and protocols exist on the workstation?"; "How well does the solution work with the common build?"; "What kinds of data exchange do you envision?"; and "What information (data) must be exchanged with other systems?"

✔ **Maintainability:** *Maintainability* deals with how easy the system is to maintain and repair. To elicit the nonfunctionals for maintainability, ask questions such as "What is the ability to change one component without affecting others?", "What effects do the maintenance activities have on customers, users, and employees?", and "Who performs system upgrades? Who is responsible for interfaces?"

Business rules are highly likely to change, so when thinking about maintainability, make sure rules aren't hard-coded.

✔ **Transferability:** *Transferability* refers to the ease with which a system can be transferred to a different hardware or software environment. Some of these concerns are lessening now that many companies are creating browser-based applications, yet these concerns have expanded with the mobile apps (like those you see on your smartphone) and the different versions and standards for e-readers. To elicit nonfunctionals, ask questions such as "Can the system be installed in a different environment (for instance, on a Mac and a PC) and in different geographies and different locations?", "What operating environment is considered the base operating system (OS)? Will the code run the same way on all platforms?", and "What government regulations need to be addressed?"

When rolling out a system to different environments, remember that each environment needs to be tested. Rolling out to two environments doubles the testing effort.

✔ **Usability:** *Usability* concerns the ways by which the user is able to learn, operate, and interpret the system results. This category includes ease of entry, learning, and handling, as well as the system's intuitiveness. Think about it this way: The reason you didn't receive training on how to use a site like Google is because the application has fantastic analysts who concentrate on usability. To elicit usability, ask questions such as "How quickly should the user be able to perform specific functions?", "How long should a particular task take?", and "What is the minimum acceptable number of mouse clicks required to perform a task?"

Stating "The system should be easy to use" isn't a valid usability requirement. You must define what *easy to use* means through metrics.

✔ **Metrics and measurements:** With any nonfunctional requirement, you must understand what measurement criteria you'll use to determine whether the requirement is successful and met. You're defining how well the solution meets the requirements. To elicit the metric, ask questions like "What are some aspects surrounding that requirement that you can measure?" and "What are the acceptable measurement time frames that are acceptable for the stakeholder?"

Documenting transition requirements

Transition requirements are temporary. They enable you to go from your current state (*as is*) to your future state (*to be*). They are temporary in nature because, after you arrive at your future state, you no longer need them.

Think about mapping out your travel in an app: You input your current position and your destination (future) position. The mapping software gives you the transition requirements (go 500 feet, make a left onto Main Street, travel 1.6 miles, make right onto Second Ave, and so on) — requirements that, once you arrive at your destination, you no longer need. In a project, when you reach your objective (the to-be state), you no longer need the directions (your transition requirements).

Examples of transition requirements include the following:

✔ **Data migration**: In data migration, you take data from one system and map and transform it into another system.

✔ **User training:** Users who will be using the new software application may not know how to use it. The training they need in order to use the system effectively has to be provided as a transition requirement.

Chapter 15 provides details on how to move from planning to implementing the solution.

Documenting technical requirements

In the technical category of the project, the BA and technical team swap authoring responsibility. The technical team writes the code, the programs, the modules, and the system documentation. You then become the reviewer to ensure that what is put in place and created meets the original intent of what the business wanted. Later, you use this documentation to make sure the solution the technical team delivers matches what was described (and signed off on) by the business users in the functional portion of the project.

Ensuring Your Requirements Have Traceability

Traceability shows you how the business requirements have been satisfied by functional requirements and ultimately through the technical requirements. Consider the *traceability matrix* in Figure 12-3. It shows the business processes on the rows, from a business perspective, and how they've been addressed with the functional requirements in the columns. With this matrix, you can ensure that each business requirement has been satisfied by a functional requirement.

Figure 12-3:
A traceability matrix helps you trace your solutions back to a requirement

Business Process	Use Case				
	UC1	UC2	UC3	UC4	UC5
1.1	✓	✓		✓	
1.2		✓			
1.3		✓	✓		
1.4					✓

Illustration by Wiley, Composition Graphics Services

Although the traceability matrix is not the only way to ensure links to other requirements, it's the most widely used. You want to be able to show that you have covered each requirement as you build upon it to the next level of requirements. It also lets you determine the impact of a change in the requirements, or helps you plan your release.

You can also use traceability when evaluating what you can do with limited resources. Suppose each use case in Figure 12-3 costs $20,000 to implement. Implementing all five use cases, therefore, costs $100,000. But the project sponsor has only $60,000 to spend. Therefore, the sponsor can't get all the business processes implemented with the amount of money available.

Now you can start looking at the traceability to determine which business requirements (listed as processes in Figure 12-3) you can address. You can implement UC1, UC2, and UC4 for $60,000. Doing so gets you 100 percent of business process 1.1 and 1.2, some functionality of 1.3, and nothing from 1.4. Or you can do UC2, UC3, and UC4, which gets you 100 percent functionality for business processes 1.2, 1.3, and 1.4, and some functionality for process 1.1 (covered in UC2). The matrix helps show how you can implement the release.

Another advantage of traceability is for analyzing impact to your scope (Chapter 10 covers determining scope). How quickly could you answer a stakeholder who asks, "What would happen if we changed process 1.1?" At this level, you can see that UC1, UC2, and UC4 are affected. By performing this impact analysis, you can analyze change requests very quickly within a project to determine the level of effort required to address a change request.

To create a traceability matrix, do the following:

1. **Write the requirement in the matrix.**

2. **Indicate the requirements that are linked to or traced to this requirement.**

   If you're using a requirements management tool, you may choose the traced requirements for those you've previously entered in the tool.

3. **Continue entering requirements and tracing them to other requirements, continuing on with test cases, program modules, and applications.**

   The more you trace your requirements, the more accurate your impact analysis is. Generally, the objectives are traced to business requirements, then to functional and nonfunctional requirements, then to test cases and test results, and then to program modules. Business rules are traced throughout as the rules affect the requirements.

Chapter 13

Defining Solutions, Part 2: Choosing the Right Analysis Technique

. . . .

In This Chapter

▶ Knowing which analysis technique is right for your requirements

▶ Determining when a text or graphical technique works best

▶ Checking out the advantages and disadvantages of each tool

. . . .

*Y*ou don't perform business analysis in a vacuum; you work with a lot of stakeholders, so keep in mind that, although you may understand the analysis and solution behind what you're doing, your stakeholder may have a difficult time wrapping his brain around it. Every person is unique, and you have to figure out how to communicate best with each individual. This chapter gives you different ways of analyzing requirements to come up with an effective solution for conveying your data — otherwise known as choosing a *data model* — in ways to best communicate the key information.

These techniques are tools to help you communicate. Each technique has its niche and analyzes a specific data best. As you go through the techniques in this chapter, understand the following:

✔ **You can perform each technique in a lot of different ways.** What kind of tool you use (computerized or hand-drawn) drives the look and feel of the technique.

✔ **You don't have to perform any of these techniques in one specific, correct way.** Because they're communication vehicles, you need to determine how you can best use them to communicate what you intend to.

✔ **Choose those techniques that are most appropriate for your projects.** That's part of planning (head to Chapter 11 for information on creating a work plan).

You can analyze requirements in many ways. If one technique doesn't express the requirements as effectively as you think it could, try another. The point is, you need to be a MacGyver of sorts and have multiple tools at your disposal.

Dealing with Data Flow Diagrams and External Interaction Textual Templates

In 1984, Stephen M. McMenamin and John F. Palmer first promoted the *data flow diagram* as a technique to understand systems by showing the data flows going into and out of a process. It's a helpful diagram that shows the parties and systems involved with a particular process, as well as the data and interfaces involved when dealing with *external agents* (those parties or systems that exchange information with the project but over which your project has no control). It's most commonly used for the project level context diagram (or scope diagram; we cover how to create that diagram in Chapter 10).

Although the data flow diagram is a graphic, as the name suggests, you can also use a text-based version called the *external interaction textual template*. The following sections describe these two options.

You use these techniques to analyze and communicate. If text communicates better to your stakeholders, use the textual template rather than the diagram.

Getting a handle on data flow diagrams

The data flow diagram consists of three basic symbols: circles, curved lines, and rectangles, as you can see in Figure 13-1. Each symbol represents something different:

- ✔ **Circles:** The circles represent the process (or the function) that actually works to transform inputs into outputs. In Figure 13-1, the process involves taking in all the information from the guest (input) and sending it off to the reservation system (output).

- ✔ **Curved lines:** The curved lines represent the data flowing into and out of the process. These bits of data aren't detailed data elements but rather a conglomeration of data called *net flow*. In Figure 13-1, dates coming from the guest into the process are arrival and departure dates (including times), but instead of getting that detailed, the diagram simply summarizes them as "dates."

- ✔ **Rectangular boxes:** The rectangular boxes represent external agents that are sources or recipients of data. Your project has no control over how these sources execute their internal processes (their work), and the project can only send data to and receive it from them. In Figure 13-1, for example, you have no idea how the reservation system processes its data, but based on what you send the system, you get the availability and price information from it.

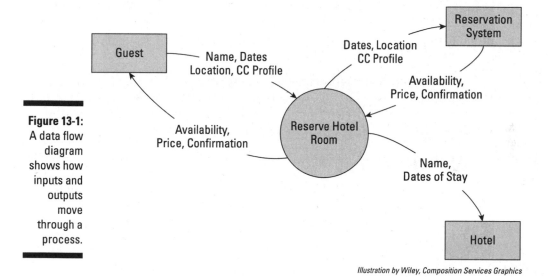

Figure 13-1: A data flow diagram shows how inputs and outputs move through a process.

Illustration by Wiley, Composition Services Graphics

Here are some examples of when you should apply this technique:

- ✔ When identifying stakeholders (those external agents!)
- ✔ When scoping your project and figuring out your boundaries

Like any analysis method, data flow diagrams have advantages and disadvantages. In the advantages column is the fact that the diagram is a very clear way to show the scope boundaries for the project so that everyone is on the same page with regard to the area being analyzed (the scope). It also highlights the items that aren't part of scope and can be documented as "out of scope."

The disadvantages primarily have to do with reader understanding:

- ✔ The diagram doesn't show sequence, so some businesspeople may have a hard time following it.
- ✔ The diagram presents the data flowing into and out of the project at a rather high level. It doesn't show all the data elements, which may be problematic for detail-oriented folks.
- ✔ The data flow has kind of fallen out of favor because, outside the scope diagram, businesspeople don't relate to the many levels of the data flow diagram. They prefer a workflow, which we discuss in the later section "Working with Workflow Diagrams."

Here's how to create a data flow diagram (for detailed instructions on using this diagram to define the scope of your project, refer to Chapter 10):

1. **Identify the process you're documenting (the circle in the middle of the diagram).**

2. **Identify all the parties and systems (the rectangles) involved in the process.**

3. **Elicit from the stakeholders the data (the curved lines) flowing among the parties, the systems, and the process.**

4. **Have the stakeholders validate your diagram.**

Examining the external interaction textual template

An external interaction textual template may sound complicated, but it's really not. You use the same information you'd use for a data flow diagram (see the preceding section) but present it in a text table rather than a graphic. A textual representation may be preferable when your stakeholders don't understand the diagram or when teaching them how to read it takes too much time.

Figure 13-2 shows a sample external interaction textual template. You can see that the left-hand column lists the external agents (the rectangles on the data flow diagram), and the middle and right-hand columns list the data itself (the curved lines on the diagram).

External Agent	Data Coming from EA	Data Coming from EA
Guest	• Request for available hotels and rooms and rates • Name • CC Information	• Availability of hotels and rooms based on dates • Confirmation of booking
Reservation System	• Room Availability • Price • Confirmation	• Request for hotels that have rooms based on dates
Hotel		• Confirmation of Name and Dates of Stay

Figure 13-2: An external interaction textual template is another way to document data flows.

Illustration by Wiley, Composition Services Graphics

ERD Is the Word: Using Entity Relationship Diagrams

If you're looking for a way to define how data is set up in your system, you're going to love the *entity relationship diagram* (ERD). True to its name, the ERD helps you organize and document the various data entities and their relationships to one another within the project. The ERD is primarily a tool to help you communicate with the data analyst on the project.

In the following sections, we explain how you can use and create an ERD and how you can modify the way the data looks with the relationship text template and entity text template to better meet the needs of your intended audience.

Getting familiar with the ERD

Like other analysis techniques, the ERD uses simple boxes, lines, and symbols to diagram the entities, attributes, and data relationships. The *entities* are the uniquely identifiable people, things, or concepts whose information is important to the business; the *attributes* are distinguishing characteristics of the entity; and the *relationships* explain how the entities share data.

You should apply this technique in situations such as the following:

✔ When you want to understand or demonstrate the relationships between the data. The relationships define business rules you'll need to know about.

✔ When communicating the data requirements to the data analyst or developer.

✔ When you need to understand all the attributes of each data element.

For instance, suppose you're working on an Internet shopping cart project. You need to document the relationships among the entities of products, orders, and line items. Figure 13-3 shows three boxes that represent the three entities involved in the shopping cart: the order, the line item, and the product. The relationship line has three symbols — the crow's feet, the circle, and the straight line — that tell you exactly how those entities relate, with a minimum and maximum value for each side. These relationships (how each entity links to another) are called *cardinalities:*

✔ The ⟨ (*crow's feet*) symbol indicates multiple entities, such as multiple e-mail addresses for one employee. You can use this symbol to show a maximum value only.

✔ The ○ symbol denotes that the item is optional — that a connection isn't required. For instance, an employee may not have a home phone number (with the advent of mobile phones, that situation is becoming more common). You can use this symbol to show that a minimum value of zero is okay.

✔ The | symbol indicates a single entry that can be used as both a minimum and a maximum value. For example, if you need a person's name, that person will have one and only one first name. This symbol shows that he must enter a first name and has a maximum of one name only.

As an example, look at Figure 13-3 and read the relationship between entities Order Line Item and Product by looking at the line between the two from left to right. The entity Order Line Item *contains / is on* (the first verb on the line) *one* (the | on the inside of the line, signifying the minimum number) and *only one* (the second | on the line, signifying the maximum) Product. To read the relationship from Product to Line Item, simply reverse the process from right to left.

Here are a few pros and cons of using this technique to consider:

✔ **Pro:** The ERD is a highly accepted standard in the data analysis world, and data analysts and developers are very familiar with how to read it.

✔ **Pro:** It's a clear description of how the data entities relate and the minimum and maximum cardinalities they exhibit.

✔ **Con:** Business people may not be familiar with the standard and may not be able to validate it without understanding the symbols.

✔ **Con:** Getting a cardinality wrong may throw off the solution design.

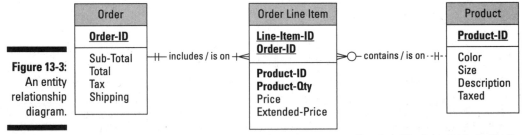

Figure 13-3:
An entity relationship diagram.

Illustration by Wiley, Composition Services Graphics

Here's how to create your ERD:

1. **Elicit from your stakeholders the information they need to capture within the scope of your project.**

   See Chapter 7 for elicitation techniques.

2. Group together the subentities and the attributes that make up the entity.

3. Draw (either in Microsoft Visio or freehand) the rectangles for the entities; put the appropriate entity name on each, and put the attributes inside.

4. Determine how you connect the entities (the relationships) and draw those in.

5. Validate your diagram with your stakeholders.

Creating database designs is way more involved than we have room to cover in this book. If you want to really get into database modeling, check out *Database Development For Dummies* by Allen G. Taylor (Wiley).

Presenting the data with entity relationship text templates

If your stakeholders (or even you) aren't comfortable with the symbols and drawings in ERD, you can use a text template instead. The *entity relationship text template* details the very same ERD information but in a text table, using a relationship between two entities as the key (in Figure 13-4, it's the relationship between Order Line Item and Product). You can read across each row based on the pairing and come up with the relationship. The advantage with this approach is that you don't need to learn the database modeling symbols, and you don't need Microsoft Visio to draw this diagram (as you may with the ERD). The disadvantage is that data analysts or developers may balk at receiving the text template. (Remember, you want to try to communicate with each audience in the language it understands.)

Figure 13-4: An entity relationship text template.

Entity Pair	Entity 1	Business Rule	At least	At most	Entity 2	Comments
Order-Line-Item – Product	An Order-Line Item	Contains	1	1	Product	If duplicate products are on the order, they will be consolidated by quantity when the order is shipped.
	Product	is on	0	Many	Order-Line-Item	

Illustration by Wiley, Composition Services Graphics

Rounding out the data: Entity text templates

The ERD and relationship text template are good, but they still don't paint a complete picture. Whether you use an ERD or entity relationship text template, you always need to document additional information about the diagram in an *entity text template.* Figure 13-5 shows the supporting information captured in the template:

- ✔ **Entity ID:** The identifier for the entity, used for tracing and reference (see Chapter 12 for info on these topics). You create this ID as you create the tracing.

- ✔ **Name:** The name of the entity. What does the business call this entity? Using the same name helps communication.

- ✔ **Unique identifier:** The ID or key that uniquely identifies an instance of the entity. For instance, the unique identifier for the entity of Order in a web-ordering project is Order-ID.

- ✔ **Number of occurrences:** How many occurrences exist today and how many that number is expected to grow by in the future. The business can probably tell you how many it has now (or if it's an existing data element, the technical people can tell you how many exist in the data structure) and what the projections are.

- ✔ **Owner:** Who owns this data? Determining ownership helps identify who makes decisions about changes in occurrences and expectations of growth.

Entity ID	Name	Unique Identifier	Number of Occurrences		Owner
			Current	Future	
E1	Order	Order-ID	15000	35000	Sales
E2	Order Line Item	Line-Item-ID	30000	68000	Sales
E3	Future	Product-ID	120000	120000	Marketing

Figure 13-5:
An entity text template.

Illustration by Wiley, Composition Services Graphics

Drilling Down a Process Decomposition Diagram

The *process decomposition diagram* (often called a *decomp*) explains the breakdown of processes within a project or business area or functional area. The purpose is to show all the processes and identify relationships and dependencies among them. Note that a decomp doesn't drill into the *how;* it merely outlines the *what*.

Take a look at Figure 13-6. If you're thinking, "That looks like an organization chart!", you're right on the money. It actually functions very similarly to an org chart in that the processes in this diagram relate to one another like the people on an organization chart relate to each other: Just as all the workers reporting to one manager make up all the work under that manager, all the processes under a higher process make up all the work of that process.

Processes that have processes underneath are called *parent processes*. Processes that report into another process are called *child processes*. Designating parent and child processes follows a couple of guidelines:

✔ If you break down a parent process, you must break it into at least two children; otherwise it's not a true parent.

✔ All the child processes together must completely describe all the activities in the parent process.

The diagram doesn't follow any defined sequence. For instance, in Figure 13-6, you don't have to check the weather before you plan the flight. Similarly, you can check the weather in any of the locations in any order; you don't have to check it from origin to en route to destination because bad weather at *any* point along the route prevents you from flying that route.

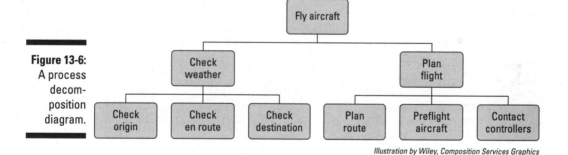

Figure 13-6: A process decomposition diagram.

Illustration by Wiley, Composition Services Graphics

Using Figure 13-6 as an example, here are some times you can apply this technique:

✔ **When you're working on a large project and need to understand the size of the work effort:** Knowing all the processes you have to document can help.

✔ **When you're validating with your stakeholders that you have captured all the processes you'll document:** Stakeholders can very easily see whether you've missed a process.

✔ **When you're eliciting processes in scope from your stakeholders:** The stakeholders are able to interact with a diagram structure they're very familiar with (in the company's org chart).

Some pros and cons to this technique include the following:

- ✔ **Pro:** The decomp diagram is useful on larger projects (those with more than five processes to study and document) because it gives you a snapshot of the big picture. On a large effort, it is easy to forget which parent each child process belongs to and how each child relates to each other. This opens the door to repeating processes for one or more parents.

- ✔ **Pro:** It's a great tool early on in the scoping phase because it gives you an idea of how many processes you have to define, which is important for time and resource estimates.

- ✔ **Pro:** It's a great technique to get your stakeholders involved in if you have sticky notes handy. Give your stakeholders the scope of what you're decomposing and a pad of sticky notes, and have them write down the processes (one per sheet) and then post them on the wall. Not only are the stakeholders 100 percent involved in the activity, but they're also team building. A side benefit is that they're doing your job for you (but we won't tell)!

- ✔ **Pro:** Stakeholders can use the diagram to find missing processes.

- ✔ **Con:** Stakeholders may get caught up in how a process is performed rather than what's being performed.

- ✔ **Con:** The diagram doesn't show solutions or sequence of processes. Let your stakeholders know you'll get there. First you have to make sure you have defined them all.

Always remember to be flexible! If your stakeholders really want to talk about sequence, let them go there. On projects where stakeholders work better talking about the details, Kupe discusses the details and then starts circling steps in a process to identify parent and child processes to build the decomp.

Step 1: Creating the process decomposition diagram

1. **Choose one of three ways to build your decomp: top-down, bottom-up, or event-driven.**

   That's right; you can use three methods to create your diagram:

   - **Top-down:** Start with the high-level processes (requirements) you identified during scoping if you have them (if you don't, elicit them from your stakeholders). From there, keep drilling down until you get to processes that contain a how; that's your stopping point. For example, Figure 13-6 states that what you have to do is "Fly aircraft" and drill down into tasks such as "Check origin" and "Contact controllers." It stops there because the next level would indicate how to do those things.

- **Bottom-up:** Think of all the detailed tasks you have to do in the area of study (or scope) and then find common groupings. For example, you may first determine all the detailed tasks such as "Preflight aircraft" and "Plan route" and then identify logical groupings such as "Plan flight." When determining the groupings, a process may fall into different headings; the goal is for the team to determine the best approach. Remember, what you want to do is make sure you don't miss any processes.

- **Event-driven:** Think of all the triggers (directives that lead to a series of actions) and the tasks that follow. In Figure 13-7, a trigger may be that a controller gives you clearance, and all the tasks you do as a pilot follow that trigger.

2. **Take notes and make a rough sketch.**

   Remember a great technique is using sticky notes to build this diagram.

3. **Build the actual diagram and validate it with the stakeholders.**

Figure 13-7:
You can build your decomp diagram by using an event-driven approach.

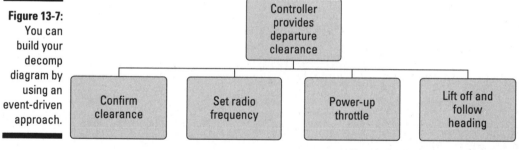

Illustration by Wiley, Composition Services Graphics

Step 2: Documenting the processes

When you have your decomposition diagram created (see the preceding section), you're only halfway done. The diagram shows you the processes, but you still have to actually document the details. For each process, you have to define what attributes and information make up each process by answering questions such as the following:

- ✔ Who are the external agents involved in the process? Who currently performs the process today? How do they do it? Who uses the output of the process?

- ✔ What causes the process to start? What is the trigger?

- ✔ What happens after the process is complete? What are the postconditions? (Get details on postconditions in the later section "The text: Use case description.")

✔ What data does the process use? Who creates the data? Is it created, read, updated, or deleted?

✔ How often is the process performed? How long does it take? How efficient is it?

The company's culture determines if, how, and where you document this information, but if you want a starting point, you can download the Requirements Package Template at www.b2ttraining.com.

Deciding on Decision Tables

You use decision tables to help analyze and communicate a company's business rules (see more on business rules in Chapter 5). They're a great way to show and clarify complicated business logic, particularly when you need to help stakeholders understand how different values work together to create a conclusion. Decision tables also help identify conditions you may not have thought out, so be on the lookout for conditions for which you have no conclusion.

A decision table contains multiple condition columns and a conclusion column, as shown in Figure 13-8. As you read across the rows, you gain more information until you arrive at your answer in the final column.

Employment History	Debt Load	Credit Rating
Poor	High	D
Poor	Medium	C-
Poor	Low	C
Poor	None	C+
Good	High, Medium	C
Good	Low	B
Excellent	High	C
Excellent	Low	A-
Excellent	None	A+

Figure 13-8: A sample decision table.

Illustration by Wiley, Composition Services Graphics

You should apply this technique in situations such as the following:

▌ ✔ When you need to make a set of complicated rules easier to understand

✔ When you want to make the stakeholder review of business decisions more quickly and easily

✔ When you want help in identifying missing conditions or conflicting conditions surrounding business logic

Keep these advantages of using decision tables in mind:

✔ **This technique helps you determine missing conditions (requirements).** By breaking out the conditions, you not only show the known conditions but also expose the unknown conditions. If those unknown conditions have no conclusion, you have uncovered a missing requirement. For instance, in Figure 13-8, what is the conclusion if a person has good employment history and no debt load? That condition hasn't been identified.

Similarly, Figure 13-8 lists conditions for people with excellent employment histories and high, low, and nonexistent debt loads, but the Debt Load column also offers a value of Medium that isn't accounted for in the excellent employment history category. This gap is an example of a missing condition (or requirement).

✔ **It's also a good tool for developers and QA people because they can use the table to design and test the system very easily from the structure of this diagram.**

Follow these steps to create a decision table:

1. **Determine the decision you want to make.**

   In Figure 13-8, that decision is assigning a person's credit rating.

2. **Figure out the variables you need answers to so that you can make that decision.**

   These variables — such as employment history and debt load in Figure 13-8 — are your conditions.

3. **Determine the valid values in each of the conditions.**

   By knowing all the valid values, you can figure out missing conclusions.

4. **Determine where the data is coming from.**

   If the data comes from a different application, you may need another decision table to demonstrate what determines the values.

5. **Set the decision from Step 1 as the last column heading and your conditions from Step 2 as the columns leading up to that.**

6. **Walk through the table, filling in the values (from Step 3) for each condition and drawing conclusions for each combination of the conditions.**

In Figure 13-8, you can see that if a person's employment history is poor and his debt load is high, he receives a credit rating of D.

Working with Workflow Diagrams

A *workflow diagram* (or *workflow*) is a visual way to show how work gets accomplished. Workflows are composed of a set of symbols that show how various workers accomplish tasks and interact with each other, as well as how information (data) flows through the business area. These diagrams have been around for a long time and come in many varieties:

- ✔ **Swimlane**: This workflow diagram focuses on interactions between organizational units and exposes bottlenecks and process inefficiencies

- ✔ **ANSI flowchart:** This style grew out of flowcharting in the 1970s and became the first standard for workflows. The symbols came out of the American National Standards Institute (hence, ANSI). Many people still use the symbols today, often inside swimlanes to show work being accomplished. For example, an ANSI flowchart may show how an employee's vacation request is approved.

- ✔ **UML Activity**: This diagram arose from UML (Unified Modeling Language). It operates like a flowchart and shows different steps and ordered tasks as well as the flow of control.

- ✔ **BPMN:** *Business Process Modeling Notation* (BPMN) is a standard created for the business rather than for application development. In other words, it focuses on graphically presenting business processes and information rather than solutions. For instance, a BPMN diagram may show the process of vacation approval overlaid on all the external agents in the process: the employee's, manager's, and company's vacation calendars.

- ✔ **Geographic diagrams:** These diagrams are commonly used in warehousing and logistics to show the placement of objects in relation to workers. For example, a geographic diagram would mandate that the least-commonly ordered products be placed farthest from the shipping dock and highest up on the racks and that the most-commonly ordered products be placed closest to the shipping station.

- ✔ **SIPOC:** *SIPOC* stands for "Supplier–Input–Process–Output–Customer." Used primarily in Six Sigma, this diagram shows who creates the data, details the high-level process, and depicts who receives the data. For example, a shipping company (supplier) provides a tracking number (input) attached to your order (the process), and a confirmation e-mail goes out (output) to you (customer, consumer). (Check out *Six Sigma For Dummies,* 2nd Edition, by Craig Gygi and Bruce Williams [Wiley] for more on SIPOC and other Six Sigma topics.)

Here are some examples of when you should apply this technique:

- ✔ When you're automating a manual process

- ✔ When you're defining responsibilities: who does what task in a process

- ✔ When you're tracking metrics for a process

- ✔ When you're trying to improve a process by looking for process ineffi-ciencies and exposing bottlenecks

TIP

This technique has its advantages — it's a very good way to see inefficiencies in the process, and it helps define the roles and responsibilities for the pro-cess — but it's also limited in that it doesn't actually solve the problem (it just documents the process). Make sure you identify the root cause of a problem before simply automating a bad process.

Decoding diagram symbols

All these diagrams use symbols to show the flow of the process as it moves through the business area within scope of your project. Each diagram uses different symbols, but they all document various aspects about the process, such as who does the work, where it is done, what data the process uses, where decisions are made, who makes those decisions, when the process starts, and what causes the process to end. You can see some of these symbol sets in Figure 13-9.

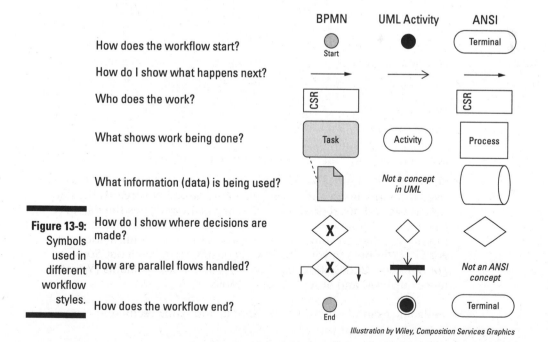

Figure 13-9: Symbols used in different workflow styles.

Illustration by Wiley, Composition Services Graphics

Creating a workflow diagram

Workflow diagramming is another one of those topics that we could write whole books about (and some people have), but for our purposes, we've pared the how-to on making a workflow down to the essentials:

1. **Determine the point of view and point in time you're diagramming.**

   Are you diagraming the process from the business' point of view or from the customers' point of view? Are you showing the way you're doing the process today (called the *as is process*) or how you want to do it with the new implementation (called the *to be process*). If you don't know, ask your stakeholders. Title the workflow appropriately as we discuss later in the section.

2. **Figure out where the process starts and where it ends.**

   This step is very important because it forms the starting point for your process activities and also identifies when it successfully (or unsuccessfully) ends. If you don't know — you guessed it — ask your stakeholders.

3. **Ask "What happens next?" or "And then what happens?" questions of your stakeholders until you understand the process from end to end.**

   Document each task and connect iy to create a flow (or path) from one task to another. When working with stakeholders, keep going down the most likely path (the one that happens most of the time) first. Then return to the alternate paths (those that don't follow the normal path). This strategy helps you avoid getting stuck in all the "what if" paths.

   As you uncover the process, listen for operative words such as *validate* or *approve;* those are your *decision points.* When you come across these words, you're going to have two paths coming out of the decision: one for the approval and one for the denial. Continue down the most common path at this point, but make sure to return to the exception path.

4. **At the decision points, figure out what information or data the worker needs in order to make a decision.**

   For each task, inquire about the data they either use (or *read,* in data language) or generate (*create*). This information leads you to requirements.

5. **Choose the type of workflow.**

   No one-size-fits-all solution works here. Your choice depends on what the company's culture is, whether the company has worked with any kind of workflow diagram in the past, and which option will best communicate to their stakeholders, as well as on your own experience and comfort level with various workflows.

Seeing a diagram in action: An example

In the BPMN workflow diagram shown in Figure 13-10, you can see how the various symbols are linked together to show how the business process works. This figure shows you some best practices for actually laying out your diagram:

✔ **Start the process in the upper left.** People tend to read from left to right, so they naturally start in the upper left. Here, the process starts when the training administrator receives a message from the student.

✔ **Title the workflow and indicate *as is* or *to be*.** You can put the title anywhere you want, but in Figure 13-10, it's in the upper right. Include "as is" or "to be" in the filename when you save the file electronically so people can more easily find the correct workflow on the shared workspace.

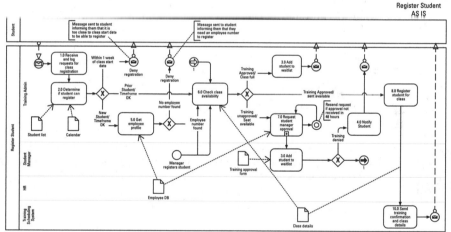

Figure 13-10:
A BPMN workflow diagram.

Illustration by Wiley, Composition Services Graphics

✔ **Don't document the process outside your control.** This one is more of a guideline than a hard and fast rule. Generally, you don't study and document what someone outside your control does. Even if you could physically document the infinite number of possibilities, finding out what those possibilities are is impossible. For instance, say you've just filled your cart on a shopping website, and the site has confirmed your order before you actually place it. What do you do then? Most likely, you click on "Submit Order," but you also may get distracted and check your e-mail, go to lunch, or respond to a text message. The point is, you can do anything at that point, and the shopping site has no control over your actions. In Figure 13-10, the student interacts with the process, but the process has no control over his actions, so the diagram doesn't document it.

✔ **Show who owns the data.** Knowing who owns the data may uncover an interface to another system or a new type of data. Notice in Figure 13-10 that HR doesn't do any work in the process, but it owns the employee database data, so it's included on the diagram.

✔ **Show which processes use the data.** This idea is the connection between the data symbols and the tasks. Orient the arrow to indicate whether the process consumes the data (arrow pointing into the task) or the task creates the data (arrow flowing to the data).

✔ **Make sure all paths resolve to an endpoint.** Having parallel paths is fine. Just ensure that all paths resolve to an endpoint.

Making a Use Case Model

A *use case model* is a presentation of the steps defining the interactions between a user (called an *actor*) and a system (usually a computer system). It details the interactions and sets the expectations of how the user will work within the system. The use case model consists of two artifacts: the *use case diagram,* which is a graphical representation showing which actors can operate which use cases, and the *use case description* (sometimes called the *use case narrative*), which is the text-based, detailed, step-by-step interactions and dialogue between the actor and the system. (The use case narrative is what people often mean when they say *use case.* Just remember there are multiple pieces that make up a use case model.)

Here, we hit on just the key points for creating the use case. For a comprehensive treatment, refer to the gold standard of use case creation in Alistair Cockburn's book *Writing Effective Use Cases* (Addison-Wesley Professional).

When is a good time to use a use case model? So glad you asked. Here are a few examples:

✔ When you're documenting detailed interactions between an actor and an automated solution

✔ When you want clear descriptions of how the user will interact with the solution

✔ When you need to get a handle on the scope of the solution

✔ When you want to identify the interfaces in the solution

Use case models are great for a variety of reasons: They give the project team a high-level view of the solution scope. They allow you and the designer to consider multiple implementation strategies. They're easy to understand (assuming they're done correctly) and make a great tool for the testers who can easily build test cases from the use case documentation. However, use case models can only do so much. Keep the following in mind:

✔ Use case models aren't well suited to capturing non-interaction-based requirements of a system (or nonfunctional requirements), such as algorithmic or mathematical requirements. These requirements are better specified declaratively elsewhere (meaning you should express what the logic is rather than how it's implemented).

✔ Use case models don't automatically make things clearer. Clarity depends on the skill of the author.

✔ Some use case relationships, such as "extends" and "includes," can be confusing to someone who hasn't received training in those aspects of use case creation.

The graphic: Use case diagram

The use case diagram is a visual scoping tool you use to plan the boundaries of the system, the expectations of the system (the use case name), and the potential user of the system.

It's a very useful diagram because it gives the project team a high-level view of the solution scope and allows you and the designer to consider multiple implementation strategies. Because it's so clear, it makes presenting the project scope information to all stakeholders easy and helps build consensus on the scope. As a matter of fact, the Paul first saw this diagram being used during a training class. Instantly, he saw the value of it in documenting project scope because it was such a clear diagram to read and understand.

A use case diagram contains the following components, illustrated in Figure 13-11:

✔ **Automation boundary:** Indicated by a rectangle in the center of the diagram, *the automation boundary* represents the system under discussion.

✔ **Actors:** These items are the stick figures documented with a descriptive name of the role of the actor. The actor represents a resource interacting with the system and can be a human or another system.

✔ **Associations:** Associations are marked by a line connecting the actor to a use case, indicating that the actor is involved with the use case. An actor can be associated with multiple use cases, and a use case can have many actors associated with it.

✔ **Use cases:** These items are represented by ovals inside the *automation boundary* and indicate the software system's goals. They contain a brief name (usually verb + noun) to describe what they do.

The use case diagram is possibly the easiest diagram to create, so the design process doesn't take much:

1. Draw the automation boundary in the middle of the workspace.

You can draw it on paper or a whiteboard or create it in Microsoft Visio or Microsoft Word (it doesn't matter).

2. **In the center of the automation boundary, identify the use cases that need to be detailed out and give them a brief description.**

   A combination of verb + noun (or noun phrase) is a very concise way to describe the use cases. In Figure 13-11, the use cases are Create Order, Pay for Order, Verify Order, and so on.

3. **Identify the actors who will be working within your system.**

   To find actors, ask "Who uses the software? Who provides the information to the software? What systems does the software interact with? Does anything happen at a predetermined time?" In Figure 13-11, you can see both human actors (Customer, Cashier, and so on) and nonhuman actors (Google Maps, for example).

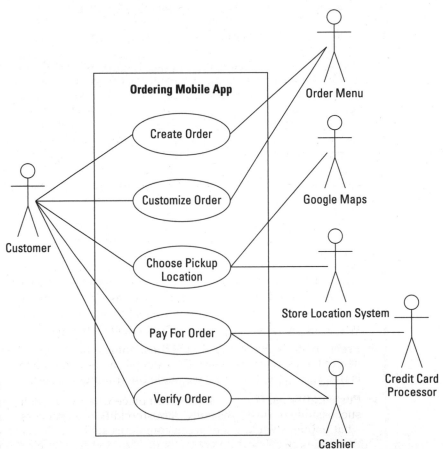

Figure 13-11:
A use case
diagram.

Illustration by Wiley, Composition Services Graphics

Because actors can be people or systems, label them by their roles rather than their specific names.

4. **Connect the actors to the use cases with the association line.**

   This line indicates which actors interact with which use cases. Anywhere an association line crosses the automation boundary, you need an interface — that is, a way for the user to communicate with the operating system. Make note of these interfaces because you have to address each one when designing the solution.

5. **Review the completed use case diagram with stakeholders to get their validation.**

   Better yet, have them participate interactively as you create the diagram.

The text: Use case description

The use case description is a written account of the sequence of steps performed by an actor to accomplish a complete business transaction. It's initiated by an actor, provides value to that actor, and is a goal of the actor working in that system. In Figure 13-12, you see a use case description that clearly documents how a student manager approves a training request from a student worker.

Most use case descriptions include the following elements at a minimum:

- ✔ **Title:** The title communicates the goal of the use case. In the example shown in Figure 13-12, the Register Student (the title) use case's goal is for the student to be able to register for a class.

- ✔ **Actors:** These folks are the people or systems who interact with the use case. Some people writing use cases also break down the actors by level within the use case: *primary* (the actor who starts the use case; in Figure 13-12, it's Student), *secondary* (the one who interacts with the use case — Student Manager in Figure 13-12), and even *off-stage* (those who don't interact directly with the use case but are involved from a business rule perspective — perhaps the department head who is requiring the student to take the training in Figure 13-12).

- ✔ **Preconditions:** *Preconditions* are those things that need to be in place before the use case can start. For example, a precondition for Figure 13-12 is that the student has to have made the training request.

- ✔ **Postconditions:** *Postconditions* are in place when you finish the use case successfully or unsuccessfully. A postcondition on success indicates what happens when the process completes successfully. A postcondition on failure is the opposite; it specifies what happens when the process doesn't complete successfully.

Primary Path

▼ 1. **Student Manager** clicks on the embedded hyperlink in the Training approval email.

2. **Registration System** navigates the **Student Manager** to the "My Training Approvals" page containing the **Student's** TRAINING-REQUEST.

▼ 3. **Student Manager** reviews the request and approves the TRAINING-REQUEST.

4. **Registration System** records the date and time of the approval, and sends notification to the **Student.**

5. ⊙ **Use Case ends with Success.**

Alternate Paths

1a. **Student Manager finds approvals on the My Training Approvals page**

1. **Student Manager** searches through the log to find a particular TRAINING-REQUEST.

➡ 2. **Registration System** chooses the desired TRAINING-REQUEST.

3. ➡ **Continue from step 2. of Primary Path.**

3a. **Student Manager denies training request**

1. **Student Manager** reviews the request and denies the TRAINING-REQUEST.

2. **Registration System** displays screen requiring DENIAL-REASON explaining why the TRAINING-REQUEST was denied.

3. **Registration System** sends notification to **Student** and copies **Student Manager** with the DENIAL-REASON.

4. ⊙ **Use Case ends with Failure.**

Figure 13-12:
A use case
description.

Illustration by Wiley, Composition Services Graphics

✔ **Path:** Also called *flow* or *story,* the *path* is the step-by-step action and interaction between the actor and the system. Paths come in three types:

- **Primary path (also known as *happy path* or *main flow*):** This route is the most commonly taken path to a successful conclusion. You can see this path documented on the top of Figure 13-12: The student manager clicks the link in the e-mail, navigates through the registration system to the training approvals page, sees the request, and approves it, triggering a confirmation e-mail to the student. It happens exactly as it should.

- **Alternate path:** This path is an alternate, less-frequented way to get to a successful conclusion. In Figure 13-12, the student manager is already logged in to the system and seeks out the pending training requests instead of accessing the system through an e-mail. After he's in, he follows the same steps as the primary path. It's a successful completion; he just didn't use the most common path to get to it.

- **Exception path:** This path is an alternate path that leads to an unsuccessful conclusion. An exception path related to Figure 13-12 can be that the student manager is unable to approve the request because she is no longer assigned as the student's manager. An error or exception message will be displayed indicating the reason.

You can add additional artifacts to the use case description to fully flesh it out:

✔ **Use case ID**: A unique identifier used for tracing.

✔ **Description**: A brief textual description of what the use case does. In Figure 13-12, a description would be "This use case description outlines the steps for a student manager to review a student request and approve or deny the request."

✔ **Created by**: The author of the use case.

✔ **Date Created and Revision History**: A chronology of the use case, which allows you to see how old the use case is (useful when doing document analysis — refer to Chapter 7),

✔ **Priority**: An indicator of this use case's importance, which is helpful in solution planning.

✔ **Frequency of Use**: An indicator of how often this use case is executed (also helpful in solution planning).

To actually put a use case description together, follow these steps:

1. **Figure out the starting point for the use case.**

   This becomes your precondition.

2. **Elicit from your stakeholders the steps you expect the user to take and what the system should do (the primary path).**

   For each step, document who performs an action and who performs a reaction (or the response).

3. **Go back and elicit the alternate ways of accomplishing the process.**

   Indicate where each alternate path starts. For instance, in the example shown in Figure 13-12, you see that alternate path 3a is taken rather than the primary path 3. Therefore, you need make sure the solution you build provides a way to deny the training request.

   Because the use case is built around the primary path, indicate how you navigate to the alternate and exception paths from that primary path. If you're using a tool to generate the use case description, it may prompt you for this information; otherwise, including a simple, "This alternate path starts after Step X of the primary path" will suffice.

4. **Document the exception flows and error messages until the description is complete.**

The finished product is a detailed list of steps the user performs and the expected system response.

Prototyping

A *prototype* is a model of a user interface (UI) in an automated system. It may be the user interface for a full system or a screen layout, report layout, or data entry form. The project team builds the prototype to demonstrate to stakeholders what the automated system will look like.

Consider the following points when designing a screen with any prototyping technique:

- ✔ **Think about the people who will be using the screen.** What are their education levels? Their skill levels? Their attitudes and motivations? Their stress levels on the job? A computer system you think is logical or useful may be confusing to someone who doesn't have the same level of expertise. How do you know what characteristics your users have? Elicit! If they're internal users, schedule an interview. If they're external customers, schedule a focus group. (You can read about these and other elicitation techniques in Chapter 7.)

  Paul was tasked with creating an application to manage and set international shipping prices. Previously, the actors set the prices by using certain formulas and then e-mailing the spreadsheets to everyone else on the project team. One way Paul's team got buy-in from the users (who didn't want to give up their spreadsheets) was to create a simulation that looked like a spreadsheet but was actually the computer application. Because the team knew the users well, it was able to craft a solution that addressed their needs and expectations.

- ✔ **Bring in the development team.** The development team has experience designing user interfaces and can be a big help. Some teams have a dedicated user experience professional. User experience professionals focus on high quality user interfaces all day long. Plus, getting the development team members' buy-in upfront (giving them a say in helping to design the UI) means they're less likely to try to change the solution when it actually gets coded. This strategy helps set expectations with the business stakeholders.

- ✔ **Remember that some prototypes are throwaways.** Prototypes are a great tool to discuss concepts and get agreement on the user experience, but the development team still has to completely create the system based on the drawing. For this reason, these drawings are sometimes called *throwaway prototypes*. (We discuss throwaway prototypes in more detail in Chapter 7).

When the proposed solution involves addition of online screens or creation of reports, business analysts (BAs) often create prototypes involving storyboards, simulations, or mockups:

✔ **Storyboards:** *Storyboards* are diagrams showing how the various screens of a system interconnect with one another. Stakeholders probably already have a vision of what they want the solution to be; with storyboards, you get to talk with stakeholders about the screens and how you move from one to the next. For each screen, you ask the users where they want to be able to navigate next. Figure 13-13 shows an example of a possible storyboard for an online shopping site.

✔ **Simulations:** *Simulations* such as the one in Figure 13-14 are creations of web pages that mimic the desired online functionality and give the users the feel of how the finished system will behave (for instance, the programmed simulation in Figure 13-14 will make an executed mockup like that displayed in Figure 13-15). Because the simulation looks and acts like their end solution, they'll get a much better experience. They can be *low-fidelity* (feels less like the real thing) or *high-fidelity* (feels very close to the real thing) — kind of like the difference between a non-retina screen and a retina screen.

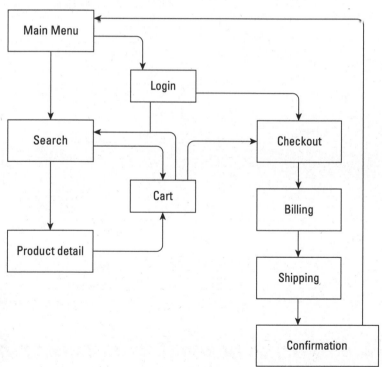

Figure 13-13:
A sample
storyboard.

Illustration by Wiley, Composition Services Graphics

Simulations enable stakeholders to confirm the solution and approve it. Although the simulation allows for users to interact with the controls and experience, it does take additional time for the BAs to create. Learning how to program simulations is a separate book (or training class) in itself; because it's so specialized, our aim here is simply to make sure you have a general awareness of them.

✔ **Mockups:** *Mockups* are drawings of a screen or report layout with its graphics, text boxes, buttons, menus, and options. Because mockups are a very common, versatile tool that you can use throughout the project without any specialized training, we walk you through them in detail in the next section.

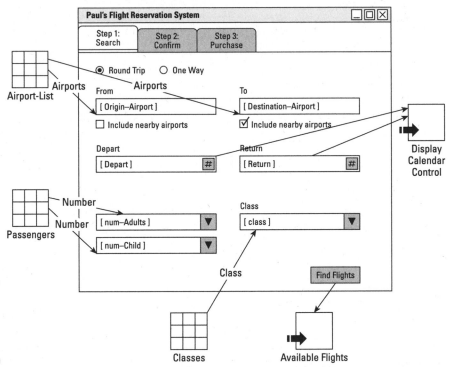

Figure 13-14:
A sample simulation program.

Illustration by Wiley, Composition Services Graphics

Familiarizing yourself with mockup basics

Mockups are sometimes referred to as *screenshots* or *wireframes*. They give you and the project team an idea of what the user interface solution will look like. When you create the mockup (whether electronically or by hand), you bring together the data requirements, process requirements, and business rules when designing the UI.

Because the mockup is only a visual representation, you still have to fully detail the requirements behind the screen in the data model or *data dictionary* (the collection of information that explains the meaning and relationships of data). You should detail the actor actions and interactions in a use case, which we cover earlier in the chapter.

Mockups make stakeholders very happy because they love seeing a picture of the solution. Figure 13-15 illustrates a mockup of a flight reservation system.

Paul's Flight Reservation System   ⬓ ▢ ⊠

| Step 1:
Search | Step 2:
Confirm | Step 3:
Purchase |

◉ Round Trip   ○ One Way

From
[   ]

To
[   ]

☐ Include nearby airports

☑ Include nearby airports

Depart
[mm/dd/yyyy   #]

Return
[mm/dd/yyyy   #]

Class

[1 adult   ▼]

[Economy   ▼]

[0 children   ▼]

[Find Flights]

Figure 13-15:
Example of
a mockup.

Illustration by Wiley, Composition Services Graphics

You can use mockups at any point in the project lifecycle where a visual rendering is required for a stakeholder to understand or validate the solution, such as the following scenarios:

➤ When designing (or redesigning) a user interface

➤ When you want to give a stakeholder a feel for the end solution you're proposing

As we note earlier, an advantage of using mockups is that stakeholders love them. However, mockups are limited. They aren't a substitute for understanding the business problem or opportunity, so be cautious about starting analysis based on a mockup.

Creating mockups

Not all BAs are screen designers, so you may find creating a mockup a bit challenging. In fact, a field of study called *human factors engineering* concentrates entirely on the interface between man and machine, which clues you in to how complex it can be.

If you can't consult a human factors engineer, use the best-in-class applications as your base. For example, if you're designing a music download application, look to Apple's iTunes as a best-in-class application.

Here's how you go about creating a mockup:

1. **Ask "why" before you even start creating a mockup.**

   That the business requested a new screen or a new interface means that it is experiencing a problem that prevents it from doing the business or wants to be able to take advantage of an opportunity. You have to figure that purpose out.

2. **Determine the number of mockups you have to create by identifying where you need interfaces.**

   Here are some guidelines:

   • **Look at your use case diagram.** Every association line that crosses the automation boundary in the diagram requires a user interface that you have to mockup.

   • **Reference your workflow diagrams.** Tasks that require a user to perform them within the system require a user interface.

   • **Look at your storyboard.** Each rectangle on the storyboard is a screen.

   Each of these documents is covered in earlier sections within this chapter.

3. **Reference your entity tables or workflow diagrams to find the data you need on the screen of the interface.**

   This info may be data displayed to the user or entered by the user when interacting with the system.

4. **Draw a rough mockup on paper, in Visio, on a whiteboard, or with a specialized tool.**

   Talk with the application development team about screen interface standards, feasibility, and design ideas.

5. Revise the design based on feedback from the stakeholders.

At this point, you need to complete the *UI specification,* which is a set of two tables — field descriptions and screen controls — that explains the details of the appearance of the screen and how everything interacts and behaves with the user, as shown in Tables 13-1 and 13-2.

Table 13-1	Field Descriptions
Screen Detail	*Description*
Name	The name of the item as it appears on the screen
Type	The type of the on-screen item, such a label, selection box, or drop-down list
Source	Where the data comes from (info that may identify other interfaces)
Description	A description of the field
Length	How long the data field is (used to compare interfaces to see whether data is getting cut off or whether a piece of data can fit within the field)
Defaults	What the field defaults to if no information is given
Req./opt.	Whether the field is required or optional
Rules	The business rules that surround this field (may be an actual rule or a cross-reference to a rule table elsewhere in the requirements package)

Table 13-2	Screen Controls
Screen Detail	*Description*
Name	Name of the control as documented on the screen (enables a cross-reference to what is on the mockup)
Control type	What the control is (radio button, button, text box, hyperlink, and so on) and how it behaves
Function description	What happens when users interact (click on a hyperlink, hover over a button, or whatever) with this control (provides detail information about the experience users will have with the system)
Enable/disable	When the button is enabled (whether it's always available to be clicked on or only enables after certain fields are filled in)
Rules	The business rules surrounding this field (may be an actual rule or a cross-reference to a rule table elsewhere in the requirements package)

Keeping It Brief with User Stories

A *user story* is a structured way to briefly describe functionality or features that will be valuable to a customer or user of a system or software solution. It's a lighter way to provide structure around the requirements and documentation (a particular plus in the agile development method — see Chapter 11 for an overview).

User stories have certain characteristics:

- ✔ **They're very brief, to the point, and written on an index card.**

- ✔ **They serve as a reminder for further requirements conversations to define details.** The extensive details for each user story will be fleshed out during development, and the user story card serves as a trigger and focal point for the conversation.

- ✔ **Test cases provide confirmation that the requirement is complete and verifiable.** We discuss user story confirmation in the later section "Confirming user stories."

- ✔ **They can be estimated.** The user story has to ride that fine line between being high-level and detailed enough that the project team can determine how long it will take to develop and being small enough to fit into a project's *iteration* (periods of time in which value is delivered to the customer). For instance, a user story of "write a book" is too large to fit into an iteration of two weeks, but you can break that down into "write Chapter 1," "write Chapter 2," and so on. We actually did that for this book!

User stories are helpful in cases like the following:

- ✔ When you want to get an idea of the users, their goal, and the value they'll receive from this goal

- ✔ When the team is able to operate without formalized documents

Advantages of using this technique include

- ✔ It's a quick way to get down and organize/prioritize the user, the goal, and the value of each requirement.

- ✔ It's a very concise description of what the users want to do.

- ✔ It's easy to transition into testing that cases are verifiable.

Of course, user stories have disadvantages as well, the main one being that, by their very nature, they're incomplete. Allow a placeholder for further definition.

Creating user stories

To create a concise (and useful) user story, you want to use a structured approach. The structure will help you identify who is getting the goal, what goal they need to realize, and why they're looking for this value. Two of the most common formats are

- ✔ "As a <user>, I want <goal> so that <value>"
- ✔ "In order to <value realized> as a <user>, I want <goal>."

The second structure starts with the value realized, so you may try using that if you're having difficulty defining a reason why the user story exists. Here is a simple example you may elicit from a marketing user: "In order for attendees to use my presentation as a reference before and/or after my presentation (the value) as a presenter (user), I want to provide a copy of my presentation slides or handouts to the attendees (goal)."

Here's how you create a user story:

1. **Determine who is requesting this functionality**.

   This information is a user role rather than the name of a specific person and goes in the <user> placeholder.

2. **Determine what they want.**

   This information is the expectation of what the user in Step 1 wants; plug it into the <goal> section of the user story structure.

3. **Determine the benefit to the user**.

   This information is the value the user will realize when the solution is put into place. It goes in place of <value>/<value realized>.

4. **Post the user story to the *project backlog* (the list of all the desired features and functions).**

After the user stories are on the project backlog, they'll be estimated as part of agile planning. This topic is covered in depth in *Agile Project Management For Dummies,* by Mark C. Layton (Wiley); and *Stand Back and Deliver,* by Pollyanna Pixton, Niel Nickolaisen, Todd Little, and Kent McDonald (Addison-Wesley Professional).

Confirming user stories

As we note earlier, you need additional information added to the user story to know when the story has been properly satisfied. This extra info provides both a starting point for unit tests and details through examples.

Just like the user story itself had a structure, so does the confirmation: "Given <precondition> when <action>, then <expected result>." The test cases (more on them in Chapter 14) then determine whether these parameters are met. For example,

- ✔ "Given *no presentation files have been associated with the presentation* when *user associates a file less than 5MB in size,* then *the file is uploaded, and the user gets a confirmation message of success.*"

- ✔ Given *no presentation files have been associated with the presentation* when *user associates a file greater than 5MB in size,* then *the system notifies the user that the file is too large to be uploaded.*"

You can test either of these conditions to ensure it meets the expected functionality.

You don't have to create all the confirmations right upfront when you create all the user stories. You can detail the test cases in a *just-in-time* fashion, when you pull them into an iteration for development.

Chapter 14

Verifying and Validating Solutions

· ·

· ·

*W*hen you bring your car into the repair shop to have a mysterious rattle in the steering wheel taken care of, one of the first things you probably do when you pick it up is to check to make sure the rattle is no longer there. If you still feel the rockin' and rollin', you know that it wasn't fixed correctly, and you turn it back over to the mechanic so she can try again. As a business analysis professional, you do the same thing with your projects: You validate that your implemented solution actually solves the original business problem(s) you identified as requirements in the beginning of your project, and you verify that it features a functionally sound design that performs as it should.

In this chapter, we clarify how verification and validation differ and explain the ins and outs of each activity. We also show you how to create test cases and a verification and validation plan and put together review requirements sessions.

Although verifying and validating mostly apply to technology-based projects, you can apply some of these techniques to non-technology–based projects as well.

Getting a Handle on Testing Basics

The purpose of testing is to make sure that what you captured from the business in terms of a requirement is what was built and ultimately what provides value to the business. During testing, you want to find defects or discrepancies at different stages before you hand the solution over to the business. The following sections clue you in on some important terminology distinctions and clarify where testing should fit into your project.

Differentiating between verification and validation

Believe it or not, verification and validation aren't the same thing. *Verification* is about making sure the design of the solution itself is well engineered and error-free. *Validation* is about ensuring that your final solution actually addresses the problems you set out to solve (the requirements). In other words, verification asks, "Did we build the system right?", and validation asks, "Did we build the right system?" You can complete validation and verification in any order, and you may even find yourself doing parts of each throughout the entire project.

In Figure 14-1, you can see how verification and validation work together. At each stage, you make sure that you've met the requirements of the previous stage. Generally, the cycle starts when the business requests a solution. Then you and the project team verify that the deliverables appropriately get to the root cause and solve the right problem. After the solution has been designed, you do more testing to verify that what you're delivering matches what was built. Finally, the business validates that you and the team built the right thing by actually using it.

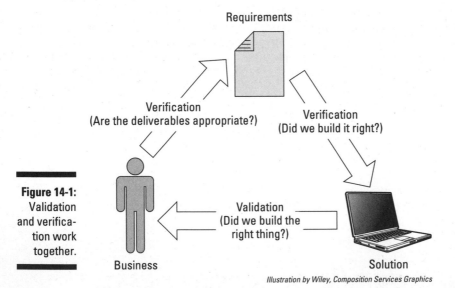

Figure 14-1: Validation and verification work together.

Illustration by Wiley, Composition Services Graphics

Making testing an ongoing activity

The simplest answer to the question "When do we begin testing?" is "As you launch the project!" You want to think about testing as soon as the project gets started so that you begin thinking about how you're going to test, what you're going to test, and so on. Another reason to think early on about testing: You can't "test in" quality; you can only build it in. That is, after the product is built, you can't add quality without returning to the build stage. Testing only verifies whether the solution was built with quality.

Figure 14-2 demonstrates exactly how testing becomes active the minute you begin and stays that way throughout the software development life cycle (SDLC) phases. When you're in the planning and scoping phases, you should start the testing effort by adding the time you need to fully test to the project plan. Continue test planning throughout the course of the project.

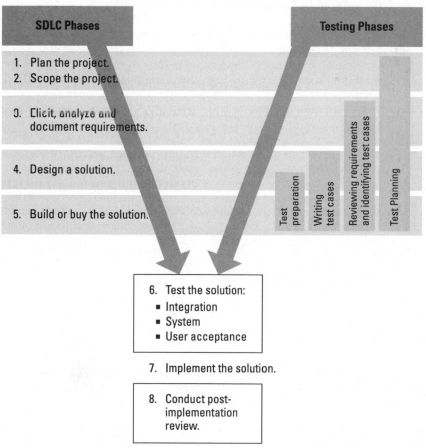

SDLC Phases

1. Plan the project.
2. Scope the project.

3. Elicit, analyze and document requirements.

4. Design a solution.

5. Build or buy the solution.

Testing Phases

Test preparation

Writing test cases

Reviewing requirements and identifying test cases

Test Planning

6. Test the solution:
   - Integration
   - System
   - User acceptance

7. Implement the solution.

8. Conduct post-implementation review.

Figure 14-2:
Testing throughout the project phases.

Illustration by Wiley, Composition Services Graphics

When the project moves into the requirements elicitation phases, the testing team validates requirements to ensure their testability and starts to identify test cases. When the solution is being designed, those performing the testing are off writing test cases. As the solution is being built or bought, the testers should be preparing for the test.

Where the two *V* paths come together, the two efforts intersect and the testing actually begins. After that, you *roll out* (implement) the system and then conduct the post-implementation review, representing the final validation.

The earlier you're involved with testing, the more defects you weed out and the bigger impact you have on build-in quality.

Verification Testing: Confirming You Built the System Right

Verification is what most people think of when they hear the word *testing* — it's the process of testing whether a solution does what it's designed to do. During verification, the testing team (which may consist of developers, quality assurance [QA] people, and some business analysts [BAs]) put the software through its paces to both confirm that it operates as expected and ensure that it conforms to the design specifications laid out earlier in the project.

Verification testing includes four phases — one pretest phase and three phases of actual testing — and each one has its own objective, participants, activities, and deliverables. Understanding the phases and the language that surround this activity helps you communicate effectively with those performing the testing, so we break down the component tests in the sections that follow.

Smoke test

Don't worry; the smoke test has been determined not to be hazardous to your health. Also called a *build verification* test, a *smoke test* is a pretest that determines whether full testing can even begin in the first place. It reveals any simple failures in the solution that may prevent you from executing the tests in the next three phases. Some project teams may link this test to unit testing (which we mention in the next section). The testing team can conduct a smoke test, using automated or manual tools.

Unit test

The *unit test* is the first actual phase of testing. It involves testing each *unit* (a small piece of code that can be independently compiled, such as an individual program or module) of the system as a stand-alone test. An example of a unit in Figure 14-3 is "Place Order." The development team (not the BA) generally performs line-by-line testing of both function and structure to find bugs within the unit before any other tests are done.

Although unit tests are performed by the development team, you should have another group (other than the development team) test in order to ensure unbiased testing.

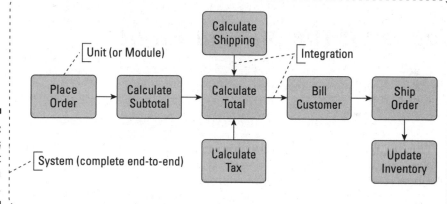

Figure 14-3: A unit is tested first by using a unit test.

Illustration by Wiley, Composition Services Graphics

Integration test

The second phase of testing, the *integration test,* ensures the individual units are playing nice in the sandbox and can actually work together. These individual units working together can be considered a subsystem (a piece of the overall system) or just linked units. The objective of this test is to find problems with how the components of the system work together, and it tests the validity of the software architecture design. The development team generally performs the integration test, although BAs may help by providing test cases and reviewing test results. (We talk about how to create test cases later in this chapter.)

Keep the following in mind about integration testing:

✔ Units aren't included in integration testing until they've successfully passed unit testing.

✔ Sometimes integration tests can have multiple levels of integration. That is, sometimes several subsystems are brought together and tested, and then those sub-systems are integrated with larger sub-systems.

Want to know how effective having independent testers can be? A BA got a call from a user who was experiencing a problem with submitting a query in a just-released application. Even after the BA walked the user through the process over the phone, the problem was still occurring, so the BA paid the user a visit. When the BA watched the user perform the task, the problem was instantly apparent. The user submitted the query by clicking on the Submit Query button with a mouse rather than pressing the Enter key on the keyboard. The project team that tested the solution was so used to only pressing the Enter key to submit the query that team members never realized they forgot to program the button, an issue that even made it through testing! Having that independent user test the system prior to release would've prevented that error.

System test

This test is the testing phase you're most involved in as a BA. The objective of the *system test* is to find problems with how the system meets the users' needs. You run this test through the entire built system from end to end, auditing all units and integrations from a linear perspective. It's the last chance for you and the project team to verify the product before it gets turned over to the users for a *user acceptance test* (see the later section "Getting users involved with a user acceptance test"). It also confirms whether the software meets the original requirements, answering the "Did we build it right?" question. (Think about how much time you spend eliciting and documenting the requirements; you don't want to waste that time, right?)

During system testing, the testing team runs quite a few tests to make sure what you turn over to the users is defect-free. As a BA, you may be involved in these testing efforts, so you want to know the lingo explained in the following sections.

Requirements validation test

This test verifies the system logic to ensure it supports the analysis requirements. Even though this work seems like it should be part of validation, it actually gets at the "Did we build it right?" question. In other words, you're verifying whether you built your system according to what your requirements dictate.

Regression test

This test is basically a retest (*regression* refers to going backward). You use this test to ensure that the changes you made to the system as part of your solution don't break what was already working. Regression usually impacts more than one program and requires more than one test.

When thinking about regression tests, you need to know what applications are impacted by the solution so you can test those applications to make sure nothing has changed. This point is where a traceability matrix (see Chapter 12) can come in handy. Also, the interface analysis elicitation technique in Chapter 7 can help you determine additional systems that the change may impact.

Dynamic test

In a *dynamic test,* you test the software to see how it performs when run under different circumstances and check the physical response from the system as those variables change with time. This test term is linked with three different types of tests:

- ✔ **Performance test:** This test measures how fast the system can complete a function. To determine whether the test passes or doesn't pass, refer to the nonfunctional requirements in your documentation that states what the response time should be.

- ✔ **Stress test:** No, this test doesn't measure how well you function on Monday morning without coffee. The *stress test* seeks to push software to its limits in terms of users, rate of input, and the speed of the response. If you have only 3 users, you probably can do this test manually; however, if you have to ensure that 2,500 users can be logged in at the same time, you're probably going to have to use an automated tool to *load* the system (simulating the stress to the system) with the number of users.

  On September 11, 2001, trying to get to CNN.com was difficult — the page simply stopped loading. Why? CNN.com experienced real-world stress on the system when millions of people tried to obtain information on the terrorist attacks in New York City. Having that many people try to access the same information at once was probably an exception condition, but it does show the impact on performance when system stress occurs.

- ✔ **Volume test:** This test checks high-volume transactions to verify the software can handle all growth projections.

Security test

You don't want the wrong people to do the wrong things in your system, right? Of course not. *Security testing* ensures that unauthorized users can't gain access to confidential data. It also certifies that authorized users can effectively complete their tasks. A good diagram to determine which users can perform which functions is a use case diagram (Chapter 13) or a security matrix (a diagram that shows which users may access which functions).

Installation test

This test makes sure the software installs on the machine as you expect it to with no problems in the installation process. When testing, make sure the requirements for the system you're installing on are stated.

Configuration test

This test determines how well the product works with different environmental configurations. For example, if your requirements state the product requires a PC or Mac with Internet Explorer's latest version or Safari, you need to test installation with both operating systems (OS) and with the configuration of the browsers on both those systems. In fact, you see configuration all the time on products' system requirements. When a software manufacturer advertises its product as working with that configuration, you can believe the company has gone through configuration tests to ensure the product meets those specifications.

Usability test

A usability test is really a validation test; however, it's sometimes done during system test time, depending on the visibility of the solution. If it's a website that millions of customers will use or see, chances are you want to bring in usability engineers to build in usability instead of waiting to test it at the end of the project. Although your project may not be a multimillion dollar release, you still need to ensure that users will be able to effectively use it.

Validation Testing: Making Sure You Built the Right System

Validation testing is your review of your project deliverables to ensure they

- ✔ Meet the project objectives or requirements and the overall needs of the organization
- ✔ Are within the project scope
- ✔ Conform to organizational standards and strategies

Of the eight phases that comprise the SDLC (shown in Figure 14-4), six of them are validation phases. These phases, circled in Figure 14-4, are where you review and inspect the deliverables to confirm that you're producing something that ultimately either solves a problem or allows the business to take advantage of an opportunity.

When you get to the phases that require you to perform validation testing, you perform three types of tests: a usability test, a user acceptance test, and a post-implementation user assessment.

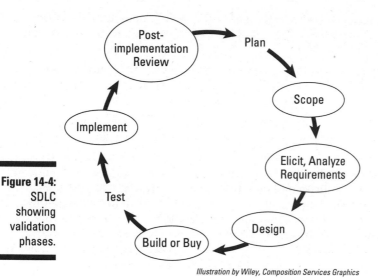

Figure 14-4:
SDLC
showing
validation
phases.

Illustration by Wiley, Composition Services Graphics

Utilizing a usability test

Usability testing occurs in the design phase. Its purpose is to show you and the project team how well the users can really use the system. You can follow ten usability heuristics to build proper usability into your design. (*Heuristics* is basically a fancy word for a hands-on learning process in which users educate themselves as they go through the program.) Consider these items more as rules of thumb than documented guidelines. The following list is based on Jakob Nielsen's ten usability heuristics:

- **Make the system status visible.** Let users know where they are within the program, keep them informed about what's going on, and give them feedback in a reasonable amount of time. A good example is the status bar that shows feedback and progress as you're downloading a program.

  How to comply: Make sure the solution continually gives the user feedback.

- **Speak in the user's terms.** Make sure the system uses the language users are familiar with; avoid system-oriented terms. Think of how Microsoft Office uses terms like *file* and *folder* rather than *electronic artifact* and *directory*, or how e-shopping sites still tell you to add your product into your "shopping cart," just like in the real world.

  How to comply: When designing a system, think about how your user would accomplish a task in the real world, and follow that convention.

- **Make backtracking easy.** When users trigger an unwanted system response, help them by providing a clearly marked way to get out. Also give them a chance for a do-over by including redo functions.

How to comply: Follow Microsoft's convention of including an undo button. Place exits in the upper-right of the screen, which has become a standard convention.

✔ **Be consistent.** Use the same terms consistently. Don't make users guess whether different words, situations, or actions mean the same thing. For example, don't interchange terms such as *save* and *store*.

How to comply: Pick one term from interchangeable options and stick with it. Make sure the term is clearly defined in your glossary and help texts.

✔ **Prevent errors.** Build in processes that stop errors from happening in the first place. Instead of merely informing a user she has misspelled the state she's shipping goods to, for example, give her a defined list from which to choose. Shipping company UPS even validates (there's that word again) the address you've entered to make sure it's a valid address. The company is preventing a delivery mistake by not allowing the user to enter an incorrect address in the first place.

How to comply: Build in processes that validate information and don't allow incorrect information to come into the system.

✔ **Use recognition rather than recall.** Don't make the user memorize a bunch of stuff; make objects, actions, and options visible. Think of how the Microsoft Office suite of products uses icons that are always displayed and shortcut menus that pop up with help for shortcut keys.

How to comply: Keep the most-used tasks and processes in front of the user instead of having her memorize how to get to them; don't bury processes multiple mouse-clicks deep. If you see users with lots of navigation sticky notes attached to their monitors, that may be a clue that the solution violates this rule.

✔ **Don't slow down the expert users.** After time with the system, a user often becomes an expert user. Give these users ways to accelerate their work by allowing them to tailor frequent actions.

How to comply: Let users program macros in the system to customize their work and perform it faster; give them shortcuts they can access when they become experts.

✔ **Display a simple user interface.** Show only the information needed at that time. Consider Google. For all the complex things the site does, the main screen is a minimalist design: just one text box and two buttons (oh, and that logo that changes with special events).

How to comply: Show only the information that's necessary to accomplish a particular transaction. If it's more than one page long, think about splitting it up into multiple steps.

✔ **Make help functions easily accessible.** Users need to know how to access good help when they need it. Make sure errors are expressed in plain language that indicates what triggered the error and how users can correct it.

How to comply: Tell users what they did wrong and how they can self-correct. For instance, suppose someone signs up online for a wine-of-the-month club and chooses a state that doesn't allow wine shipments. Instead of the error box saying, "You've made an invalid selection, please try again," it should state, "You've chosen a state that doesn't allow incoming shipments of wine. Please choose another state or select a non-alcoholic product."

Using software developer error codes may help the developer when performing unit testing, but they're of little to no value for the user. For instance, the error message "You've triggered an ORA-6439 Error. Contact System Administrator" means nothing to an end-user and can even create additional confusion. Telling her instead that "You've entered your flight dates/times out of order. Please change your dates so you leave before you return" not only scores you points because you helped her out but also prevents a call to your company's customer service department.

In the early stages of your project, define what characteristics your users have, including skill level, previous experience, and education level. During usability testing, select testers who match your demographics to work through the system to see whether it has good usability among your target audience.

Getting users involved with a user acceptance test

The purpose of the *user acceptance test* (UAT) is to show adherence to the project objectives, not to find bugs or software defects. It's the final phase of testing, where users submit the software to real-world scenarios to verify it meets their needs.

Follow these steps to perform the user acceptance test:

1. **Get an agreement with the customer/user on the test parameters.**

   Make sure you and the user are on the same page regarding the following items:

   - **Set of acceptance test cases and pass criteria:** As the BA, you typically assist by providing test cases and test scenarios to the people performing the UAT.

   - **Test environment:** You may want to test off-site or at a remote location if that environment is the real world in which the users operate. For example, remote salespeople are often in their cars or at Wi-Fi hotspots, so testing a solution for them may need to occur in one of those locations.

- **Test procedures:** Confirm how users are going to test through the conditions.

2. **Turn over any information about known defects in the system.**

   This step is beneficial for two reasons. One, your being upfront and honest is better than the users finding out on their own. Two, you can have a mitigation plan and explain to users when they'll have a fix for the defects.

3. **Let the users test the system according to the plan.**

4. **Have users sign off on the system, thus accepting it.**

   Getting users to sign off on the user acceptance test not only indicates acceptance; it's also a major project milestone.

Receiving feedback with a post-implementation user assessment

Although you as the BA should accept feedback about a system any time it's given, you should also perform an official post-implementation assessment after the users have gotten training on and used the product for some time — usually about 3 to 6 months after implementation.

The real test of whether a system successfully meets its objective is whether the users are still using it several months after implementation. If so, the solution was successful and is meeting the need. If not, the process broke down somewhere, or the solution otherwise failed to meet that need.

Here's how to perform a post-implementation user assessment:

1. **After the initial 3-to-6-month usage period, schedule a session with the business users to conduct a post-implementation assessment.**

2. **During the session, elicit feedback either through observation or a facilitated workshop.**

   Get the users talking. Pay particular attention to their superlatives and get them to explain those statements. If they say the system is useless, drill down into why it's useless. If they tell you it's always crashing, ask them what actions they perform right before it crashes. After all, you want to understand their concerns because they can turn those into future requirements! (You can find details on the observation and facilitated workshop techniques in Chapter 7.) *Note:* Some of your observations may be the metrics (measurements of time, effort, or quality) surrounding a process. Make sure you're familiar with the expectation and come prepared with a stopwatch!

3. **Record your observations and users' answers to your questions.**

4. **Provide the participants with your documentation and have them validate your information.**

5. **Make final changes based on users' feedback.**

6. **If necessary, make recommendations for the next steps, which may be a new project, a maintenance fix, or a change in the process.**

The post-implementation assessment isn't a complaint session ("the system is horrible") or a *lessons-learned* session (which concentrates on how you can improve the project processes). It's designed to be a report-back of the product and whether/how well the product meets the business needs.

Preparing for the Test

Testers use two main documents when designing the test documentation: the *requirements package* (what the BA creates) and the *project plan* (what the project manager [PM] creates). The requirements package details what needs to be tested; the project plan tells you how much time you have to test it. In Figure 14-5, you see how those two documents feed into the creation of the *test plan.* Coming out of the test plan document, you have multiple test cases designed to verify the system, and each one of those test cases has one or more procedures designed to prove compliance.

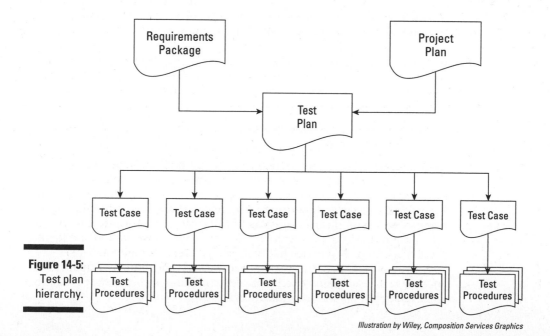

Figure 14-5:
Test plan
hierarchy.

Illustration by Wiley, Composition Services Graphics

Creating test cases

Test cases are step-by-step instructions, including specific inputs and conditions, that testers follow to validate the system's functionality. They also include the expected result. You and the project team can create hundreds — if not thousands — of test cases when supporting the testing effort. The larger the project, the more test cases you create. To create a test case, do the following:

1. **Identify the test items.**

   Read through whatever project artifacts you have available to identify the test items. These documents may include the scope diagram, use case diagram, user stories, workflow diagrams, prototypes, and so on. If you're working on a program to search for airfares, the use case diagram may tell you that passengers are able to search for flights, which means you want to be able to test search for flights to ensure passengers can do it.

2. **Create the input and output specifications.**

   Use the artifacts you reviewed in Step 1 to determine what data you need to put into the test and what the expected result is. When searching for flights, what inputs do you need to have in order to get the output? The answer may be something like the flight dates and times and the origin and destination locations.

3. **Define the environmental needs.**

   These items come primarily from your nonfunctional requirements (see Chapter 5). For example, you may have a configuration requirement that states the solution must be able to run on iOS 5.1 and iOS 6. So you create a test case to operate under the iOS 5.1 environment and another for the iOS 6 environment. You may also need to consider whether this new flight searching system works only on regular computers or is being rolled out as an app for tablets?

4. **List any special procedural requirements.**

   If you need to process anything special, such as if you have to go outside the test to set something up prior to continuing the test procedure, list that here. For example, suppose the interface with the master list of all flights isn't working; in that case, you fake the test by mocking up flights in the master flight database between the steps for submitting the flights and receiving the results.

5. **Document any inter-case dependencies.**

   List any other test cases or other artifacts that the test case must include to be complete. The flight searching system may contain dependencies on the list of airports and airlines in the system.

6. List any approvals.

Include who needs to approve the test case.

Test case writing is an *iterative* process, which means you go through it one piece at a time. Walk through the steps with one artifact (say, the use case diagram) and get the information out of that. Then, go through the six steps again with another artifact (such as the prototype) to uncover more test cases. If you're having a hard time uncovering test cases for any requirements or artifacts it may be because they aren't written clearly or in enough detail. You may have to go back and redefine the requirement.

When creating test cases, think of both the positive (the expected value) and the negative (a value that leads to an exception condition) test conditions.

Putting together the verification and validation plan

The *verification and validation test plan* describes how a software product will be tested. Writing one can be a challenge if you've never done it before. But have no fear — you can create a great test plan by including the following sections.

Introduction

Start off by explaining the test and describing the objective of the project. Remember to keep it short like your elevator speech (that is, as though you could deliver it by the time an elevator ride ends). Make sure to include any references to other documents here. For example, if you're creating a system to track hotel stays for a frequent traveler, you'd state that here.

Test items

Define the items — those documents that explain the functionality of the system — that you're going to test. They may be the requirements documentation or design documentation. Your company may have different names for these documents, but no matter their names, what you test comes out of these documents. The tests surrounding a frequent traveler points program would be derived, for example, from the business requirements document and the functional specification document.

Features to be tested

List the software features you're going to test. As you think about this list, think about the data you need in order to test. If one of the features you're testing is a frequent traveler being able to view her historical stays, you need login information, date range options, and hotel stay details such as number of nights, location, and dates. For example, a feature tested would be to reward 50 percent bonus points to a Platinum Elite traveler.

Features not to be tested

Including features you aren't going to test seems counterintuitive in a testing document, but doing so immediately sets up appropriate expectations; users won't have any misconceptions about what they'll have tested. A feature that likely would not be tested in the frequent traveler program (perhaps to the surprise of stakeholders) is integration with billing.

Test data necessary

You have to figure out not only what tests you need to run but also what data needs to be in place for the test. This step is important. *Remember:* A test has planned inputs, so you need to think about what the expected results are based on those inputs.

Here's how to find test data:

1. **Look through the test cases to see which requirements you're going to test.**

2. **For each one of those test cases, figure out what the expected result is.**

3. **Determine what data you need to input in order to get the expected result.**

4. **Document the data needed in order to produce the expected result.**

For instance, suppose you're working on a project in which you need to calculate frequent traveler's level within the program based on the number of nights stayed in hotels. You organize the data values as the input specifications, as shown in Figure 14-6, so that you're able to test the test cases.

Test Case	Expected Result
Purchase a product that is taxed	Product should have the sales tax calculated and added to it at purchase time.
Purchase a product that is not taxed	Order is calculated without sales tax being applied to the product.
Purchase multiple items, some taxed, some not taxed	Sales tax should only be applied to the taxed items on the order.

Figure 14-6: Document the data you need inputted before testing.

Illustration by Wiley, Composition Services Graphics

Approach

This section explains the approach the testing team is going to use to verify the requirements. It states any testing cycles and tools, manual and automatic. In the frequent traveler example, the system test is made up of three system test cycles: 3 weeks for the first one, 2 weeks for the second, and 1 week for the third.

Item pass/fail criteria

Have a clear definition of what makes a test case pass and what makes it fail. Defining this guideline upfront in the validation and verification plan can prevent confusion later. An example of pass criteria may be completing all test procedure steps until no unresolved defects remain that prevent you from moving forward in your testing process (referred to as *showstoppers*).

Suspension and resumption criteria

If you've ever been involved with testing before, you know that sometimes your tests reveal showstoppers. This section of the plan details how you handle these defects in your testing process, such as the fact that you'll stop the testing if a test procedure can't be run and resume when a new software build is provided.

Testing tasks

The section is a listing of what tasks, such as defining testing schedules and creating test cases, need to be completed in order to carry out the testing. The results of the testing tasks will be the test plan, test design specifications, test cases, test procedures, test logs, test results, and defect logs.

Environmental needs

In this section, you detail the specific environment in which the test is to be conducted — perhaps in a test lab with a specific machine setup or on an assembly line — to show how the solution works in the environment. Look to the nonfunctional requirements to determine test needs such as volume test, stress test, configuration test, and so on.

Knowing where the tests are conducted is important to developing the test plan. Consider the following questions when creating the test plan:

- ✔ Is the test in a lab? What are the lab conditions?

- ✔ Do any special environmental concerns affect the test? Can you simulate them if they're not in the actual test area? For instance, if the application is being rolled out to a subzero environment, are you testing in that environment or in a lab with regular temperatures? (Some may say computer labs are cold enough as it is!)

✔ Are the tests in a central area accessible to the testers, or do testers have to travel to test the system?

Document your findings in the test plan so everyone who is involved in the test knows the location and can plan appropriately. For example, in the frequent traveler program, you must be able to test registering a traveler into the frequent traveler program.

Responsibilities

Who performs which set of tasks? For example, maybe the senior QA analyst creates the test plan and a QA analyst creates the test cases with input from the BA.

You need to understand who's involved in testing so you can plan appropriately for the test. Here are some questions and concerns to explore:

✔ What kind of experience do the testers have with the project?

✔ What kind of experience do they have with the system?

✔ Do they need to be trained prior to testing? If so, you know you need to add time into the project plan.

✔ Are the testers independent? If not, can they avoid making assumptions (which is a risk because they built the system)?

✔ Do they have testing criteria? Are they looking to you to create testing scenarios and test cases?

✔ Are they located on-site? Are they traveling? How does that travel affect the project plan?

✔ What time commitments do they have outside of the project? Is it 10 percent or 50 percent?

If you're managing other BAs and need to move some of your people around, testing is one of the best times to do so. You get a resource that can perform testing independently, and moving a BA into a new business area to support a new application gets her to understand the new system quickly, which builds skills for the future.

Staffing and training needs

If the testers need to be trained on the system, you include that information here. If you need additional staff or have to requisition staff from the QA pool, you need to mention that in this section as well.

Schedule

Talk about the dates for the tests, as well as any testing cycles and when they may take place. If this information is detailed in a project plan, you may want to just include a hyperlink or reference to the project plan to avoid getting dates out of sync.

Single-source it! Whenever you have a chance to, you should provide one source for the information. For instance, the more you manually document the same information in multiple places, the greater chance that when updates happen, one of those documents will be out of sync with the rest. Figure out which document the data should reside in and then link to that document from the others.

Risks and contingencies

Outline any risks associated with the test and include any contingencies that address them. Similar to the schedule, if these testing risks are located in a different document, referencing that document here is fine.

By understanding the degree of risk in the various areas of a solution, you're in a much better position to understand where to spend your testing energy. Suppose testing goes on longer than expected, and you need to cut some out to save time. Knowing what your highest-risk testing areas are allows you to focus on them to make sure you get the most return on your testing investment.

For instance, if you're creating an online shopping cart, the business would probably be at greater risk if the cart didn't calculate order totals properly than if it had a problem with the feature that shows similar items customers may also want to buy. The latter malfunction may merely lead to some strange cross-selling, but the former can put you out of business — obviously, a huge risk. Understanding which risk areas are higher means you can test appropriately and make choices if necessary.

To establish risks, do the following:

1. **Look through the project documentation to find risks that have been documented.**

2. **Identify which tests relate to the risks (particularly to the riskiest areas).**

3. **Schedule those tests that relate to the riskier areas early in the testing process.**

   This way, the highest risks get addressed, giving the team plenty of time to correct the product before it goes out the door.

Approvals

The people who sign off on the verification and validation plan are those involved in proving functionality and validating suitability. Those performing the tests (developers, BAs, PM, QA) sign off and in doing so indicate that they're aware of what is in scope for the tests. Those accepting the system (clients and customer) may need to sign off, as well, indicating awareness of what will be and will not be tested.

Conducting a Requirements Review

A *requirements review* is a structured audit where participants ask questions, make suggestions, and improve the quality of the product being reviewed. When multiple people play a role in improving the quality of the artifacts under review, the result is a better product. You can conduct a requirements review at anytime during the course of the entire project.

Requirements reviews have several benefits:

- ✔ **Finding missing requirements:** Because multiple people are involved in a review, you have multiple brains that can clarify textual descriptions and identify and correct inaccurate representations of the material.

  You want everyone on the project team to come to a single interpretation of the requirements, so clarifying a misunderstanding in the requirements document early on (as opposed to after it has already been programmed into a product) is a huge benefit.

- ✔ **Identifying quality improvements:** Remember, you can't test in quality, so you have to figure out where to build in quality as you create your product.

- ✔ **Educating other team members on other parts of the project:** This process can help with knowledge transfer because more people understand the entire project rather than just their own small components of it.

Requirements reviews are great ways to find defects in a document. Look for areas in the document where you state the same information in different ways, such as in the text and in a graphic. Make sure both sources of information say the same thing. For instance, if an *entity relationship diagram* (ERD) (a logical map of the data structure — see Chapter 13) says a particular field is mandatory, make sure the corresponding text table doesn't say that it's optional.

At any point in the project, you can perform a requirements review on any artifact or deliverable in the project. Here's what you should ensure when you review some of the most common artifacts:

✔ **Business requirements:** They're testable and support the original project objectives.

✔ **Software requirements (sometimes called *detail design* or *software requirements specifications*):** They align with the functional design and business requirements.

✔ **Program walkthroughs:** The program code is efficient and no interfaces are forgotten. In addition, you should make sure the code is the most efficient it can be and that it features industry best practices.

✔ **Test case:** All the requirements are being tested. Additionally, this area is one in which the team needs to determine what data should be in place for testing.

✔ **Post-implementation user assessment:** The product that was produced as the solution is actually being used.

Conducting a step-by-step review of the artifact

A formal requirements review follows several steps:

1. **Schedule the time with the participants.**

   Figure out who needs to be in the reviews and then determine when they can all meet. Some participants' attendance may be mandatory, but other people may be optional participants. Make sure you find a time that works for everyone and officially schedule it (versus playing it by ear).

2. **Deliver the review materials.**

   Determine how much time prior to the meeting people need to review the materials and send them out accordingly to the meeting participants. Generally, distributing review materials two business days beforehand is a good guideline, but project timelines and review material size may dictate a longer or shorter time frame.

   If project time is tight, you can deliver review materials on a Friday for a Monday meeting. This setup gives you two days to review the materials before the review session. We don't recommend making this strategy a habit because not many people like doing project work over the weekend. However, if you're stuck, it does allow you to recapture some lost project time and still deliver materials with enough time to read them.

3. **Review materials prior to session.**

This step is the responsibility of all review session participants. They need to review the materials prior to coming into the working session (and we don't mean five minutes prior).

4. **Conduct the session.**

This point is where the participants get together and make suggestions. We provide some pointers later in this section.

5. **Record all the changes to be made to the review materials.**

These notes include all the items you'll make changes to following the review session.

6. **Update the material.**

Refer to your review notes and make changes according to what was requested.

7. **Conduct a second review if necessary.**

If the meeting produced a lot of changes or reviewed an artifact in the middle of a project, conducting a second review to verify the changes were applied properly is a good idea.

Recruiting participants

Who participates in the reviews depends on whether the review is formal or informal and on what kind of data/information you want feedback on. The following sections break down some considerations for each kind of review.

We mention a lot of different potential meeting participants in the following sections, but managers are nowhere to be found. In most cases, managers shouldn't attend review sessions because

- ✔ **They can change the behavior of a room.** People may not voice their opinions because they're afraid of management retribution. If the managers in your organization have this power, it's best to keep them out of a room.

- ✔ **They may use it as a chance to review the BA's job performance.** The review is designed as a way to improve the artifact, so it isn't effective as a grading session for the BA anyway.

We aren't saying that managers absolutely, positively can't be at a session. Some managers can provide a great deal of knowledge and have a great oversight of system interfaces and other parallel projects. Also, you want them in the room reviewing the deliverable; just ensure their presence doesn't disrupt the flow of the meeting.

Informal reviews

An informal review is a great sanity check for a BA. You can pass a document — such as meeting minutes, business requirements, or a scope document — to any other team member and ask her for feedback. The point of the informal review is to improve the overall quality of the document. You don't even need to review an entire document. You can just meet with someone to get feedback on a particular area of the document.

For example, if you need feedback on test cases, meet with a QA analyst — because these folks deal with testing all day long, they're in the best position to review your work. If you want feedback on a prototype, meet with a software application developer.

A great way to mutually improve your document and feed yourself at the same time is to have lunch with another BA on another project and swap documents for peer review. Not only do you improve the quality of each other's documents, but you also gain insight into each other's projects, interfaces, and requirements. Based on the review, you may wind up finding a missing interface!

Formal reviews

A formal review is structured and has defined participants. Each participant plays a role in the review, but not all of them may participate in every review. The list of participants is as follows:

- ✔ **Author:** This person is the creator of the product being reviewed. The author is the one who can clarify what a particular statement within the documentation means, so she needs to be available to answer questions.

- ✔ **Recorder:** The *recorder* is the person making detailed notes about the changes to be made in the document being reviewed. Generally, this participant should be someone other than the author because the author is busy explaining what certain areas of the document mean. However, more and more companies are leaving this role to the author as well.

When Paul oversaw a team of BAs, he acted as the recorder in review sessions for them. The BAs could take their own notes if they wanted to, but the detailed outline of the changes and modifications was recorded by Paul. This approach alleviated work for the BAs so they could concentrate on the meeting and not the note-taking.

- ✔ **Facilitator:** This person conducts or moderates the session, calling on participants for comments and questions and directing the flow of conversation. Ideally, the facilitator should be someone other than the author, but this hat often gets put on the author's head as well.

✔ **Peers:** *Peers* are people who hold the same job and/or title as the author and can critically review the product and offer suggestions. For example, if the document is a business requirements document, you want other BAs as peers in the review session to help ask questions about what a BA needs to include in the document.

✔ **Reader:** The *reader* reads the document aloud during the session and prompts participants for their comments and suggestions on each section. This optional role generally ends up falling to the author or facilitator.

✔ **Additional reviewers:** This category is basically anyone else on the project team who can provide input on different aspects of the documentation. For instance, a usability engineer or lead developer may make quality suggestions on a prototype and the user experience.

The wider the range of viewpoints, the greater the comments, so invite enough people to the session in order to get the feedback you need. Just make sure it's not so many that you overwhelm yourself.

Chapter 15

Transition: Moving from Planning to Implementing

. . . .

In This Chapter

▶ Realizing why transition requirements are key to the success of your project

▶ Identifying transition requirements in existing project requirements

▶ Understanding the components of a good rollout strategy

. . . .

Simply put, the word *transition* refers to moving from one stage to another. Transition as it relates to analysis projects is all about moving from the development and test environment, where you're building the solution, to the production environment, where the users are actually using it. Think about a sports team that adds a new play to its playbook. First, the coach designs the play and has the players test it out in practice (the development and testing environment). When the coach feels the players are ready, he lets them try it in a game — the equivalent of the production environment. This chapter describes how to move your project from the practice field to the game field.

This transition brings change to the organization, including impacting how staff members do their jobs. In general, people struggle with this change, even if they ask for it by hiring you as a BA. This chapter outlines specific tasks you should complete to make change easier for those impacted by the transition: reviewing the requirements components, assessing organizational readiness, fostering stakeholders' motivation and competency, and designing a rollout strategy.

Preparing for the Transition

You should always have some sort of role in discovering transition requirements and overseeing the transition in general, even though the task may not always fall solely on your shoulders (some project teams have other roles that are responsible for ensuring a smooth transition of the solution). Even if you aren't the only responsible party, stay involved in the transition requirements; as the BA, you're very close to the details of the project and the user community, so your input is critical.

You don't so much develop transition requirements as you discover them by analyzing items already created (such as your stakeholder analysis plan, scope documentation, and process documentation), which means you don't have to wait until the solution is complete to start determining the transition requirements. You can elicit and capture the necessary information through-out the project and then finalize the requirements before rollout. We go into detail about this process in the following sections.

Transition requirements: The basics

Unlike most other requirement types, *transition requirements* are temporary; you don't need them after you implement the solution. Despite their disposable nature, though, they may just be the most important of all requirements because they help ensure that the people you're building the solution for will actually use it. People are more likely to use the solution if the transition from the development environment to the working environment is smooth.

Transition requirements are part of every type of project. They're the final steps in a project that you need to take in order to get the organization from its current to desired future state, all laid out in a *rollout plan.* These steps can include data conversion, software installation, user training, and a plan for phasing out the old system and switching to the new one. You need to have a complete understanding of what the final solution will look like in order to discover your transition requirements. For example, a company implementing a new accounting software system has to determine what information or data needs to be brought over from the old system to the new system, when the best time to stop using the old system and start using the new one is, and how much training the users need on the new process and features.

Reviewing the requirement components

Successfully implementing a change in an organization requires planning and analysis. To start things off, you should review the requirement components, which means understanding all the systems and people being impacted by the change (more on requirements components in Chapter 8):

- ✔ **Information/data:** Depending on the project, data may have to move from an old system to the new system you're implementing, which may require converting the data from one form to another. For example, an old system may contain just one address field, while the new system offers address line 1 and address line 2. Moving the data requires the team to split one field into two fields. Your transition requirements need to include what data from the old system needs to be in the new system, when this transfer takes place, and who is responsible.

✔ **Processes:** Are you implementing new procedures with your project? Does your project add to or change how people do their work? These kinds of changes require communication about and training on the new process.

✔ **External agents:** *External agents* are the people and systems impacted by the project. The people that manage the systems your project impacts need to be notified so they're ready when you implement your system. For example, say your project is a web application where people can sign up for the company's newsletter. After you get the information from the web app, it needs to be sent to another system (such as a company database) where someone on staff tracks sign-ups. To make sure your project is successful, the people managing the database need to be ready to accept the information before you make the web application live.

In order to extract all the transition requirements in these areas, you simply do a gap analysis on all these components. You can read about gap analysis in Chapter 8.

Assessing organization readiness

Another aspect of successful implementation is assessing how ready the organization is for change and how the organization handles change in general. This is sometimes referred to as *change management*. Some questions to consider include the following:

✔ **Is the organization comfortable and experienced with change?** If you've been involved in other projects at the organization before, use your past experience to answer this question. If not, ask someone who has. How did people handle change? Why did it go well or not so well? Learn from the past; try not to make the same mistake twice, and if something worked well in a previous project, include that strategy in your current project.

✔ **Do the people impacted by the change know why the project is being implemented?** Knowing why the change is coming helps prepare people for a change.

✔ **Are the people impacted looking forward to the change?** People who are looking forward to a change are more open to accepting it.

✔ **Are the people resisting the change?** Listen for the resisters of the change and try to get them involved in the team and included in the design of the solution. Getting them involved in the team helps gain their buy-in to the change.

Some changes result in job losses. If you anticipate changes to jobs or loss of jobs, work with management to put a plan in place that addresses how to handle those discussions that may come up during the project.

Understanding the users — specifically, their experience on previous projects and their emotional commitment to the project — gives you insight into how they may handle change. Flip to Chapter 11 for information on getting to know the people on your project.

Fostering stakeholders' motivation and competence

Regardless of how great your solution is, the individuals impacted by it determine the success or failure of your project, so a big part of your change management plan is managing stakeholders' experience with change. Failing to address the human side of change can easily result in a failed project.

Many books and experts focus on change management. As a business analysis professional, you can help get stakeholders on board for the change in two key areas: motivation and competence. Individuals who possess the motivation and competence for the change not only are accepting of the change but also help drive its implementation in the organization.

Motivation

In order to achieve project success, the intended users of your solution must feel driven to implement the change. They're truly the only ones who can ultimately put it into action, so you need them to be invested in the solution. Motivated individuals become project supporters and help others become more motivated for the change.

Here are some things you can do to foster stakeholder motivation:

✔ **Make your project personal to the stakeholders.** Communicate to them how the change will improve their efficiency, make their job easier, or potentially free up some of their time.

✔ **Make sure they know upfront why it's happening.** Individuals who know why the change is being made will be more motivated to implement it. Make sure all stakeholders are clear from the get-go on the reasons behind the project. Everyone should be aware of the project's goals and of the business value the project delivers.

This process starts on day one. You should be driving the team toward this information in scoping (which you can read about in Chapter 10).

✔ **Don't be afraid to continually remind people of the why.** If necessary, wear a sandwich board with the goals and business value of your project around the office!

✔ **Empower stakeholders to be part of the change.** Give them a voice on the project by including them in elicitation sessions. If they have a say in how the change will be implemented, they're more motivated to implement it.

Competence

Individuals who possess the knowledge and skills for the change are more open to accepting it. You can start to gauge competence (or lack thereof) toward the end of the project as the solution is being completed. To avoid having stakeholders understand the why but not the what, get them involved early. Let them touch and feel the new solution as soon as possible. The more time people have to prepare, the better.

Depending on the magnitude of the change, formal and/or informal training on the new software, hardware, processes, and policies may be necessary to give the right level of competence to the impacted stakeholders.

Other ways to build competency include the following:

✔ **Ensure that full and active executive support is in place.** An executive somewhere is paying for the efforts behind your project, but that's only one piece of the support puzzle. Active executive support also includes visible actions at the executive level. Does the executive promote the project, communicate its importance for the business, and help convince the resisters that it's best for the business?

Kupe was on a project that was helping build the business analysis competency at a company. The executives had approved the effort, but their actions didn't really support it. Kupe and his team came up with new procedures and guidelines that changed how people did their business analysis work. Come rollout time, however, the executives didn't fully support the effort with their actions. Managers didn't hold individuals accountable to try the new guidelines or to adhere to standards put in place. The change didn't fully take hold because when it came down to it, management didn't require anyone make the change.

✔ **Overcommunicate.** You can't overdo communication about the project, its rationale, and its impact. Communicate early and often during the project. By doing your stakeholder analysis (refer to Chapter 3), you can identify who needs to be involved and how to best communicate with them.

✔ **Have a training plan in place.** Make sure you have a training plan set up to help ensure that everyone knows how to use the new solution before it's implemented. Training shouldn't stop when the project is over, either. On larger initiatives, consider having formal training reference material available, as well as knowledgeable individuals in place for support after the solution is live. Those folks may be people on the team or users with a deep understanding of the system (often referred to as *power users*.)

✔ **Develop procedures for feedback:** To help guarantee people will be on board with a change, you need to make sure their voices are heard. Early in the project, set up some mechanism for people to share their concerns, thoughts, and ideas. As part of this system, you also need a way to respond. Depending on the size of the project and number of impacted people, responding can take time, so make sure resources are assigned to this task. The worst thing you can do is ask for feedback and then not respond to it.

Regardless of the size of the project and the number of impacted stakeholders, you should put some form of each of these aforementioned items in place — even on small initiatives.

As a business analysis professional, you may or may not have all the skills necessary to ensure a smooth transition. Transition is a critical step in the project, so if you don't have the skills, work with your team to ensure someone focuses on the change management.

Rolling Out Your Strategy with the Right Approach

After you've discovered your transition requirements, assessed the organization's readiness, and addressed motivation and competency, you're ready to choose the approach you want to use to roll out your strategy and actually implement the solution. Note that this phase of the project includes the entire team; it's not just you and the users of the new solution. You can choose from three different approaches: parallel processing, piloting, and single cutover. In this section, we discuss the components, advantages, and disadvantages of each.

If you're dealing with a large project, your upfront strategy may be to create solutions in phases, in which case each one of the phases would be released in one of these manners.

Trying parallel processing

In *parallel processing*, users continue to use the current process and software while also using the new processes and software. Consider this approach a real-world test with a safety net provided by the current system.

Parallel processing works best when your project involves automating a manual process. You should use this approach for a set amount of time to verify that the new system is working as anticipated. The user can continue to perform the process manually while a software system does the same thing automatically. Then you can compare the results of both and make sure the new automated solution is working as anticipated. And if an issue pops up with the new system, you have the results of the manual process as a backup.

Additional advantages of this approach include the following:

- ✔ It provides an easy rollback strategy if the system doesn't work as anticipated.
- ✔ Any issues discovered with the new system don't negatively impact the business because the old system is still being used.

However, parallel processing has its disadvantages:

- ✔ Users have to use both systems, which adds time to operations. The additional time can be costly and reduce productivity.
- ✔ The system administrators need to support both systems during the parallel processing.

You don't have to use parallel processing with all users of the new solution; you can do it with a subset of the users. After the subset is satisfied with the new system, you can make full transition to the new system

Picking piloting

Piloting the solution means that you're implementing the new solution for only a small group of people. For a period of time, they use the new system while others use the current system to evaluate whether the solution is working as anticipated. If so, the team can decide to roll it out to the rest of the community or pick another pilot group and continue until all groups are on the new solution.

You've most likely seen some examples of piloting, such as when restaurant chains offer a new menu item in certain stores to test interest from customers or when retail chains implement system updates in stores close to the home office to ensure they work as anticipated before they roll it out to all stores nationwide.

The pilot approach works best when a company is trying to roll out a new product, particularly when the team suspects that users will find the change difficult. The team can use a test market for the new product to determine what's effective.

You can help your team come up with appropriate pilot subgroups based on what you've learned about the different stakeholder groups. You'll have a sense of which groups are more open to the change and thus make good pilot groups.

Advantages of this approach include the following:

- ✔ It comes with a low risk for the initial run of the new product. Only a small group is impacted if issues arise. The team can more easily address issues for a small group than for a large group.

- ✔ Fewer users need training at one time.

- ✔ Because the team is working with small groups, each group gets more attention, which helps stakeholders accept the change.

Here are some disadvantages of piloting:

- ✔ The rollout takes longer than with other approaches, which keeps resources from working on other solutions.

- ✔ The system administrators need to support both systems during the pilot phase(s).

Selecting single cutover

Using the *single cutover approach* means that you stop the current process and go right to the new solution that's replacing it. This method is like ripping off a bandage in one quick motion. Users are using the current system one day and the new system the next.

A single cutover approach works well for small enhancement projects. These projects usually don't involve many changes, so the abrupt switch to the new system is fairly easy for the users to handle. In addition, this approach comes in handy for large initiatives where parallel processing is too difficult or costly, such as the transition of a customer relationship management system for a sales team. Having a sales team manage the customer base in two systems may be too cumbersome, and it may even result in inaccurate data and poor customer service. In this scenario, sticking with single cutover (perhaps after piloting it on a small group first) is a better bet. (We cover the parallel processing and piloting approaches in the preceding sections.)

Often, this approach includes everyone on the team being ready as soon as the new system is turned on. Single cutovers usually occur during a slow time, such as in the middle of the night or weekends, to help minimize business disruption. We've been involved in many cutovers on Saturday or Sunday. Having coffee, donuts, and pizza helps (at least in terms of morale)!

The single cutover approach offers advantages such as the following:

- ✔ It provides a clean transition for system administrators. They don't have to support multiple systems.
- ✔ The user community doesn't have to work in multiple systems like it does in the parallel process approach.
- ✔ Everyone cuts over at one time, so the project team doesn't have to manage multiple rollouts as it does in the pilot approach.

Disadvantages of this approach include

- ✔ Any problems with the solution mean a high risk of severe customer/ business impact.
- ✔ The business may experience a reduction in productivity during the learning curve for users.
- ✔ Single cutover requires more planning and coordination of all resources impacted than other approaches do.

Examining the Components of Your Rollout Plan

No matter what rollout approach you choose (see the preceding sections), you should include certain must-have components in your rollout plan before cutover to help ensure the smoothest transition possible. (***Note:*** In this section, we use *cutover* in a generic way to refer to the moment when you fully transition from the old system to the new system. Refer to the earlier "Selecting single cutover" section for info on using a single cutover as a specific rollout approach.)

You should discuss each component with your team and then record the results in a master rollout plan that outlines all the details of the transition. The example in Table 15-1 shows a rollout plan that covers all of these must-haves:

- ✔ **Handling of reporting and work-arounds:** You need to determine how the users should give feedback on issues with the new system to the team. Also, figure out who's responsible for correcting the system and providing a work-around for the user in the meantime to minimize productivity issues.

- ✔ **Data conversion/migration:** Know what data needs to be converted and/or migrated to the new system and when this shift needs to happen to ensure that the new system includes accurate information.

- ✔ **Security access setup:** Users for the new system may need to have access to the new system prior to cutover. Some systems may require users to create their log-in, but most internal company systems give access to users and provide log-in information for them. Having that user list and log-in information prepared is necessary.

- ✔ **Training plan:** Depending on the complexity of the new system features, you should put a training plan in place. Map your new features for the people who will be using them and develop training for them. The training can be as simple as doing a demonstration of the new features. If the features are such that they may be difficult to understand by a demonstration alone, you may need to create training materials and have hands-on workshops with the users so they're comfortable with the new features.

- ✔ **Rollback plans:** Your system administrators need to come up with a plan for rolling back to the old system if issues with the new system have a critical and negative impact on the business that makes continuing with the new system impossible until the issues are resolved.

- ✔ **Success criteria for rollout:** These criteria can include running specific functions without issue. If users using the new system successfully complete certain processes, the rollout has succeeded.

Table 15-1	Sample Rollout Plan		
Date/Time	Task	Responsible Person	Rollback/Contingency
Friday, March 20–Wednesday, April 1	Train all users on new system.	Tim – BA	N/A
Friday, April 3	Apply security settings for all users.	Jane – System administrator	N/A

Date/Time	Task	Responsible Person	Rollback/Contingency
Friday, April 3, Noon	Ensure all users are logged out of existing system.	John – Business area manager	If all work can't be finished by noon, have employees keep a paper backup of information that can be entered into new system after the cutover.
Friday, April 3, 1 p.m.–2 p.m.	Back up database.	Jim – Database administrator	This step has to be complete to move forward; otherwise, roll back to earlier iteration. Anticipated time: 30 minutes.
Friday, April 3, 2 p.m.–4 p.m.	Convert production data to new system.	Donna – Developer	This step has to be complete and tested before moving forward; otherwise, roll back to earlier iteration Anticipated time: 1 hour.
Saturday, April 4, 10 a.m.	Cut over to new system.	Donna – Developer	Test to ensure users can log in to new system; if they can't, rollback to previous iteration.
Saturday, April 4, 11 a.m.	Test that new system runs as anticipated.	Tom, Sue, Mary – User representatives	Complete processes agreed upon; otherwise, roll back to earlier iteration.
	Respond to issues with test.	Tim – BA Donna – Developer	If the issue is a training issue, resolve; otherwise, roll back to earlier iteration. If the issue is a system error, determine the root cause.

Turning Your Solution Over to Operations

The final step after the new system is in place — regardless of the rollout approach you use — is to hand the new solution over to the company's operations staff, release the project team to work on other projects, and ensure that ongoing support for the system's users is provided (by you or someone else).

Issues may come up as people use the new system. The organization most likely has a plan for ongoing support. Some companies even have dedicated support teams to handle any problems users have with the system. As a consumer, you've probably interacted with a team like that when, say, your cellphone malfunctioned and you called a toll-free number to speak with a customer support representative. The support team typically remains in place for the life of the system.

Smaller organizations don't have separate groups for projects and ongoing support, so business analysis professionals often play the role of customer support; after all, they have a deep understanding of the systems being implemented and the business area using the systems. Allocating your time can be very challenging because predicting how many support questions you'll receive is so difficult. If you're the one responsible for ongoing support, a good practice is to allocate a majority of your support time for the period just after the cutover. The amount of time you need to allot may be 1 day or 2 weeks; it just depends on the complexity of the new system and how many users are impacted. More-complex systems and larger user groups mean you should allocate more time. The users need to feel they have the support they need so they can build confidence in the new system.

Regardless of the support team's size, you as a business analysis professional should ensure that your support staff (whether it's a team or an individual) is aware of the features of the new system. You can include the support group in the user training you have or give a specific training session for them where you can discuss potential issues that may arise and how to handle them.

Part V
The Part of Tens

For a bonus business analysis part of tens chapter, head online to www.dummies.com/extras/businessanalysis.

In this part . . .

- ✔ Stay on top of your business analysis skills in a fast-paced environment by uncovering ways to interact with other business analysts and further your business analysis education.

- ✔ Prepare yourself (and your schedule) to jump into a new project.

- ✔ Discover favorite analysis techniques of various experts in the business analysis field.

Chapter 16

Ten Ways to Keep Your Business Analysis Skills Sharp

In This Chapter

▶ Finding ways to interact

▶ Attending extracurricular activities

▶ Using business analysis techniques outside of the office

No book on business analysis would be complete without a discussion of ways to keep yourself at the top of your game. The ideas in this chapter are a good starting point, but every person is unique, so your "keeping sharp" list may not be the same as your coworker's. Combine the information in this chapter with your own abilities and situation, and you can come up with a grand strategy for keeping yourself sharp as a business analyst (BA).

Participate in Social Media

Sure, you may consider social media to be the realm of younger generations, but when you think about how many millions of people see those funny cat videos and celebrity Twitter posts, you can see why social media outlets are actually good places to interface with other BAs. If you have a question about how to work with a difficult stakeholder in a project planning meeting, pose the question on a chat forum or on Twitter.

Groups on LinkedIn that deal with business analysis are great for posing questions (and reading what has been written about your particular topic). Some of our favorites include "BA Forum," "IIBA," our local General Atlanta chapter of the International Institute of Business Analysis, and of course, "B2T Training"! Follow business analysis hashtags on Twitter (*hashtags* categorize topics and begin with the pound sign: #). One of our favorites is #baot ("business analysis on Twitter"). You can see what people are reading, what BA topics and challenges are current, and where trends are going.

Make sure to put in your 2 cents on these forums; don't just sit there quietly lurking. When you add something to the discussion, you become part of the virtual community.

Always be professional when you post (which may mean keeping certain details confidential if you want to share a story or get advice about a client). And when you're participating in forums, make sure you do your research first by using the site's search functions to look for previous discussions on your topic. Someone may have posed the same question earlier and sparked a lengthy discussion. You don't want to re-ask the same question and go over the same information previously discussed. If you do pose a similar question to one already discussed, make sure you differentiate it from the prior discussion and let people know you've done your research.

Network with Peers

Another great way to keep your skills sharp is to network with other BAs at a convention, a party, or even a local chapter meeting of the IIBA. (Explaining what you do as a career to outsiders can be tough, so imagine finding another BA at a party and having a great conversation!) Getting together with other BAs has several benefits:

- **Establishing future employment contacts:** By talking to other BAs, you create a pool of resources you can go back to in the future. If you're ever looking to pick up extra work, you can reach out to your network to see about opportunities for employment and growth. You may even find out through your grapevine about a really interesting job proposition before it hits online job sites.

- **Creating a positive reputation:** People see you as having interest in business analysis. It's more than just a 9-to-5 job for you, and you show interest in improving your skills.

- **Finding people you can commiserate with and learn from:** Other BAs have similar troubles and skills as you have and would be happy to share their success stories with you. Who doesn't want to help someone else by sharing her experiences?

When networking, try to make a point to meet at least one new person each time you go to a BA function. Follow up afterward with a personal note showing your interest in keeping in contact.

Get/Be a Mentor

Mentoring relationships are probably one of the most overlooked ways to stay sharp, and they offer advantages for both the mentor and the mentee. The mentor/mentee relationship is two-sided. The mentee gets knowledge and wisdom from the mentor. He can bring the mentor difficult situations and issues he needs help working through. The mentor's job isn't to solve all the mentee's problems; rather, she shares with the mentee her own experiences and ideas and prods him to think through how he can solve them on his own.

The mentor benefits from learning of the challenges and difficulties in another colleague's business area and from the satisfaction of imparting knowledge to another BA. And a mentee usually ends up teaching a mentor something! Additionally, mentoring may also lead to promotional opportunities and open up management positions.

When looking for a mentoring relationship, make sure you and the potential mentor or mentee are compatible with each other. Just because one of you has a lot of wisdom doesn't mean that person will make a great mentor for the other.

Leverage Peer Reviews

Sometimes you get so close to a document or a subject that you can't see past a certain point or you make internal assumptions that others don't follow. The easiest way to get past your internal assumptions is to have someone who is unfamiliar with the material read through it. Ideally, try to find someone who performs the same job you do, because she'll know what to look for within your document (such as the proper way to structure project objectives) and give you constructive feedback. Just remember, fair is fair. If someone peer reviews your document, you owe her the same service. Offer to peer review one of her documents.

If you have a chance to peer review, help out the other BA by asking probing questions to get her to think about her document rather than simply giving her the answer. For instance, if you find an objective stating, "Increase sales," ask her questions such as "By how much? Dollar amount? Percentage?" and "By when? Year end? Fiscal or calendar year?" Questions help the BA by making her think about the issue rather than just capturing your response to it.

Attend Formal Training

Formal business analysis training isn't just helpful; it's also required if you're a member of the IIBA looking to apply (and recertify) for its Certification of Competency in Business Analysis (CCBA) and Certified Business Analysis Professional (CBAP) certification levels. The benefits of training include the following:

✔ **It lets you discover new techniques.** You can perform many tasks in a lot of different ways, and formal training gives you new ways to tackle a problem.

✔ **It promotes standardization of techniques and approaches.** If your entire team goes through the training, you'll all know the same techniques and can read and interact with each other's *artifacts* (documents).

Even if you're a crack BA or someone managing BAs, attending training helps you understand the techniques other BAs (even temporary ones) in your organization are learning. Knowing the techniques they use can help you understand their requirements so that you can offer tips and guidance.

✔ **It keeps you fresh.** Often, senior BAs have been doing work for 10 to 15 years at one company and are very comfortable with their standard approaches. Training keeps them from being complacent and helps them implement fresh ideas.

Present on Business Analysis Topics

Yeah, we know. Many people fear public speaking more than dying. But we recommend presenting a business analysis topic in front of others anyway because doing so pays back huge dividends:

✔ **You learn from your research.** When you present, you'll probably do a lot of research on the topic ahead of time (or at least we hope you do). So in addition to providing a lot of information on the topic to those attending your presentation, you find out a lot yourself just in doing the research.

✔ **You gain communication skills.** With every presentation, you become more comfortable speaking in front of people, which is an important skill for a BA to have. Communication is at the core of everything a BA does, and the more you present, the more you become skilled in giving information to and receiving information from various audiences.

✔ **You foster networking contacts.** A hidden benefit to presenting is networking. The topic you present is probably something someone in the audience is struggling with; your talk may provide her with more insight and possibly a solution to her problem. You've helped her out, which is good for your peer relations and the industry's growth and camaraderie. Following the presentation, you may exchange business cards or contact information with people in the audience. These are great networking opportunities. (We touch on networking earlier in this chapter.)

Read Books (Like This One!)

Whether you read on paper or an e-reader, reading is a great way to discover different approaches to solving a problem, particularly if you branch out from business analysis books. Remember, as a BA, you interface with a lot of different people who speak a lot of different languages. Understanding more about their worlds can help you when you communicate with them. Here are some genres to consider:

✔ **Business analysis books:** These books can help you find new modeling techniques, elicitation techniques, or ways to communicate requirements.

✔ **Business books:** This kind of book can help you understand the missions of different businesses and why they do things a certain way. Reading books about other businesses and business strategy helps you learn from others' experiences — both good and bad.

✔ **Technology books:** These books can help you understand software applications and software architecture structures, among other things. Although BAs don't need to know all the technology surrounding an application, they do need to know enough to talk to the technology partners.

✔ **Change management books:** Much of what you do as a BA centers around change, so understanding why people and organizations change, how change affects people, and how to manage change can be helpful.

Have Lunch with Business Partners

Lunching with business partners has a bonus: Not only are you feeding yourself, but you're also establishing a relationship. We can't speak for all business partners, but we've found that lunch is a great time to establish relationships with many of them and understand their worlds.

Breaking bread with business partners can improve your interactions with them in the following ways:

- ✔ **You earn considerable respect.** The partners see that you're trying to understand their lives and challenges within the business. By showing interest in understanding their challenges, processes, and issues, you're showing you care.

- ✔ **You become educated in the business and in what they specifically do.** It's no longer just a project; you know more about the business because you understand what the partners have to accomplish and see how certain applications or processes hinder or help them.

- ✔ **You put your name on their radar.** No longer are you just "that BA on that project"; you have a name and a relationship with the business partners. Chances are that when you need something from them, you won't just end up in their inbox as an unanswered e-mail. They'll want to help you out because they know you're listening to them.

- ✔ **You become a trusted advisor.** This trust isn't automatic, of course, but the more you work with them and the more you understand about their business problems and hindrances, the greater chance you can start offering helpful suggestions.

Rotate to Multiple Business Domains or Applications

A big value of a BA is as a liaison between business and technology who can understand each side to create a solution that solves a business problem or takes advantage of an opportunity. But here's the catch: If you're stuck in one area, you tend to see all the problems solved in a particular way. That can lead to stale solutions.

The more you know not only about the application and business domain you work in but also about other business domains and how they interact with yours, the more valuable you become. You can understand how different systems interact or how a business rule is shared (and implemented) in different areas of the business.

You can also see how data interacts among multiple systems and determine duplicate data sources. The more systems and business processes you support within your company, the more you can see impacts or help one business area leverage a process or action from another business area.

Use Business Analysis Techniques at Home

The connection between business analysis and home may not seem that obvious, but you can incorporate business analysis techniques into everyday life, which just helps them become second nature to you. No, we're not talking about giving your children a business process diagram on how they should clean their rooms (although that would be nice). Here are some more-practical favorites:

✔ **Facilitation:** As a parent, be a facilitator with your children. Help them through situations and get them to work through disagreements. Suppose your children are having an argument over which movie to watch. Shannon wants to watch *Lord of the Rings* and Fiona prefers *The Princess Bride* (one of Paul's favorite films). Instead of siding with one over the other or choosing a compromise (like watching *Star Wars*), think of what each of them really wants.

If you know Shannon would rather read a book anyway, let her read a book while Fiona watches her movie choice. Then, when the movie is finished, they can switch places. Getting the kids to agree on a solution is very similar to finding consensus among stakeholders in business: You get them to agree to support a solution, which may mean that one stakeholder gets her requirements in phase 1, the other in phase 2.

✔ **Requirements:** When making a major purchase (such as a house) do you prioritize your "requirements?" What is more important, three bedrooms with a good school system and a short commute, or four bedrooms and a bigger house but a 45-mile commute? It's the same kinds of decisions you go through with your projects.

✔ **Business cases:** Make a business case for decision options. If you're looking at alternatives for a vacation, list out the advantages and disadvantages of each one and then make a recommendation to your spouse. And then when you get the response, you may have to use facilitation!

✔ **Communication:** Practice your communication skills. Don't assume that your spouse will pick up the right kind of orange juice on the way home simply because you sent a text message saying "orange juice." If you want the correct product, specify exactly what your expectations are. To make it simple, use your smartphone to send a picture of the old container!

Chapter 17

Ten Ways to Prepare Yourself for a New Project

In This Chapter

▶ Figuring out your starting point

▶ Fostering communication with all parties involved

*N*o matter what the variables are on a project — size, type, stakeholders involved, or whatever — taking a few particular steps before you jump in is always a good idea. In this chapter, we present ten smart things you should always do to get yourself ready to start a new project.

Hit the Ground Running and Get Up to Speed

The best thing you can do for yourself after you're assigned to a new project — even if you're not going to start for a few weeks — is to begin the ramp-up process. No matter what stage of a project you accept a business analysis role in, you're already a touch behind and have some catching up to do. Unless you conceived the project, someone ahead of you has already identified the issues and business drivers, determined the solution, made the case for the project, or started building or executing the project plan. Therefore, at a minimum, you've got some background and context to catch up on!

Even if you don't know much about your new project, you can use your fabulous elicitation skills and techniques to do a little research. Try the following:

✔ First, look at the *domain area* — your stakeholder's key problem or solution space, such as human resources, the finance practice, retail management, or information research — and determine where you may need to bolster your knowledge.

✔ If you don't yet know the problem your project is focusing on, just look for information to learn more about the basic roles, responsibilities, or overall processes of the domain. What do people do? What do they have trouble with?

✔ You may also want to brush up on your technology skills or knowledge (such as web, reporting, or client-server solutions). Get to know what terminology and issues are common in your type of project.

If you're a consultant coming in from the outside, you have an extra step: learning the company's culture and organization. Hit the company's website to find out about and its mission, values, and what makes it tick. You don't want to show up your first day in a suit and tie when they're all in jeans and T-shirts (or worse, in jeans and T-shirt when they're all in suits and ties).

Clear Your Calendar and Your To-Do List

Anything you can do to free up time and make room on your plate before you start on a project really helps you focus on your work. People often say being new to a project feels like drinking from the fire hose because new project assignments frequently create a situation where you have too much to do too quickly. Whether you're a rookie team member or you've worked with this team on other projects before, figuring everything out still takes you twice as long as you (and your sponsor) want. Clearing your calendar of other obligations allows you the time you need to spend on this project.

In an effort to help bring you up to speed, your team or project manager will likely invite you to every single meeting that goes on in your first few months on the project regardless of whether you actually need to be there. Therefore, you need to have room on your calendar to accommodate all the new meeting invitations you're going to get.

Before you start working on the new project, be sure to close the door on any old projects or outstanding deliverables. The mountains of documents and information you're likely to receive for your new project are going to take some time to read through and analyze — which leaves no time for finishing up other commitments.

Take a Vacation!

Before you start your assignment or the work really gets nuts, take a break. Get away with your sweetie or just take a few days to sleep in, do some laundry, and hide out at your favorite coffee shop with a great book (maybe one on your new domain so you can hit the ground running as we suggest earlier in the chapter).

Getting ready to work by not working may sound odd, but you should get some rest and enjoy some down time before you have to rev that engine, because fitting a break in mid-project can be pretty difficult. Think about it:

- ✔ Projects often have unrealistic (or at least really tight) deadlines.

- ✔ When project managers or sponsors are building a new team or adding team members to an existing team, they want to get the kickoff meetings done and get the work going! The timeline is set, the meetings scheduled, and the deliverables queued up.

- ✔ The scope is always too big (and if it's not, that scope creep guy from Chapter 10 is guaranteed to show up anyway).

- ✔ You're frequently on the *critical path* for much of the work; that is, every day you delay one of your activities, it pushes the project out that much longer). As the project gets closer to key milestones or delivery time frames, the overtime starts to kick in. Many a project team has been known to have a "typical late night" or an occasional weekend when work just has to get done and personal time gets asked to take a backseat.

So take time now to energize yourself and come in fresh!

Get Organized

Congratulations! You're now the proud parent of a brand-new set of requirements, which is sort of like having a new baby. Everybody wants to see them and touch them. Like babies, requirements get changed frequently and grow bigger and bigger every day.

Don't allow your requirements to get into a position where they start to crawl — or run — away from you. Do the business analysis version of *nesting* (what people often do to prepare their homes a new baby): Plan and get prepared for your soon-to-be-growing responsibility.

Documenting and managing all the requirements for the project in the most efficient, effective, and transparent manner possible usually falls to you as the business analyst (BA) even if your company has invested in a fancy requirements tool. Your team members and stakeholders need to be able to find and access the most current, up-to-date set of requirements possible; to provide them with that capability, you have to create an organizational plan and structure that supports this need and lets you feel confident that what everyone is reading is in fact correct.

Have an organizational plan before you dive in and keep it maintained after you start. Ask yourself the following questions:

✔ Is a centralized (preferably electronic) location available where you can store documents, diagrams, and an index or table of contents so you can guide stakeholders to the latest-and-greatest content?

✔ What about when things change? Does your team have a way to *version control* documents or information; that is, can you indicate what's current, what's old, and what's a new draft in progress?

✔ What's your mental model for the project information and its requirements? How will you organize all the content? You need to keep it updated but not duplicated, and others need to understand it and know where to look for things. Consider organizing requirements either by level of analysis (business, stakeholder, solution, and the like) or by process or function. You can even do both!

If these capabilities and systems don't exist, get or create them. The other team members are going to ask you, and if they can't find what they're looking for, the team will quickly spiral into confusion. You hold the key to their sanity (or their insanity).

Identify What's Been Done So Far

At whatever point in time you join a project, the first thing you need to do is take a little look around to see exactly where you are and what's left to be done. When you understand this aspect, you can start planning how to get that stuff done.

You are where you are. The team may have wanted or expected to be in a certain place by the time you joined or some other specific point in time, but that target may not the reality of the situation.

Take the time to make sure you know about everything that's already been analyzed, completed, prototyped, or documented. In trying to hit certain milestones, the team may have overlooked some important things. When you need information for a critical decision, you don't want to discover that key inputs are currently open or questions are left hanging in the air. That doesn't mean you have to go back to the beginning and redo things that have already been done; just figure out whether you have gaps to fill.

Color in the Solution

Coloring a solution requires you to understand what character people expect or need it to have. The character and color that people expect from the solution shape and define the solution's goals and criteria for success.

The decisions your team needs to make on design, functionality, processes, and technical features over the course of the project depend on what success looks like to the business you're working for. Therefore, the steps you need to take to deliver on any of those particular solutions are different for each business.

Defining success requires getting an understanding of your stakeholders' perspectives — what success on this project means to them. Ask them these questions:

✔ "What are you going after?"

✔ "What are you not going after?"

✔ "When the solution is in place and really performs successfully, what does that look like?"

✔ "Overall, what does success for this solution look like to you?"

Define Everyone's Roles, Responsibilities, and Deadlines

Every person on a project team has a role of some sort, and making sure everyone is on the same page about what those roles entail is crucial for a successful project. Your team may include a BA, a project manager (PM), a developer, a business stakeholder, a subject matter expert (SME), a quality assurance person — whomever you have on the team and whatever their roles are, don't just review roles or titles and leave it at that. Have a conversation with your colleagues about specifically what's included in each role's responsibilities so you can negotiate any gray areas or identify the need for any additional team members.

Follow these steps:

1. **Ask each team member, "What specifically do you see as included in your role?"**

2. **Explain what you see as being included in your role — what you're accountable for and what work you plan to do.**

3. **Talk about how you'll help each other.**

Teams need to talk about hand-offs, expectations, and deadlines (though they often don't). Make sure you tackle what work and deliverables you'll give to and get from each other and what you'll do together (and by when).

Get to Know the Core Team

The *core team* comprises the folks that are going to work with you on the core of the project, day in and day out. You interact with these people most frequently, communicating on a ridiculously regular basis (likely far above and beyond how often you communicate with the extended team members in the following section.) If you're working on an agile project, you may even be locked in a room with them all day, every day! (For details on agile projects, flip to Chapter 11.)

Follow these suggestions to get to know the core team:

- ✔ As quickly as you can, identify who's on the team.
- ✔ Get to know what people's roles are (as noted in the preceding section), understand what each person generally does from a focus or discipline perspective, and get a sense for what skills individuals bring to the table.
- ✔ Discuss the percentage of time they've dedicated to the work of the project and ask about what else they're working on.

This information helps you understand what's been done, who may have done it, and the level of expertise they applied while doing it.

Extend a Hand to the Extended Team

Your *extended team members* are those players, stakeholders, and various participants that may work on the project less frequently than the core team members in the preceding section. They're important, but the amount of work they have to do may be light. Extended team members may include centralized roles such as a security analyst, a legal SME, a regulatory special-ist, or a liaison to the project management office. They may have an area of expertise and need to provide input on certain requirements, but they don't have a regular or full-time role.

Clue extended team members in: Tell them the goals and give them the road map so that they're aware and feel like they're a part of the team. Maybe they want to contribute but have no idea how to because they don't know what's needed or aren't really sure what's expected of them. You need to have that same conversation about roles with the extended team members as you do with the core team members so that everyone knows what he's supposed to do and what the expectations are; that way, you lessen the risk that work won't get done.

Collaborate

You need to collaborate with people on and around your team. Your role as a business analyst includes bridging the gap between stakeholders and team members; you need to put a hand out and make sure you shake theirs. Help each other. Do what you can to get work done together. Maybe you pick up the slack for somebody else once in a while, and maybe he picks up the slack for you. The goal is to work off each other.

Look beyond just getting work done and focus on doing it efficiently and effectively, coming to better solutions than you may have been able to on your own. Find that spark.

When the team members are really working well together and playing off each other, great accomplishments happen as a result.

Chapter 18

Ten Experts Chime In

*L*ike doctors practice medicine, business analysts (BAs) practice business analysis. With every experience, you gain knowledge that improves your skills for your next interaction or project. Direct experience isn't the only teacher, however. You can also learn a lot from others' experience in the field, like where they think a technique is best used or how they adapt the technique for different situations. For this chapter, we ask nine experts to chime in on their favorite techniques and explain how they use them to add value to their work, and Kupe throws in an extra tip at the end.

The Three Pains Approach to Better Elicitation (Hans Eckman)

According to Hans Eckman, a technology workstream manager at SunTrust Bank in Atlanta, Georgia, one challenge foils most projects: elicitation. "Stakeholders often represent their wants as needs in elicitation sessions and simply rattle off a wish list of solutions, when they should be talking about problems, causes, and necessities," says Eckman. "An approach called *the three pains* can help you uncover the true business needs. During your elicitation sessions, ask variations of 'What three things are causing the most pain?' This focuses the conversation on the core problem, not the proposed solution."

Here are some sample questions you can ask, courtesy of Eckman:

✔ Tell me about the three most frustrating things you have to deal with.

✔ What three things about your daily tasks would you change?

✔ What three steps of the process cause the most errors or problems?

As you elicit with the three-pain questions, Eckman recommends that you listen for red flags such as the following and drill down into them to get at the real problems and needs:

✔ Processes with long wait times.

✔ Times when a person makes a decision without the information she needs.

✔ Systems where the person has to go somewhere else to make a change.

✔ Answers like "That's just how we do it here" or "We've always done it that way."

Context Diagram (Ali Ibarguen)

The Context Level Data Flow Diagram (what we call a *scope diagram* in Chapter 10) is a great visual representation of the scope and complexity of a project. Ali Ibarguen, senior instructor of B2T Training with 20 years of business analysis experience, says the following:

"It succinctly shows the interactions the solution will have with external entities, like systems, people, and vendors. It should be developed at the start of a project during scoping but should be used and referred to all along the life of the project to ensure adherence to approved scope. The context diagram is so valuable for a variety of reasons:

✔ It gives a big-picture look at the data interactions of the potential solution, as well as a high-level look at all the data (business information).

✔ It helps you make sure you have covered all your solution's data requirements throughout the life of the project.

✔ It helps you identify the entities or parties involved in the project from whom you need to elicit detailed requirements.

✔ It shows all the systems external to yours with which you have to build or update system interfaces.

✔ It clearly shows what's not in scope of your project."

For detailed information on how to create and use a scope diagram, head to Chapter 10.

Affinity Diagram (Jonathan Babcock)

Jonathan Babcock, senior manager at Jabian Consulting in Atlanta, Georgia, loves the affinity diagram technique for generating ideas and dialogue around a project topic, particularly during the early discovery and idea generation phases. He says, "The *affinity diagram* is not what you typically think of when you think of a diagram. It's not a drawing at all, but rather a simple way to elicit, organize, and prioritize ideas or requirements. It's also a great way to ensure that everyone gets to participate in the conversation. Finally, it makes it easier for the analyst to keep the conversation out of the weeds by focusing on themes rather than details while still providing an early feel for the range of possibilities and scope boundaries."

Here's how to use the diagram:

1. **Introduce the topic.**

   Clearly describe the topic of discussion, goal of the exercise, and technique.

2. **Brainstorm for 2 to 5 minutes.**

   Ask all participants to think freely and quietly write down as many ideas as they can think of on the topic on note cards or sticky notes. The submissions may pertain to the problem to be solved or possible solutions.

3. **Post and read the ideas.**

   Ask participants to post their idea notes on a central, open space — generally a wall, whiteboard, or open desk. You can then either have participants read the ideas as they're posted or as you organize them after they're posted.

4. **Clarify and group the ideas.**

   Ask for clarification as needed. As the ideas are shared, logical groupings or categories begin to emerge. You or participants may suggest heading names for the groupings and arrange similar ideas under the topic headings.

5. **Prioritize.**

   When the ideas are organized, ask team members to vote for those they find most worthy of investigating in greater depth. Give each participant some adhesive stickers or stars (typically three to five), and have them mark the ideas they prefer. After everyone has voted, arrange the ideas with the highest number of votes at the top under their respective headings.

6. **Recap.**

   Recap what the group learned during the session and conclude after the ideas have been gathered, organized, and prioritized. Convene separate, targeted sessions to develop ideas in depth.

Process One Pager (Robin Grace)

Robin Grace — principal consultant, business analysis, of IndigoCube in Johannesburg, South Africa — shares a tool he designed: "In an attempt to make my process analysis more efficient, I created what I call my *Process One Pager*. The One Pager is a very simple and easy way to see an entire process described on one page because you use only high-level description, as opposed to including all the how-to details. Subject matter experts understand the One Pager, can give input on it quickly and efficiently, and easily review it for approval. To make the One Pager, focus a small stakeholder group in a workshop on a single process (rather than the whole workflow) and elicit normally." (For detailed instructions on elicitation, flip to Chapter 6).

According to Grace, you can adapt the symbols to match the methodology that is popular at any given time. For example, in Figure 18-1, you can see how the One Pager can be applied to the *Business Process Modeling Notation* (otherwise known as *BPMN*, a standard that focuses on graphically presenting business processes and information as opposed to solutions).

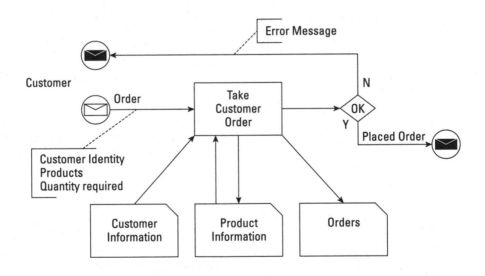

Figure 18-1: Example Process One Pager.

Illustration courtesy of Robin Grace.

On this one page, you can see who or what event triggers the organization to do this specific piece of work, as well as the specific names used by the organization to describe the work. It also shows what underlying information the process requires. Notice that it uses different types of directional arrows to illustrate whether this information is created, read, updated, or deleted.

Data Modeling (David Morris)

From the simplicity of the visual glossary to the sophistication of a fully dressed class diagram or entity relationship diagram, data modeling helps describe, visualize, and analyze the things you develop, enhance, or create to replace and improve processes and products. David Morris — senior consultant, BA Practice Management, of Redvespa Consultants Limited in Wellington, New Zealand — expands:

"When you work in information technology, you simply cannot ignore the 'information angle;' however, I find more and more that data modeling and data analysis have become a lost art to business analysis practitioners, who see data as the sole responsibility of database administrators and report designers. Understanding and modeling data helps you gain a truer, holistic view of the product or process in focus; it complements the process and interaction design views and often helps drive out additional processes or functionality not covered in requirements stated by customers or other key stakeholders. As one of the vital elements of my business analysis practice, I use data modeling at every stage of a project:

- ✔ **Right at the beginning of scoping a new product or process:** When we're bringing together a glossary of terms, I often turn it into a conceptual data model, or 'visual glossary.' At this stage, it is often just the terms shown in boxes, with lines joining any terms that are related.

- ✔ **When I integrate a new product or process concept into the associated business requirements:** At this point, I discard any terms that are simple definitions and focus on whatever represents the elements being worked on, any artifacts involved, or the key stakeholders involved. I also identify any obvious attributes and behaviors.

- ✔ **In specifying the product or process:** The nature of new product development is often that you will not know all the features and capabilities you need until you start delivering it. After a project has been approved and work is fully underway, the data model will be reviewed and updated as further detail is uncovered."

Facilitated Session (Shelley Ruth)

Shelley Ruth, senior BA at Cornell University in New York, shares this advice: "I find that using a facilitated elicitation session is very useful when bringing a big diverse group (usually comprised of cross-functional stakeholders) together. This technique also works perfectly at the start of a new project. Hosting facilitated sessions is not just about getting the information. It's also about building relationships for success. I find that when I bring the larger group together, we get everyone on the same page and start setting the foundation for collaboration."

To use Ruth's elicitation session process, do the following:

- **Allow enough prep time.** The rule of thumb for time needed to plan a facilitated session is to double the actual session time. So for a 4-hour session, allow a minimum of 8 hours for preparation time.

- **Before having a facilitated session, perform the proper planning and buy-in.** Have individual phone calls, e-mails, or in-person meetings around the project topic. The participants should feel heard and be kept informed.

- **Always follow through with your action items and continually share progress.** Doing so demonstrates credibility and helps build trust in your constituents.

- **Host the session.** Consider making the session 3 to 4 hours long, which allows you (and your team) to get more requirements elicited during a concentrated block of time. Elicit the high-level objectives, success criteria, and high-level needs of the stakeholders, and then home in on pieces and make a plan to break those items into achievable chunks.

- **Document and share the outcomes of the session with your participants.** Don't keep all of the information to yourself. Give participants a chance to review the content and add any additional thoughts to make sure you captured the information correctly before you continue with the project.

In some cases, more than one facilitated session is necessary. Don't feel like everything has to be captured in one session. Depending on the subject matter and time you have, adding another session or doing follow-up interviews is perfectly okay.

Root Cause Analysis (Kathy Claycomb)

Root cause analysis is one of Kathy Claycomb's favorite techniques because it can help make sure your project gets off on the right foot. (Read about root cause analysis in Chapter 8.) Claycomb is a senior instructor at B2T Training in Dallas, Texas, and she says that you can use root cause analysis to

✔ **Solve the right problem.** Performing root cause analysis lets you discover the real problem rather than be distracted by symptoms masquerading as the real problem.

Says Claycomb, "I fielded a phone call from an angry salesperson one morning. While I was still on the phone with him, my VP of Sales came storming into my office. It seems that my proposal team had missed a key response deadline, and we were no longer in the running for a potentially lucrative sale. Both the salesperson and the VP had all sorts of suggestions for how I needed to fix 'my problem.' They went so far as to tell me that my proposal analyst was incompetent and should be fired. Afterward, I called the analyst and asked the key question: Why had we missed the deadline? It turns out that our only high-quality color laser printer had failed as they were printing. There was no backup printer, the embedded graphics wouldn't print on any of our other printers, and there was no time to go to a local printing shop before the shipping deadline. I asked why we were doing this so close to the deadline, giving us no time to deal with a failure. It seems that the same salesperson who had been burning up my phone line had missed his deadline for sending pricing details to the proposal team.

"Bottom line: None of the sales team's suggestions, including firing the analyst, would have solved the problem: the initial delay of the key data. By doing a little root cause analysis, we were able to identify and solve the real problem instead of just addressing the symptoms."

✔ **Realize that more than one cause may exist.** When you uncover something that is contributing to a problem, focusing on that cause and not looking for others may be tempting. But a problem often has multiple causes, and good root cause analysis can help you identify all of them.

✔ **Intelligently select the cause(s) you want to address.** In a complex problem, you may not be able to fix all the underlying causes. Teams may decide not to address an underlying cause because it's out of their control, it's too expensive, it'll take too long, or it won't have a significant impact on the overall problem.

Requirements Traceability (Russ Pena)

Requirements traceability is a critical subdiscipline of requirements management; basically, it's the process of directionally linking requirements and requirements artifacts to a business request called *business features.* (Flip to Chapter 12 for details on traceability.) Russ Pena, first vice president and senior BA at SunTrust Bank in Atlanta, Georgia, says that traceability serves analysts in several ways:

- **Tracing requirements:** Traceability ensures that all requirements support the stated business goals (system features). It also assists in identifying missing or unnecessary requirements and helps with analyzing the impact of changes to requirements.

- **Managing relationships among requirements:** Traceability prevents your analysis from slipping into a dangerous *scope creep* (changes and increases beyond the project's original mission) by proving that your product does not exhibit any capabilities that have not been asked for by the project sponsors.

- **Linking requirements in a hierarchical fashion:** Traceability supports any impact analysis that you need to do as part of requested modifications to requirements and artifacts by identifying the effect on the project.

- **Tracking requirements to the source request:** Traceability helps the consumers of your requirements provide the project with more substantiated test and design coverage analysis.

In order to establish an environment where traceability is successfully adapted, Pena suggests you do the following:

- **Embrace a consistent process for trace management.**

- **Establish a requirements approach discussion that occurs prior to the requirements management effort.**

- **Decompose tracing in a single direction.**

Functional Decomposition Diagram (Greg Busby)

One of the most important tools in the kit of Greg Busby, lead BA at Cornell University in New York, is the *functional decomposition diagram* — a visual representation of processes that uses colors and shapes. He says, "This deceptively simple tool helps focus the entire project team and, with a few tweaks, can lead to storyboards, guide user role discussions, and provide a framework for scoping and phasing discussions. Set up correctly, it can also lead to an understanding of where various systems overlap and provide guidance for your business and technical architects.

"Doing a functional decomposition diagram is pretty simple. Just work with the subject matter experts to create the diagram, starting at the highest level. Then iteratively expand (decompose) each of the processes (or functions) that the system must automate until you're down to the point where you can envision a screen (or a related few screens) that will deliver the needed functionality. Usually, this stage will be two to three levels deep, except in the largest of systems. Then repeat this process for each of the functions, and you're done. I've found this task can largely be completed in a single session, often in a couple of hours. Of course, it's easy to expand the diagram if something is discovered later on as well. The right time to use a decomp diagram is early in the project, during high-level discussions of what the system should do; however, it's also an excellent way to analyze systems that are already deployed but that you are looking to replace or enhance."

Figure 18-2 shows an example of a functional decomposition diagram.

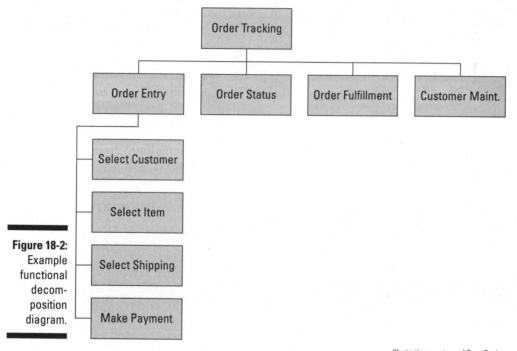

Figure 18-2: Example functional decomposition diagram.

Illustration courtesy of Greg Busby.

It's All About the Communication! (Kupe Kupersmith)

The phrase "It's the economy, stupid" was created and used by the 1992 Bill Clinton presidential campaign. According to the story, James Carville wrote this statement on a whiteboard to help the campaign get focus. He wanted the campaign to stress how Clinton's opponent, George H. W. Bush, did a poor job with the economy during his first term in office. This focus was a very simple and clear direction for the campaign. It helped campaign workers make decisions on how to answer questions from reporters and when creating and delivering campaign speeches. It's a big reason why Clinton went on to win the election.

My (Kupe's) take on this phrase for business analysis is "It's all about the communication!" In my unscientific research, I found a large theme among top analysts is that they constantly ask themselves "Will what we're doing help communicate the business need and/or solution requirements?" That question is the backbone of how they plan their work and make decisions related to their work during a project.

Make and post a sign with this phrase on it in a place where you see and read it every day. Keep the sign until the concept is a part of who you are as a business analysis professional. When your actions start to follow the meaning of the sign, you can pass the sign to another BA in need.

Index

• C •

• S •

About the Authors

Paul Mulvey has been around analysis in some way, shape, or form since 1985. When promoted from technical writer to business analyst in 1994, his question, "What do business analysts do?" was answered with, "We're not sure, but they write a lot of stuff and run meetings." If only he had this book back then, he would've had a ready-made career path. Instead, he went through a lot of trial-and-error.

Thankfully, Paul figured it out, rising in the BA ranks to be chosen by UPS to create its global business analysis competency model. During that time, he also earned his CBAP designation, published articles on websites (beginning with batimes.com) and eventually on his own blog at www.b2ttraining.com. He is an often-requested speaker and teacher. You can connect with him at www.linkedin.com/in/paulmulvey.

Kate McGoey has more than 20 years of direct and consulting experience in different application development and lifecycle process roles in the management consulting, publishing, life sciences, aeronautics, and business services industries. After evaluating her career, she found business analysis was her passion and professional center of gravity, so she transitioned into instructional design and training. Kate is Director of Client Solutions at B2T Training.

Winner of the requirements.net inaugural Requirements Lifecycle Award, Kate has broad internal back-office and commercial software product development experience. She has performed principal BA or PM roles on technology and improvement projects and has also led shared service teams, BA CoEs, and PMOs. Originally a charter member of the IIBA NYC chapter, Kate now attends Atlanta chapter meetings and serves on BABOKv3 writer and reviewer teams. She has been a panelist and featured speaker at business analysis industry conferences, various Professional Development Day sessions, and local IIBA chapter meetings. She welcomes connections at www.linkedin.com/in/kmcgoey or twitter.com/kate_mcgoey.

Kupe Kupersmith is president of B2T Training and has more than 15 years of experience in practicing business analysis. He has served as lead business analyst and project manager in various industries. In 2006, Kupe was part of the first group of BAs to earn their certified business analysis professional (CBAP) designations. His passion for business analysis and will to gain worldwide recognition for business analysis led him to run for, and be elected to, a board position with the International Institute for Business Analysis (IIBA).

As president of B2T Training, Kupe uses his business analysis skills to help manage the day-to-day operations of the company and to define and implement strategic initiatives. His career progression backs his belief that those practicing business analysis are the future leaders of companies. Kupe is a requested speaker in the business analysis field. To connect with Kupe, visit www.linkedin.com/in/kupetheba/.

Authors' Acknowledgments

We want to thank you, our readers. If it weren't for you, we'd have no reason for a book! As a group, we want to thank the B2T Training family. To all of our B2T instructors, thank you for helping us formulate and share our ideas through your instruction of our courses. To the entire staff, thanks for chipping in whenever you could while we were writing this book. Finally to Tina, our CEO, thank you for believing in us and sponsoring this effort. We are thankful for our team at Wiley: Stacy Kennedy, Tracy Barr, Sarah Sypniewski, Tracy Barnes, and Megan Knoll for making it such a rewarding experience.

Paul Mulvey: I mostly want to thank my family for giving up family time hours so I could write this book. To Shannon and Fiona, my daughters, for keeping me informed of the latest pop culture and for participating in all the crazy adventures that make life worth living. To my mom and dad, who gave me a sense of adventure to go out and chase what I really want to do. And finally, to my wife, Kathleen, who had to endure months of my banging away on my MacBookAir instead of candlelight conversations so I could make the editorial deadlines on the book. Cheers to you all!

Kate McGoey: Kudos to the #baot and IIBA chapter groups connecting me with Kupe, Angie Perris, and Tina Joseph, whom I value and thank for the B2T opportunity, their confidence, and the surprise opportunity to coauthor this book! I must "bang out" thanks to Paul and Kupe for such flexibility and encouragement. Gratitude to critical inspirers who may not know it: '95–'99 Mercury-ObjS, taught and stoked BA fire; super-smart CoE co-lead, LRashes; QA goddess CZaglin; stretch-oppy's BButtacavoli; collabtv DSS, CLP, BP; TE; and dynamo's EBG! Love to my parents, gen-twin, and HomeOps Mgr Joan! Special Bryan and Reilly, you overwhelm me with love and your smarts! To Dennis, my heart and devotion. Your love for our family inspires me most.

Kupe Kupersmith: I want to thank my coauthors in this endeavor; you made it fun. A big thanks goes to Tina Joseph, Barbara Carkenord, and Angie Perris for bringing me in to B2T Training and giving me the opportunity to solely focus on business analysis. Without this, I wouldn't be in the position I'm in today. I want to thank my parents for always believing in me even when others didn't. To my kids, Jordan, Evan, and Rachel, you may feel I'm always pushing you to do your best: "We don't try in this family — we do!" You do the same for me. And to my wife and best friend, Janine. You inspire me, you push me, you love me, and you support me. Plain and simple, without that, I couldn't accomplish what I do.

Publisher's Acknowledgments

Acquisitions Editor: Stacy Kennedy

Project Editor: Tracy L. Barr

Copy Editor: Megan Knoll

Technical Editor: Tracy E. Barnes

Special Help: Sarah Sypniewski

Project Coordinator: Patrick Redmond

Cover Image:
© Alex Slobodkin / iStockphoto.com

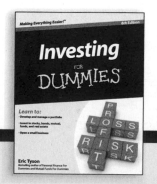
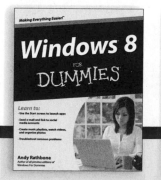

Math & Science

Algebra I For Dummies,
2nd Edition
978-0-470-55964-2

Anatomy and Physiology
For Dummies,
2nd Edition
978-0-470-92326-9

Astronomy For Dummies,
3rd Edition
978-1-118-37697-3

Biology For Dummies,
2nd Edition
978-0-470-59875-7

Chemistry For Dummies,
2nd Edition
978-1-1180-0730-3

Pre-Algebra Essentials
For Dummies
978-0-470-61838-7

Microsoft Office

Excel 2013 For Dummies
978-1-118-51012-4

Office 2013 All-in-One
For Dummies
978-1-118-51636-2

PowerPoint 2013
For Dummies
978-1-118-50253-2

Word 2013 For Dummies
978-1-118-49123-2

Music

Blues Harmonica
For Dummies
978-1-118-25269-7

Guitar For Dummies,
3rd Edition
978-1-118-11554-1

iPod & iTunes
For Dummies,
10th Edition
978-1-118-50864-0

Programming

Android Application
Development For
Dummies, 2nd Edition
978-1-118-38710-8

iOS 6 Application
Development For Dummies
978-1-118-50880-0

Java For Dummies,
5th Edition
978-0-470-37173-2

Religion & Inspiration

The Bible For Dummies
978-0-7645-5296-0

Buddhism For Dummies,
2nd Edition
978-1-118-02379-2

Catholicism For Dummies,
2nd Edition
978-1-118-07778-8

Self-Help & Relationships

Bipolar Disorder
For Dummies,
2nd Edition
978-1-118-33882-7

Meditation For Dummies,
3rd Edition
978-1-118-29144-3

Seniors

Computers For Seniors
For Dummies,
3rd Edition
978-1-118-11553-4

iPad For Seniors
For Dummies,
5th Edition
978-1-118-49708-1

Social Security
For Dummies
978-1-118-20573-0

Smartphones & Tablets

Android Phones
For Dummies
978-1-118-16952-0

Kindle Fire HD
For Dummies
978-1-118-42223-6

NOOK HD For Dummies,
Portable Edition
978-1-118-39498-4

Surface For Dummies
978-1-118-49634-3

Test Prep

ACT For Dummies,
5th Edition
978-1-118-01259-8

ASVAB For Dummies,
3rd Edition
978-0-470-63760-9

GRE For Dummies,
7th Edition
978-0-470-88921-3

Officer Candidate Tests,
For Dummies
978-0-470-59876-4

Physician's Assistant Exam
For Dummies
978-1-118-11556-5

Series 7 Exam
For Dummies
978-0-470-09932-2

Windows 8

Windows 8 For Dummies
978-1-118-13461-0

Windows 8 For Dummies,
Book + DVD Bundle
978-1-118-27167-4

Windows 8 All-in-One
For Dummies
978-1-118-11920-4

Available in print and e-book formats.

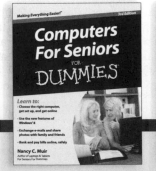